THE PENGUIN POETS

D108

THE PENGUIN BOOK OF
RESTORATION VERSE

Harold Love was born in Brisbane, Australia, in
1937. He went to the Church of England Gram-
mar School in Brisbane, then gained first class
honours in English from the University of
Queensland. He was awarded his Ph.D. for a
thesis on Restoration drama from Pembroke
College, Cambridge, and is now Senior Lecturer
in English at Monash University, Melbourne.
Dr Love's principal diversion is music of the
sixteenth and adjacent centuries. He is married
and has three children.

THE PENGUIN BOOK OF

Restoration Verse

EDITED WITH AN INTRODUCTION
by Harold Love

PENGUIN BOOKS

Penguin Books Ltd, Harmondsworth, Middlesex, England
Penguin Books Inc., 7110 Ambassador Road, Baltimore, Maryland 21207, U.S.A.
Penguin Books Australia Ltd, Ringwood, Victoria, Australia

—

First published 1968

—

Copyright © Harold Love, 1968

—

Made and printed in Great Britain
by Hazell Watson & Viney Ltd
Aylesbury, Bucks
Set in Monotype Garamond

Wit, sacred Wit, is all the bus'ness here.

APHRA BEHN

Contents

INTRODUCTION 21

A NOTE ON THE TEXT 31

ACKNOWLEDGEMENTS 33

The Libertines

THOMAS FLATMAN
The Unconcerned 37

ABRAHAM COWLEY
From Upon Liberty 37

SIR JOHN DENHAM
Natura Naturata 39

ALEXANDER RADCLIFFE
As concerning Man 40

CHARLES COTTON
Clepsydra 41

JOHN OLDHAM
From A Satyr against Vertue 42

SIR CHARLES SEDLEY
Out of French 45

JOHN WILMOT, EARL OF ROCHESTER
The Maim'*d Debauchee* 45

ALEXANDER RADCLIFFE
The Ramble 47

JOHN OLDHAM
The Wolf and the Dog 52

JOHN WILMOT, EARL OF ROCHESTER
From A Satyr Against Man 55

SIR CHARLES SEDLEY
The Doctor and his Patients 56

CONTENTS

JOHN DENNIS
The Two Friends 57

JOHN WILMOT, EARL OF ROCHESTER
Grecian Kindness 58

SIR CHARLES SEDLEY
Song ('Drink about till the Day find us . . .') 58

CHARLES COTTON
Anacreontick 59

SIR CHARLES SEDLEY
To *Julius* 60

CHARLES DARBY
From Bacchanalia: Or a Description of a
Drunken Club 60

JOHN WILMOT, EARL OF ROCHESTER
Upon Nothing 63

Moralists and Visionaries

JOHN MILTON
The Creation of Man *from* Paradise Lost 69

THOMAS TRAHERNE
The Salutation 70

THOMAS TRAHERNE
The Vision 71

SIR RICHARD BLACKMORE
Description of Chaos *from* Prince Arthur 73

JOHN MILTON
Description of Chaos *from* Paradise Lost 74

JOHN BUNYAN
Three Songs from The Pilgrim's Progress 76

JOHN NORRIS
The Reply 78

THOMAS TRAHERNE
Blisse 79

JOHN DRYDEN
From Religio Laici 80

CONTENTS

SIR WILLIAM DAVENANT
From The Philosopher's Disquisition directed to
the Dying Christian   81

WILLIAM WYCHERLEY
From To the Duke of *Buckingham*   84

MATTHEW PRIOR
To the Honourable *Charles Montague*, Esq.   84

JOHN WILMOT, EARL OF ROCHESTER
Plain Dealing's Downfall   86

EDMUND WALLER
Of the last Verses in the Book   87

The Chroniclers

ANDREW MARVELL
From A Poem upon the Death of His late
Highnesse the Lord Protector   91

SIR JOHN DENHAM
News from *Colchester*   93

ROBERT WILD
From Iter Boreale   96

ORINDA (Katherine Philips)
On the Fair Weather just at the Coronation   97

ALEXANDER BROME
The Cavalier   98

THOMAS FLATMAN
The Retirement   99

JOHN DRYDEN
From Annus Mirabilis   101

ANON
London mourning in Ashes   102

JOHN DRYDEN
The Rebirth of London *from* Annus Mirabilis   107

ANDREW MARVELL
The Dutch in the Thames *from* The Last
Instructions to a Painter   109

CONTENTS

ANON
A Lampoon ('Good people draw neare . . .')   112
ANDREW MARVELL (?)
A Ballad call'd the Hay-Markett Hectors   114
ANDREW MARVELL
Upon Blood's attempt to steale the Crown   116
JOHN OLDHAM
From Satyr II ('Upon the Jesuits')   116
JOHN OLDHAM
Loyola's Instructions to his Followers   117
JOHN WILMOT, EARL OF ROCHESTER (?)
On *Rome*'s Pardons   118
JOHN DRYDEN
From Absalom and Achitophel   119
RICHARD LANGHORN
From The Affections of my Soul, after Judgment
given against me   119
JOHN OLDHAM
The Careless Good Fellow   121
RICHARD DUKE (?)
A Panegyrick upon Oates   122
ANON
The State of the Nation   125
CHARLES SACKVILLE, EARL OF DORSET
My Opinion   126
JOHN DRYDEN
From The Medal   127
ANON
On Algernon Sidney   128
SIR CHARLES SEDLEY
A Ballad to the Tune of *Bateman*   129
ANON
On *K.W.*3^d   131

CONTENTS

Reasons of Love

JOHN MILTON
The Creation of Woman *from* Paradise Lost   135

JOHN DRYDEN
Song from Tyrannick Love   136

JOHN WILMOT, EARL OF ROCHESTER
Song ("'Twas a dispute 'twixt heav'n and
Earth . . .')   137

SIR CHARLES SEDLEY
To Cloris ('*Cloris*, I cannot say your Eyes . . .')   137

CHARLES SACKVILLE, EARL OF DORSET
A Song ('Methinks the Poor Town . . .')   138

SIR CHARLES SEDLEY
Song ('*Phillis*, Men say that all my Vows . . .')   139

THOMAS FLATMAN
The *Slight*   140

JOHN WILMOT, EARL OF ROCHESTER
Song ('My dear Mistress . . .')   140

JOHN WILMOT, EARL OF ROCHESTER
Song ('While on those lovely looks I gaze . . .')   141

JOHN WILMOT, EARL OF ROCHESTER
Song ('All my past Life . . .')   141

JOHN OLDMIXON
To Cloe   142

SIR CHARLES SEDLEY
To Cloris ('*Cloris*, I justly am betray'd . . .')   143

JOHN WILMOT, EARL OF ROCHESTER
A Song ('Absent from thee I languish still . . .')   143

ANON
The Kind Mistress   144

SIR WILLIAM DAVENANT
Song from The Rivals   146

JOHN WILMOT, EARL OF ROCHESTER
The Mistress   147

JOHN OLDHAM
The Parting   148

CONTENTS

ORINDA (Katherine Philips)
To Mris. M[ary] A[wbrey] upon Absence   149

CHARLES COTTON
The Tempest   150

SIR CHARLES SEDLEY
Song ('Love still has somthing of the Sea . . .')   151

SIR CHARLES SEDLEY
Song ('Smooth was the Water, calm the
Air . . .')   152

JOHN DRYDEN
Rondelay   153

ANON
An Amorous Dialogue between John and his
Mistris   154

CHARLES SACKVILLE, EARL OF DORSET
From the Latin   157

NATHANIEL LEE
Song from Theodosius   157

JOHN DRYDEN
Song from An Evening's Love, or the
Mock Astrologer   158

CHARLES SACKVILLE, EARL OF DORSET
The Advice   159

CHARLES COTTON
Ode   160

JOHN DRYDEN
Song from The Spanish Fryar   161

SIR CHARLES SEDLEY
Song ('Phillis, let's shun the common Fate . . .')   161

JOHN WILMOT, EARL OF ROCHESTER
To a Lady in a Letter   162

THOMAS SOUTHERNE
Song from Sir Antony Love, or the Rambling
Lady   163

ANON
No true Love between Man and Woman   164

JOHN WILMOT, EARL OF ROCHESTER
Song ('Love a Woman! y'are an Ass . . .')   166

CONTENTS

ANON
The Women's Complaint to *Venus*   167

RICHARD DUKE
Caelia   168

THOMAS FLATMAN
The Batchelor's Song   169

SIR CHARLES SEDLEY
Constancy   169

SIR CHARLES SEDLEY
Song ('Seel *Hymen* comes; How his Torch
blazes!')   170

ALEXANDER BROME
A Wife   171

ANON
Song ('To friend and to foe . . .')   172

CHARLES COTTON
Sonnet   174

THOMAS FLATMAN
Love's Bravo   174

JOHN DRYDEN
Song from Marriage A-la-Mode   175

WILLIAM WYCHERLEY
Song from Love in a Wood   176

CHARLES COTTON
Forbidden Fruit   176

SAMUEL BUTLER
From Hudibras   177

JOHN WILMOT, EARL OF ROCHESTER
Song ('*Phillis*, be gentler I advise . . .')   180

MATTHEW PRIOR
Verses by Mr *Prior*   180

CHARLES SACKVILLE, EARL OF DORSET
The Fire of Love in Youthful Blood   182

ANON
Fading Beauty   183

JOHN WILMOT, EARL OF ROCHESTER
A Song of a young Lady to her Ancient Lover   183

CONTENTS

ANON
One Writing Against his Prick 184
ANON
The *Old Man's* Complaint 185
ANON
The Maid's Answer 185
SIR CHARLES SEDLEY
Advice to the Old Beaux 186
APHRA BEHN
And forgive us our Trespasses 187

The Translators

JOHN OLDHAM
An Ode of *Anacreon*, Paraphras'd 191
JOHN WILMOT, EARL OF ROCHESTER
Upon his Drinking a Bowl 192
THOMAS CREECH
The Cause of Thunder *from* Lucretius, Book VI 193
JOHN DRYDEN
Lucretius, The Fourth Book: Concerning the
Nature of Love 196
JOHN DRYDEN
Horace Lib. *I.* Ode *9* 199
WILLIAM CONGREVE
An *Ode* In imitation of *Horace,* Ode IX. Lib. I. 200
SIR FRANCIS FANE
To a *Perjur'd Mistress:* the 8th. Ode of *Horace,*
lib. II Imitated 202
SIR CHARLES SEDLEY
The Eighth Ode of the Second Book of *Horace* 203
JOHN DRYDEN
From *Horace* Ode *29* Book *3* 204
GEORGE VILLIERS, 2ND DUKE OF
BUCKINGHAM
Part of an Ode of *Horace* Paraphras'd 205

CONTENTS

JOHN DRYDEN
  From The Sixth Book of the *Aeneis*   206

THOMAS CREECH
  Ovid, Amores, *I. viii*   208

JOHN DRYDEN
  Ovid, Amores, *II. xix*   209

JOHN DRYDEN
  The Vices of Women *from* The Sixth Satyr of
  Juvenal   211

Portraits and Histories

CHARLES COTTON
  Resolution in four Sonnets, of a Poetical
  Question put to me by a Friend   215

JOHN DRYDEN
  The Enemies of David *from* Absalom and
  Achitophel   217

JOHN DRYDEN
  From The Second Part of Absalom and
  Achitophel   222

JOHN WILMOT, EARL OF ROCHESTER (?)
  Pindarick   224

ANON
  A Panegyric   225

JOHN DRYDEN (?)
  On the Dutchess of *Portsmouth*'s Picture   228

ALEXANDER RADCLIFFE
  Upon Mr. *Bennet*, Procurer Extraordinary   228

JOHN SHEFFIELD, DUKE OF BUCKINGHAMSHIRE
  The Characters of the Wits *from* An Essay on
  Satyr   229

JOHN WILMOT, EARL OF ROCHESTER
  My Lord All-Pride   232

ANON
  A Dialogue between *Fleet Shepard* and *Will*
  the Coffee Man   233

CONTENTS

CHARLES COTTON
On *Rutt* the Judge   234

SIR CHARLES SEDLEY
To *Scilla*   234

HENRY NEVILE PAYNE (?)
A Character of the Dutch *from* A Description of Holland   235

SAMUEL BUTLER
The Character of Sydrophel *from* Hudibras   236

SIR SAMUEL GARTH
Portrait of a Physician *from* The Dispensary   240

THOMAS HEYRICK
On an *Indian* Tomineios, the Least of Birds   241

Town and Country

CHARLES COTTON
The Morning Quatrains   245

JOHN OLDHAM
The Streets of London *from* A Satyr in Imitation of the Third of Juvenal   247

ALEXANDER RADCLIFFE
Wrote in the Banquetting-House in *Grayes-Inn-Walks*   250

JOHN WILMOT, EARL OF ROCHESTER (?)
Satyr ('What *Timon* does old Age begin t'approach . . .')   250

GEORGE VILLIERS, 2ND DUKE OF BUCKINGHAM
On the London Fire's Monument   256

ALEXANDER RADCLIFFE
A Call to the Guard by a Drum   256

CHARLES COTTON
New Prison   262

THOMAS DURFEY
Second Dialogue between *Crab* and *Gillian from* The Bath, or the Western Lass   264

CONTENTS

CHARLES COTTON
From Epistle to *John Bradshaw Esq.*   266

THOMAS DURFEY
A Ballad of *Andrew* and *Maudlin*   268

CHARLES COTTON
To my Friend Mr. *John Anderson*   270

THOMAS HEYRICK
The Battle between a *Cock* and a *Capon*   272

THOMAS TRAHERNE
Walking   275

CHARLES COTTON
Elden-Hole *from* The Wonders of the Peak   277

RICHARD DUKE
An Epistle from Mr *Duke* to Mr *Otway*   283

SIR CHARLES SEDLEY
On a Cock at Rochester   284

Poet and Public

WILLIAM WYCHERLEY
Advice to a Young *Friend* on the Choice of his
Library   289

SIR CHARLES SEDLEY
To Nysus   290

JOHN OLDHAM
A Dissuasive against Poetry *from* A Satyr   290

SAMUEL WESLEY
The *Beggar* and *Poet*   293

ROBERT GOULD
To *JULIAN* Secretary to the Muses   294

JOHN WILMOT, EARL OF ROCHESTER
An Allusion to Horace   296

JOHN DRYDEN
First Prologue to Secret Love, or the Maiden Queen 300

WILLIAM WYCHERLEY
To Sir *George Etheridge*   301

CONTENTS

JOHN OLDHAM
  From A Letter from the Country to a Friend in
    Town   301
ANDREW MARVELL
  On Paradise Lost   302
THOMAS FLATMAN
  On Dr. *Woodford*'s Paraphrase on the *Canticles*   304
CHARLES SACKVILLE, EARL OF DORSET
  On Mr *Edward Howard* upon his *British Princes*   305
JOHN OLDHAM
  Upon the Author of a Play call'd *Sodom*   306
SIR CHARLES SEDLEY
  Song A-la-Mode   308
JOHN DRYDEN
  Mac Flecknoe   309
WILLIAM WYCHERLEY
  The Envious Critick   315

Mors Omnibus Communis

THOMAS FLATMAN
  Song ('Oh the sad Day . . .')   319
JOHN NORRIS
  The Meditation   319
JOHN NORRIS
  Superstition   320
JOHN WILMOT, EARL OF ROCHESTER
  Seneca's *Troas*, Act 2. *Chorus*   322
RICHARD BAXTER
  The Death of Dives *from* Madness   322
JOHN NORRIS
  A Wish   325
JOHN BANKS
  From The Innocent Usurper   325
THOMAS HEYRICK
  From The Submarine Voyage   326

CONTENTS

JOHN BANKS
  Description of a Sea-battle *from* The Unhappy
    Favourite   327
JOHN CROWNE
  From The Ambitious Statesman   328
ROBERT GOULD
  From To the Society of the Beaux-Esprits   328
JOHN DRYDEN
  To the Pious Memory of Mrs Anne Killigrew   329
CHARLES COTTON
  An Epitaph on *M.H.*   335
JOHN DRYDEN
  To the Memory of Mr. *Oldham*   336
FLEETWOOD SHEPHERD (?)
  Epitaph on the Duke of Grafton   337
ALEXANDER RADCLIFFE
  An Epitaph upon the Worthy and truly Vigilant,
    Sam. *Micoe* Esq.   338
ALEXANDER RADCLIFFE
  Epitaph on Mr *John Sprat*   339

Envoi

ANON
  The Leather Bottel   343
JOHN HOPKINS
  To *Amasia*, tickling a Gentleman   345
SAMUEL WESLEY
  To the Laud and *Praise* of a *Shock Bitch*   345
JOHN WILMOT, EARL OF ROCHESTER (?)
  Rochester to the Post Boy   348
MATTHEW PRIOR
  On Fleet: Shepheard's takeing away a child's
    bread and butter   348
ANON
  On Melting down the Plate   349

CONTENTS

BIOGRAPHICAL NOTES   351

INDEX OF AUTHORS   373

INDEX OF FIRST LINES   375

Introduction

THE men of the Restoration have stood up to the moralists much more resolutely than they ever did to the Dutch. Two and a half centuries of unceasing reminders that their political behaviour was brutal and corrupt, their distrust of idealism shallow, their sexual mores gross, and their art trivial have managed only to obscure, not diminish, the degree of our reliance on them. Today we may even feel that we have more to learn about our own particular predicament from the generation of Newton, Locke, Wren, Hooke, Bunyan, Boyle, Shaftesbury, Purcell, Pepys, Rochester and Dryden than from almost any other. If they were only seldom visited with the divine discontents of their grandfathers, the Jacobeans, they were able to deal with the problems facing their society in a much more realistic and effective way. If they lacked something of the balance and urbanity of their successors, the Augustans, they were able to dare more greatly and to persist more energetically. Because we recognize this, it is no longer essential, as it was in the nineteenth century, to demonstrate in detail that the poets and dramatists of the period really had something to say: the point at issue in recent discussions has been rather how successful, and how honest to themselves, they were in the saying. One of the aims of the present anthology is to offer material for an informed reconsideration of this question.

A second and more fundamental aim has been to gather from the very large body of printed and manuscript verse surviving from the years between 1660 and 1700 a selection of the best poetry written about the things that meant most to the poets. What those things were does not take much finding out. Restoration poetry is concerned almost exclusively with the familiar, the immediate, and the explicable. It does not often undertake the exploration of a private world or the anatomization of a particular personal experience, and when it does so will usually present its discoveries in a generalized, publicly accessible way:

> What ever is to come is not,
>   How can it then be mine?
> The present Moment's all my Lot,
> And that as fast as it is got,
>   *Phillis*, is wholly thine.

The self-conscious formality of the Augustans and the intensity of feeling of Donne and his followers are both foreign to it, the second, naturally, more so. Its most fruitful moods are the companionable, the ironic, the denunciatory, the deliberative, the jocular, the grave and the lustful. Its subjects are not very different from those of the modern daily newspaper – sex, politics, people, places, drink, sport, death, and a little religion. Individual poems and poets escape triumphantly from these restrictions but most are perfectly content to remain within them. Its language, as we would expect, sticks close to the rhythms and vocabulary of everyday speech: even its exercises in the high style are usually far less artificial in their syntax and diction than those of the poets of the eighteenth century. The virtues of this language – fatally easy to overlook in comparisons with more tightly organized verse – were clear enough to Coleridge when he praised 'not a few' poems of Cotton for being

... replete with every excellence of thought, image, and passion, which we expect or desire in the poetry of the milder muse; and yet so worded, that the reader sees no one reason either in the selection or the order of the words, why he might not have said the very same in an appropriate conversation, and cannot conceive how indeed he could have expressed such thoughts otherwise, without loss or injury to his meaning.

(*Biographia Literaria*, xix)

They were equally evident to a poet of a very different kind, Gerard Manley Hopkins, who wrote of Dryden in a letter to Bridges that 'his style and his rhythms lay the strongest stress of all our literature on the naked thew and sinew of the English language'. The poetry the Restoration wanted to write and read had to be natural, lucid and vigorous, and to make it so the poets had to work much harder than is normally appreciated. Effortlessness was a quality of style, never a recipe for composition.

Naturally such poetry is limited. It addresses itself to too few human capacities to be able to rise more than occasionally to greatness. But what it does within its limits can be extraordinarily agreeable, and not infrequently exciting. A considerable proportion of the present volume is taken up with light verse – songs, ballads, epigrams, lampoons – representing a verse counterpart to popular music which has come close to disappearing from our own culture. An even larger proportion consists of what we might call applied (or at least applicable) poetry – prologues, poems of commendation and congratulation, propaganda poems, amorous persuasions, funeral elegies – verse which was brought into existence in order to perform a specified social function and was as integral a part of the current of daily life at the time as the advertising jingle – the only real contemporary analogy, and hardly a very reassuring one – is in ours. Verse of this type draws its vigour and interest from the life it portrays rather than from any intrinsic energizing principle and because of this will not always succeed in becoming art. It will rarely fail, however, to exhibit a highly accomplished matching of means to ends which can bring its own special delight. No age has produced quite so lively a crop of journeyman poets.

Ultimately Restoration poetry is a reflection of the men who made it and for whom it was made. The contemporaries of Dryden, for all their energy and shrewdness, are narrower, coarser, more predictable in their responses and more tolerant of cliché than the Jacobeans had been. It is almost as if in positing a universe in which it was far more easy for man to know and accept his place they had removed the imperatives that had forced Shakespeare and Donne, less certain of their moral bearings and less confident of their ability to rediscover them through reason alone, to learn to feel to their full capacity and, equally important, to observe themselves feeling. Here it is worth remembering that the Jacobeans had been such great explorers both in the flesh and the spirit partly because they found things so thoroughly unsatisfactory at their points of embarkation. Donne, to take the most obvious example, belonged to an age whose ideas and institutions were still predominantly medieval, and which, as a result, offered few meaningful opportunities for practical, public self-expression to a mind which was in many essentials a modern one. The age of Dryden, who was born in the year Donne died, was able to disregard not only the sixteenth-century world view (as represented by scholastic logic, Aristotelian science, Ptolemaic astronomy, patristic divinity, Ciceronian rhetoric etc.) but also many of the inherited social and political institutions which had exacted such superstitious reverence from even the best minds among the Jacobeans. Charles II brought back the monarchy, law French and the Book of Common Prayer, but no one, except perhaps the most fanatic of his Tory supporters, was ever going to be persuaded again that these were part of the order of nature. Freed from the encumbrances of the old, and with more faith in the future than had been possible during the closing years of the interregnum, the Restoration set out with immense energy and inventiveness to replace the medieval civilization shattered by the Puritans with one that would be both sounder, because conceived in full awareness of human needs, and truer, because tested at every stage by the infallible rule of common sense. Some of its enterprises – its attempt to revolutionize the institution of marriage, for instance – failed, but a high proportion were splendidly successful. The sciences were re-thought according to mechanistic principles and the movement of the heavens reduced to rule and expressed in terms of an accurate mathematical model. The old metaphysics gave way to the new psychological atomism of Locke. The language of music felt the directing force of tonality, that of poetry the antithetical rhetoric of the closed couplet, discriminating between notion and notion, word and word, with the exactness of a chemist's balance. Prose first became a thoroughly effective means for the disciplined analysis of ideas and the communication of fact. In politics, the resolute experimentation of the previous thirty years continued – the Restoration itself being, in a sense, the most daring of the experiments – and the solution reached in 1689 was, like most Restoration solutions, a durable one. Lastly, and this the grandest enterprise of all, from the smouldering ruins of Elizabethan London a new city grew.*

> More great than human, now, and more *August*,
>   New deifi'd she from her fires does rise:
> Her widening streets on new foundations trust,
>   And, opening, into larger parts she flies.

The spirit of Dryden's lines was already abroad before the fire. Even Milton, hostile in so many ways to his age, was able to detect it and to express it in blank verse which comes unusually close for its author to the balance and economy of the heroic couplet:

> Then staid the fervid Wheeles, and in his hand
> He took the golden Compasses, prepar'd
> In Gods Eternal store, to circumscribe
> This Universe, and all created things:
> One foot he center'd, and the other turn'd
> Round through the vast profunditie obscure,
> And said, thus farr extend, thus farr thy bounds,
> This be thy just Circumference, O World.
> Thus God the Heav'n created, thus the Earth ...

If we have to have a phrase for the age, we might call it an age of builders (this being its principal difference from the

---

* For an interesting collection of the verse inspired by the destruction and rebuilding of London, see R. A. Aubin's anthology *London in Flames: London in Glory* (New Brunswick, 1943).

age of Pope which is pre-eminently an age of occupiers). Its proper emblem is not the Merry Monarch sauntering with Nell Gwyn and Louise de Kerouaille, but something that nobody ever bothered to paint – the surveyors among the rubble of the old London re-determining, and, where possible, rationalizing boundaries, measuring, judging and planning. And the poets who inhabited the new city were, for better or worse, the poets of an age of builders.

What were the consequences of this? For the professional poets – Dryden, Shadwell, Settle, Tate, Otway, Behn – they must have been clear enough, though never of course formulated. The poet was to be a full participant in the great reconstruction, and was to perform the tasks of celebrating its goals, expounding and, where necessary, criticizing its methods, neutralizing its opponents, and diverting the planners and workers in their hours of leisure in a way that would not distract them from their toil. Pepys (an administrator of genius) is from this point of view the ideal Restoration playgoer: he never once came away from the theatre with what we would call an idea. Insofar as the poet was involved in politics – and at times it was impossible for him not to be – he would naturally be a party writer, but he would take good care, however fierce the controversies in which he was engaged, not to disturb the gentlemen's agreements which had been reached about the big, intractable questions that had set the previous generation to apostolic blows and knocks. Those who, like Milton, insisted on keeping these questions open did so at the risk of neglect and ridicule. Even Marvell's generous commendatory poem on *Paradise Lost* does not altogether escape a patronizing note.

Luckily most of the writers were not professionals, and even the supreme professional had enough spare time to produce a *Mac Flecknoe*, the one major poem that Dryden seems to have written for no other purpose than his own pleasure. The amateur was free within certain limits to react against the age. He might follow Sedley in erecting a cult of elegance and writing poems whose virtue lies almost solely in the impeccability of their tailoring. Or he might follow Cotton in rejecting the values and manners of the town for those of his Derbyshire neighbours and tenants. He might, again, follow Rochester whose more strenuous reaction against the ethos of an age of builders led to what was virtually a cult of vandalism. Whether or not he was a professed 'libertine' (here used in its seventeenth-century sense, which is closer to the modern 'anarchist' than 'sensualist') he would almost inevitably write in praise of love, wit and wine, this being his most effective way of asserting the claims of the personal life against those of the corporate. Whether he found anything else to write about would depend on whether he had any new values to put in the place of those he rejected, a requirement that few of the amateurs could meet and that condemned a discouragingly large proportion of them to grossness, stridency or the belief that writing was only a diversion. (All of the major literary talents of the Restoration except Dryden's and Bunyan's were patently under-exercised.)

A few were able to escape the trap. A Rochester, dis-enchanted with the age, could struggle heroically to establish values of some kind, and eventually find himself a Christian and almost a Whig. A Dryden (whose non-official verse hints at strong Hobbist sympathies) could find a moral basis for the rather squalid social role of professional consulting poet in his consciousness of membership of an ideal senate of wits whose lawmakers were not Clarendon and Shaftesbury but Horace and Virgil. Most poets, however, lacked such resources, and only one, Oldham, can be said to have mounted a genuinely effective social critique from a libertine point of view. Sooner or later the amateurs made their peace with the age, or with God, or destroyed themselves in heroic attempts to live out the imaginings of their mighty minds in frailer flesh. The rake Sedley survived to write a long and tedious panegyric in heroic couplets on the joys of marriage. Oldham was dead at thirty, Rochester at thirty-two. Lee had drunk himself into insanity at thirty-four. Etherege, Wycherley and Congreve simply stopped writing. The poetry of pleasure remains uncritically celebrative, and in this represents an artistic as it may also a moral dead end. It is an assertion of independence from the age, not a coming to terms with it, and the same must also be said of the relatively slim body of religious poetry which was not just a restatement of what had already been better said by Donne, Herbert and Quarles. Even the malcontents did not want to rock the boat too much. Only Rochester, and perhaps Bunyan, would have comprehended the savage dissatisfaction with human society which finds expression in *Gulliver's Travels*. The attitude of the wits was essentially that of Shadwell's Bruce in *The Virtuoso*: 'Say what we can, the Beastly, Restive World will go its way; and there is not so foolish a Creature as a Reformer.'

The Restoration poets, in short, had two choices. They either promoted the basic assumptions of the age of builders or they advertised their independence of them. They hardly ever analysed these assumptions critically, nor is there any reason to believe that they did not accept them as fundamentally desirable. Those of them who did have objections to make were rarely prepared to put any serious effort into the business of enunciating them. Here it is relevant to note that even the two poets who were best equipped to understand the nature of their alienation from the age, Rochester and Oldham, never once turned against the poetic language it had enjoined upon them, never once sinned against clarity and common sense. Neither they, nor their contemporaries, were prepared either to play or to dare with words. Speech as they saw it was designed to ensure communication in a society whose most urgent enterprises were cooperative. Irresponsible in so many ways, they never once neglected their self-imposed responsibility to be directly intelligible even to uneducated readers, and if we have any difficulty in understanding them today it will be because of their allusions, not their syntax or vocabulary. One consequence of this was that their linguistic resources became perilously restricted. In his middle period Dryden had almost entirely abandoned metaphor: his return to it in a few poems of his final years is made in a holiday spirit and with the professed aim of out-doing Donne at his own (by now thoroughly misunderstood) game. The narrowness of the emotional range of Restoration poetry may easily be due, in fact, as much to the unavailability of the expressive means necessary to go beyond that range as any lack of awareness that there was something to be expressed. That this is so is suggested strongly by the dramatic verse of Lee, Otway and Southerne which strains continually for true passionate utterance without ever being able to maintain it for more than a line or two.

But I have said more than enough about the limitations. So much less daring in their visions than the great Jacobeans, the Restoration poets have gained a command of a whole range of skills unknown to them: the ablest have been abundantly successful at, in Saintsbury's phrase, 'recognizing the eclipse of the Moon and utilizing the opportunities of the Earth'. We have lost the catachresis but gained the sentence, and, in the particular field of satire, a command of the rhetoric of insolence that makes earlier English satirists sound like ranting buffoons or whining schoolboys. There were things after all that Dryden could do standing on his head which were beyond the reach of Shakespeare.

Donne, to make the comparison for the last time, had been a poet of transcendence. His central preoccupation is a wholeness of contact with another being – a mistress or a God – which can only be achieved by the calculated abuse of reason, sense and appetite. His senses are alert for the purpose of circumventing sense; his reason keen in order to confound reason. The Restoration poets are poets of the current and familiar. They prefer to rest imaginatively in the immediate experience and because they lack any sense of the uniqueness of the experience, or of the validity of relative points of view, they do not feel the need to express it in a felt or even a particularized form. They are rootedly hostile to any attempt to turn instinct or the senses into stepping stones to transcendental awareness. They are disgusted by sins against logic; so much so as to be quite prepared to put at least as much energy into the refinement of their grammar as the metaphysicals had into the devising of conceits.* The result of all this is that their poetry will stand or fall by the vigour and conviction it can impart to a generalized enunciation of shared apprehensions, a process which in a bad poet can end in a deadly nothingness (e.g. the endless, indistinguishable 'Songs' that litter the miscellanies) but which at its best can rise to a magisterial gravity, an unspectacular but completely satisfying 'rightness', or an exhilarating revitalization of the commonplace and the familiar. If we feel, in turning from the pages of Donne to those of Dryden, that words have become duller, more ordinary things, we will never feel as Dryden himself felt when reading Chapman's *Bussy D'Ambois*:

When I had taken up what I supposed a fallen star, I found I had been cozened with a jelly: nothing but a cold, dull mass, which glittered no longer than it was shooting; a dwarfish thought, dressed up in gigantic words, repetition in abundance, looseness of expression, and gross hyperboles; the sense of one line expanded prodigiously into ten; and, to sum up all, uncorrect English, and a hideous mingle of false poetry and true nonsense; or, at best, a scantling of wit which lay gasping for life, and groaning beneath a heap of rubbish.

This is, in effect, a definition by negatives of the Restoration poetic achievement. It is not an achievement to be overlooked lightly.

* Anyone doubting this should consult the two specimens of close verbal analysis which have come down to us from the period, the *Notes and Observations on the Empress of Morocco* (1674) by Dryden, Crowne and Shadwell, and the reply of the same year by Elkanah Settle, *Notes and Observations . . . Revised*. The tests which the authors apply in a completely frivolous spirit to the lines of their rivals are exactly those they were in the habit of applying under more sober circumstances to their own.

A Note on the Text

COPY-TEXT for the poems contained in this anthology is normally that of the earliest authoritative source whether printed or manuscript. Departures from this principle are specified in the bio-bibliographical notes at the end of the volume. Where possible I have collated all other early texts that I had reason to believe might contain authorial revisions and have incorporated variants from these when I was satisfied that they were, in fact, the author's. When poems have been heavily revised, I have sometimes preferred to print either the earlier or the later version as it stood.

For many of the political poems and much of the verse of the court wits there are no authoritative texts, only a number printed or manuscript (the latter being, as a rule, far more reliable), each separated by several copyings from the archetype. Many of these texts are contained in manuscript miscellanies which were produced on a commercial basis by clandestine scriptoria and survive in relatively large numbers. As it was impossible for me to consult all the manuscripts, I made the arbitrary decision to restrict my collations to the texts preserved in the two largest repositories, the British Museum and Bodleian Libraries, and in five individual manuscript miscellanies belonging to the Yale, Harvard and Nottingham University Libraries, the National Library of Scotland, and the Victoria and Albert Museum. I have at no time approached private owners of manuscripts. Texts arrived at in this way will still retain a certain degree of scribal corruption, but may be relied on to represent the author's intentions better than those generally current in his own day or, in some cases, at any time since.

Editorial method must always be conformable to the aim of the edition and the convenience of its readers. Although convinced an old-spelling text was essential, I did not consider myself obliged to be as reluctant about making alterations to copy-text as would have been the case had I been preparing a critical edition. I have therefore felt free to modernize or otherwise modify the spelling, punctuation, capitalization and italicization whenever I considered that there was a danger of a reader unused to seventeenth-century orthography being misled, confused or seriously distracted. In particular, to give examples of some of my more systematic alterations, I have added apostrophes to nouns in the possessive case, given such spellings as 'then' (= than) and 'humane' (= human) their modern form, pruned a number of carelessly printed texts, especially those taken from the 1680 edition of Rochester's *Poems on Several Occasions*, of superfluous or inappropriate italics, deprived some unimportant words of unwarranted capitals, and removed the comma used quite mechanically by some scribes and compositors after the first of two nouns joined by 'and' (though not when I felt that a pause was appropriate to the context). Where issues of comprehension and emphasis were not concerned, I have left the copy-text exactly as I found it.

I have tried to keep footnotes to a minimum, partly to avoid distraction and partly because to produce an adequate gloss for every contemporary allusion in verse so rich in references to the life of its time would have meant a substantial reduction in the number of poems which could be included. Readers requiring more detailed information about the persons and incidents mentioned should consult the Yale University Press Poems on Affairs of State series (general editor George de Forrest Lord), the first two volumes of which, along with D. M. Vieth's *Attribution in Restoration Poetry*, have always been within reaching distance during the preparation of this volume.

Acknowledgements

MY greatest obligations in preparing this anthology have been to the libraries which provided me with the materials for it. My preliminary source-hunting was done in the British Museum, Bodleian, and Cambridge University Libraries, the Baillieu Library, Melbourne University, the State Library of Victoria, the Australian National Library and the University of Sydney Library. I owe a particular debt to the two last named for giving me free run of their valuable collections of Restoration literature, the first assembled by David Nicol-Smith, the second by Hugh Macdonald. For the microfilms and photostats from which most of my texts were prepared I must thank, besides the libraries already named, the Folger Library, the Newberry Library, the Henry E. Huntingdon Library, the Chicago, Harvard, London, Nottingham, Texas and Yale University Libraries, the Library of Congress, the National Library of Scotland, the Victoria and Albert Museum, the Pepysian Library, Magdalene College, Cambridge, and the Derby Public Library. The unfailing promptness and efficiency with which my requests were met has made my work immeasurably easier.

Of my more particular obligations, the most substantial has been to Norma Bolton who typed most of the manuscript from difficult copy with remarkable speed and accuracy. I must also thank W. J. Cameron, Laurence Davies, Dennis Davison, Joan Elvins, Leba M. Goldstein, Ken Goodwin, W. A. G. Scott, Bruce Steele, Iain Topliss and John Wallis for much appreciated help in assembling, identifying and checking my texts, and Monash University for financial aid.

Lastly I must thank my wife Rosaleen who, among countless other indirect contributions to these pages, has supplied me with running accounts of her progress through several dozen recent novels, which might otherwise have tempted me to forego the delights of the Matchless Orinda and the Doctor's Patient Extraordinary.

Clayton, Victoria

The Libertines

The Unconcerned

Now that the world is all in amaze,
    Drums and Trumpets rending heav'ns,
Wounds a bleeding, Mortals dying,
    Widdows and Orphans piteously crying;
Armies marching, Towns in a blaze,
    Kingdomes and States at sixes and sevens:
    What should an honest Fellow do,
Whose courage and fortunes run equally low?
    Let him live, say I, till his glass be run,
    As easily as he may;
Let the wine, and the sand of his glass flow together,
    For Life's but a winter's day;
    Alas from Sun to Sun,
The time's very short, very dirty the weather,
    And we silently creep away.
Let him nothing do, he could wish undone;
And keep himself safe from the noise of a Gun.

THOMAS FLATMAN

From *Upon Liberty*

He's no small Prince who every day
    Thus to himself can say,
Now will I sleep, now eat, now sit, now walk,
Now meditate alone, now with Acquaintance talk.
This I will do, here I will stay,
Or if my Fancy call me away,
My Man and I will presently go ride;
(For we before have nothing to provide,
Nor after are to render an account)
To *Dover*, *Barwick*, or the *Cornish* Mount.
    If thou but a short journey take,
    As if thy last thou wert to make,

Business must be dispatch'd e're thou canst part,
 Nor canst thou stirr unless there be
 A hundred Horse and Men to wait on thee,
And many a Mule, and many a Cart;
 What an unwieldy man thou art!
 The *Rhodian Colossus* so
 A Journey too might go.

Where Honour or where Conscience does not bind
 No other Law shall shackle me,
 Slave to my self I will not be,
Nor shall my future Actions be confin'd
 By my own present Mind.
Who by Resolves and Vows engag'd does stand
 For days that yet belong to Fate,
Does like an unthrift Morgage his Estate
 Before it falls into his Hand,
 The Bondman of the Cloister so
All that he does receive does always owe.
And still as Time comes in, it goes away
 Not to Enjoy, but Debts to pay.
Unhappy Slave, and Pupil to a Bell!
Which his hours' work as well as hours does tell!
Unhappy till the last, the kind releasing Knell.

If Life should a well-order'd Poem be
 (In which he only hits the white
Who joyns true Profit with the best Delight)
The more Heroique strain let others take,
 Mine the Pindarique way I'le make.
The Matter shall be Grave, the Numbers loose and free.
It shall not keep one setled pace of Time,
In the same Tune it shall not always Chime,
Nor shall each day just to his Neighbour Rhime;
A thousand Liberties it shall dispense,
And yet shall mannage all without offence;
Or to the sweetness of the Sound, or greatness of the
 Sence;

Nor shall it never from one Subject start,
    Nor seek Transitions to depart,
Nor its set way o're Stiles and Bridges make,
    Nor thorough Lanes a Compass take
As if it fear'd some trespass to commit,
    When the wide Air's a Road for it.
So the Imperial Eagle does not stay
    Till the whole Carkass he devour
    That's fallen into its power.
As if his generous Hunger understood
That he can never want plenty of Food,
    He only sucks the tastful Blood.
And to fresh Game flies cheerfully away;
To Kites and meaner Birds he leaves the mangled
  Prey.

ABRAHAM COWLEY

Natura Naturata

What gives us that Fantastick Fit,
That all our Judgment and our Wit
To vulgar custom we submit?

Treason, Theft, Murther, all the rest
Of that foul Legion we so detest,
Are in their proper names exprest.

Why is it then thought sin or shame,
Those necessary parts to name,
From whence we went, and whence we came?

Nature, what ere she wants, requires;
With Love enflaming our desires,
Finds Engines fit to quench those fires.

Death she abhors; yet when men die,
We are present; but no stander by
Looks on when we that loss supply.

Forbidden Wares sell twice as dear;
Even Sack prohibited last year,
A most abominable rate did bear.

'Tis plain our eyes and ears are nice,
Only to raise by that device,
Of those Commodities the price.

Thus Reason's shadows us betray
By Tropes and Figures led astray,
From Nature, both her Guide and way.

SIR JOHN DENHAM

As concerning Man

To what intent or purpose was Man made,
Who is by Birth to misery betray'd?
Man in his tedeous course of life runs through
More Plagues than all the Land of *Egypt* knew:
Doctors, Divines, grave Disputations, Puns,
Ill looking Citizens and scurvy Duns;
Insipid Squires, fat Bishops, Deans and Chapters,
Enthusiasts, Prophecies, new Rants and Raptures;
Pox, Gout, Catarrhs, old Sores, Cramps, Rheums and
    Aches;
Half witted Lords, double chinn'd Bawds with Patches;
Illiterate Courtiers, Chancery Suits for Life,
A teazing Whore, and a more tedeous Wife;
Raw Inns of Court men, empty Fops, Buffoons,
Bullies robust, round Aldermen, and Clowns;
Gown-men which argue, and discuss, and prate,
And vent dull Notions of a future State,
Sure of another World, yet do not know
Whether they shall be sav'd, or damn'd, or how.

'Twere better then that Man had never been,
Than thus to be perplex'd: *God save the Queen.*

ALEXANDER RADCLIFFE

*Clepsydra**

Why, let it run! who bids it stay?
  Let us the while be merry;
Time there in water creeps away,
  With us it posts in Sherry.

Time not employ'd's an empty sound,
  Nor did kind Heaven lend it,
But that the Glass should quick goe round,
  And men in pleasure spend it.

Then set thy foot, brave Boy, to mine,
  Ply quick to cure our thinking;
An hour-glass in an hour of Wine
  Would be but lazy drinking.

The man that snores the hour-glass out
  Is truly a time-waster,
But we, who troll this glass about,
  Make him to post it faster.

Yet though he flies so fast, some think,
  'Tis well known to the Sages,
He'll not refuse to stay and drink,
  And yet perform his stages.

Time waits us whilst we crown the hearth,
  And dotes on Rubie Faces,
And knows that this Career of mirth
  Will help to mend our paces:

He stays with him that loves good time,
  And never does refuse it,
And only runs away from him
  That knows not how to use it.

*A water clock.

He only steals by without noise
  From those in grief that waste it,
But lives with the mad roaring Boys
  That husband it, and taste it.

The moralist perhaps may prate
  Of vertue from his reading,
'Tis all but stale and foisted chat
  To men of better breeding.

Time, to define it, is the space
  That men enjoy their being;
'Tis not the hour, but drinking glass,
  Makes time and life agreeing.

He wisely does oblige his fate
  Does chearfully obey it,
And is of Fops the greatest that
  By temp'rance thinks to stay it.

Come, ply the Glass then quick about,
  To titillate the Gullet,
Sobriety's no charm, I doubt,
  Against a Cannon-Bullet.

CHARLES COTTON

From *A Satyr against Vertue*

Vertue! thou solemn grave Impertinence,
Abhor'd by all the Men of Wit and Sence!
Thou damn'd Fatigue! that clogst Life's journy here,
Tho thou no weight of Wealth or Profit bear!
Thou puling fond Greensicknes of the Mind!
That mak'st us prove to our own selves unkind,
Whereby we Coals and Dirt for Diet chuse,
And Pleasure's better Food refuse!
Curst Jilt! that leadst deluded Mortals on,
Till they too late perceive themselves undone,

Chows'd* by a Dowry in Reversion!
    The greatest Votarie thou ere couldst boast†
(Pitty so brave a Soul was on thy Service lost!
    What Wonders he in Wickednes had done,
Whom thy weak Pow'r could so inspire alone?)
    Tho long with fond Amours he courted thee,
Yet dying did recant his vain Idolatry;
    At length, tho late, he did Repent with shame:
Forc'd to confess thee nothing but an empty Name.
    So was that Lecher‡ gull'd, whose haughty love,
Design'd a Rape on the Queen regent of the Gods above.
    When he a Goddes thought he had in chase,
    He found a gawdy Vapor in the place,
    And with thin Air beguil'd his starv'd Embrace;
    Idly he spent his Vigor, spent his Bloud,
And tir'd himself t'oblige an unperforming Cloud.

    If human kind to Thee ere worship paid,
        They were by Ignorance misled,
That only them devout, and Thee a Goddes made:
Known haply in the World's rude untaught Infancy,
Before it had outgrown its childish Innocence,
        Before it had arriv'd at Sence,
Or reach'd the Manhood and Discretion of Debauchery:
    Known in those ancient godly duller Times,
    When crafty Pagans had ingrost all Crimes:
    When Christian Fools were obstinately Good;
    Nor yet their Gospel-Freedom understood;
Tame easy Fops! who could so prodigally bleed,
To be thought *Saints*, and dy a Calendar with Red!
    No prudent Heathen ere seduc'd could be
        To suffer Martyrdom for Thee;
Only that arrant Ass, whom the false Oracle call'd wise,§
    (No wonder if the Devil utter'd Lies)
That sniveling Puritan, who spite of all the Mode
        Would be unfashionably Good,

*Duped, defrauded.   †Brutus.   ‡Ixion.
                §Socrates.

And exercis'd his whining Gifts to Rail at Vice;
    Him all the Wits of Athens damn'd,
    And justly with Lampoons defam'd;
But when the mad Fanatick could not silenc'd be
    From broaching dangerous Divinity,
The wise Republique made him for Prevention dy,
And quikly sent him to the Gods and better Company.

    Let fumbling Age be grave and wise
    And vertue's poor contemn'd Idea prize
Who never knew, or now are past the Sweets of Vice,
    While we, whose active Pulses beat
    With lusty Youth and vigorous Heat,
Can all their Beards and Morals too despise:
While my plump Veins are fill'd with Lust and
    Blood,
    Let not one Thought of her Intrude,
    Or dare approach my Breast;
    But know 'tis all possest
    By a more welcom Guest;
And know I have not yet the Leisure to be Good:
    If ever unkind Destiny
    Shall force long Life on me;
    If ere I must the Curse of Dotage bear,
Perhaps I'll dedicate those Dregs of Time to her,
And come with Crutches her most humble Votary.
    When sprightly Vice retreats from hence,
    And quits the Ruins of decayed Sence,
    She'll serve to usher in a fair Pretence
And varnish with her Name a well-dissembled Impotence!
    When Ptisick, Rheums, Catarrhs, and Palsies seize,
    And all the Bill of Maladies,
Which Heav'n to punish overliving Mortals sends;
Then let her enter with the numerous Infirmities,
Her self the greatest Plague, which Wrinckles and grey
    Hairs attends.

JOHN OLDHAM

Out of French

Dear Friend, I fear my Heart will break;
In t'other World I scarce believe,
In this I little pleasure take:
That my whole Grief thou may'st conceive;
Cou'd not I Drink more than I Whore,
By Heaven, I wou'd not live an Hour.

SIR CHARLES SEDLEY

The Maim'd Debauchee

As some brave Admiral in former War,
Depriv'd of force, but prest with courage still;
Two Rival-Fleets appearing from afar,
Crawles to the top of an adjacent Hill;

From whence (with thoughts full of concern) he views
The wise and daring Conduct of the fight,
Whilst each bold Action, to his Mind renews,
His present glory, and his past delight;

From his fierce Eyes, flashes of Ire he throws,
As from black Clouds, when Lightning breaks away,
Transported, thinks himself amidst his Foes,
And absent, yet enjoys the Bloody Day;

So when my years of impotence approach,
And I'm by Pox and Wine's unlucky chance,
Forct from the pleasing Billows of debauch,
On the dull Shore of lazy temperance,

My pains at least some respite shall afford,
Whilst I behold the Battails you maintain,
When Fleets of Glasses sail about the Board,
From whose Broad-sides Volleys of Wit shall rain.

Nor let the sight of Honourable Scars,
Which my too forward Valour did procure,
Frighten new listed Souldiers from the Warrs,
Past joys have more than paid what I endure.

Shou'd hopeful Youth (worth being drunk) prove nice,
And from his fair Inviter meanly shrink,
'Twill please the Ghost of my departed Vice,
If at my Councel, he repent and drink.

Or shou'd some cold complexion'd Sot forbid,
With his dull Morals, our Night's brisk Alarmes,
I'll fire his Blood by telling what I did,
When I was strong, and able to bear Armes.

I'll tell of Whores attacqu'd, their Lords at home,
Bawds' Quarters beaten up, and Fortress won,
Windows demolisht, Watches overcome,
And handsome ills by my contrivance done.

Nor shall our Love-fits *Cloris* be forgot,
When each the well-look'd Link-Boy* strove t'enjoy
And the best Kiss was the deciding Lot,
Whether the Boy us'd you, or I the Boy.

With Tales like these, I will such thoughts inspire,
As to important mischief shall incline.
I'll make him long some Antient Church to fire,
And fear no lewdness he's call'd to by Wine.

Thus States-man-like, I'll sawcily impose,
And safe from danger Valiantly advise,
Shelter'd in impotence, urge you to blows,
And being good for nothing else, be wise.

JOHN WILMOT, EARL OF ROCHESTER

*Torch-bearer.

The Ramble

While Duns were knocking at my Door,
I lay in Bed with reeking Whore,
With Back so weak and Prick so sore,
                              You'd wonder.

I rouz'd my Doe, and lac'd her Gown,
I pin'd her Whisk, and dropt a Crown,
She pist, and then I drove her down,
                              Like Thunder.

From Chamber then I went to dinner,
I drank small Beer like mournful Sinner,
And still I thought the Devil in her
                              Clitoris.

I sate at *Muskat*'s in the dark,
I heard a Trades-man and a Spark,
An Atturney and a Lawyer's Clark,
                              Tell Stories.

From thence I went, with muffled Face,
To the Duke's House, and took a place,
In which I spu'd, may't please his Grace,
                              Or Highness.

Shou'd I been hang'd I could not chuse
But laugh at Whores that drop from Stews,
Seeing that Mistris *Marg'ret Hewghs*
                              So fine is.

When Play was done, I call'd a Link;
I heard some paltry pieces chink
Within my Pockets, how d'ee think
                              I'employ'd 'em?

Why, Sir, I went to Mistriss *Spering*,
Where some were cursing, others swearing,
Never a Barrel better Herring,
                    Per fidem.

Seven's the main, 'tis Eight, God dam' me,
'Twas six, said I, as God shall sa' me,
Now being true you cou'd not blame me
                    So saying.

Sa' me! quoth one, what Shamaroon
Is this, has begg'd an Afternoon
Of's Mother, to go up and down
                    A playing?

This was as bad to me as killing,
Mistake not Sir, said I, I'm willing,
And able both, to drop a shilling,
                    Or two Sir.

Goda'mercy then, said Bully Hec–
With Whiskers stern, and Cordubeck
Pinn'd up behind his scabby Neck
                    To shew Sir.

With mangled fist he grasp'd the Box,
Giving the Table bloody knocks,
He throws – and calls for Plague and Pox
                    T'assist him.

Some twenty shillings he did catch,
H'ad like t'have made a quick dispatch,
Nor could, Time's Register, my Watch
                    Have mist him.

As Luck would have it, in came *Will*,
Perceiving things went very ill,
Quoth he, y'ad better go and swill
                    Canary.

We steer'd our course to *Dragon Green*,
Which is in *Fleetstreet* to be seen,
Where we drank Wine – not foul – but clean
                Contrary.

Our Host, y'cleped *Thomas Hammond*,
Presented slice of Bacon Gammon,
Which made us swallow Sack as Salmon
                Drink water.

Being o'er-warm'd with last debauch,
I grew as drunk as any Roch,
When hot-bak'd-Wardens* did approach,
                Or later.

But oh! the damn'd confounded Fate
Attends on drinking Wine so late,
I drew my Sword on honest *Kate*
                O'th'Kitchin;

Which *Hammond*'s Wife would not endure,
I told her tho' she look'd demure,
She came but lately I was sure
                From Bitching.

We broke the Glasses out of hand,
As many Oaths I'd at command
As *Hastings*, *Sabin*, *Sunderland*,

                Or *Ogle*.†

Then I cry'd up *Sir Henry Vane*,
And swore by God I would maintain
Episcopacy was too plain

                A juggle.

*Pears baked in the embers.
†Robert Spencer, second Earl of Sunderland, and 'Mad' Jack Ogle
were both officers of the horse-guards at the time the poem was written.
I have been unable to identify either Hastings or Sabin.

And having now discharg'd the House,
We did reserve a gentle Souse,
With which we drank another rouse
                           At the Bar.

And now good Christians all attend,
To Drunkenness pray put an end,
I do advise you as a Friend,
                           And Neighbour.

For lo! that Mortal here behold,
Who cautious was in dayes of old,
Is now become rash, sturdy, bold,
                           And free Sir;

For having scap'd the Tavern so,
There never was a greater Foe,
Encounter'd yet by *Pompey*, No
                           Nor Cæsar:

A Constable both stern and dread,
Who is from Mustard, Brooms and Thread,
Preferr'd to be the Brainless Head –
                           O'th'People.

A Gown 'had on by Age made gray,
A Hat too, which as Folk do say,
Is sirnam'd to this very day
                           A Steeple.

His Staff, which knew as well as he,
The Bus'ness of Authority,
Stood bold upright at sight of me;
                           Very true 'tis.

Those louzy Currs that hither come
To keep the King's Peace safe at home,
Yet cannot keep the Vermin from
                           Their *Cutis.*

Stand! stand! sayes one, and come before –
You lye, said I, like a Son of a Whore,
I can't, nor will not stand, – that's more –
D'ye mutter?

You watchful Knaves, I'll tell you what,
Yond' Officer i'th May-pole Hat,
I'll make as drunk as any Rat,
Or Otter.

The Constable began to swell,
Altho' he lik'd the motion well:
Quoth he, my Friend, this I must tell
Ye clearly,

The Pestilence you can't forget,
Nor the Dispute with *Dutch,** nor yet
The dreadful Fire, that made us get
Up early.

From which, quoth he, this I infer,
To have a Body's Conscience clear,
Excelleth any costly cheer,
Or Banquets.

Besides, (and 'faith I think he wept)
Were it not better you had kept
Within your Chamber, and have slept
In Blanquets?

But I'll advise you by and by;
A Pox of all advise, said I,
Your Janizaries† look as dry
As *Vulcan*:

---

* The constable refers to De Ruyter's raid up the Medway.
† The standing army of the Ottoman Empire, famed for their impetuosity in attack.

Come, here's a shilling, fetch it in,
We come not now to talk of Sin,
Our Bus'ness must be to begin
                              A full Can.

At last, I made the Watch-men drunk,
Examin'd here and there a Punk,
And then away to Bed I slunk
                              To hide it.

God save the Queen! – but as for you,
Who will these Dangers not eschew,
I'd have you all go home and spue
                              As I did.

ALEXANDER RADCLIFFE

The Wolf and the Dog

From *A Satyr address'd to a* Friend,
that is about to leave the University,
and come abroad in the World

One time, as they walk'd forth e're break of day,
The Wolf and Dog encounter'd on the way:
Famish'd the one, meager, and lean of plight,
As a cast Poet, who for Bread does write:
The other fat and plump as Prebend was,
Pamper'd with Luxury, and holy Ease.
    Thus met, with Complements, too long to tell,
Of being glad to see each other well:
    How now, Sir Towzer? *(said the Wolf) I pray,*
Whence comes it, that you look so sleek and gay?
While I, who do as well (I'm sure) deserve,
For want of Livelihood am like to starve?
Troth Sir (replied the Dog) '*thas been my Fate,*
I thank the friendly Stars, to hap of late

*Possibly a hit at Charles II's director of propaganda, Sir Roger
L'Estrange, who was attacked by the Whigs under this name.

On a kind Master, to whose care I owe
All this good Flesh, wherewith you see me now:
From his rich Voider every day I'm fed
With Bones of Fowl, and Crusts of finest Bread:
With Fricassee, Ragoust, and whatsoe're
Of costly Kickshaws now in fashion are,
And more variety of Boil'd and Roast,
Than a Lord Mayor's Waiter e're could boast.
Then, Sir, 'tis hardly credible to tell,
How I'm respected, and belov'd by all:
I'm the Delight of the whole Family,
Not darling Shock* more Favorite than I:
I never sleep abroad, to Air expos'd,
But in my warm apartment am inclos'd:
There on fresh Bed of Straw, with Canopy
Of Hutch above, like Dog of State I lie.
Besides, when with high Fare, and Nature fir'd,
To generous Sports of Youth I am inspir'd,
All the proud shees are soft to my Embrace
From Bitch of Quality down to Turn-spit Race:
Each day I try new Mistrisses and Loves,
Nor envy Sovereign Dogs in their Alcoves.
Thus happy I of all enjoy the best,
No mortal Cur on Earth yet half so bless'd:
And farther to enhance the Happiness,
All this I get by idleness and ease.

    Troth! (said the Wolf) I envy your Estate;
Would to the Gods it were but my good Fate,
That I might happily admitted be
A Member of your bless'd Society!
I would with Faithfulness discharge my place
In any thing that I might serve his Grace:
But, think you, Sir, it would be feasible,
And that my Application might prevail?

    Do but endeavour, Sir, you need not doubt;
I make no question but to bring't about:
Only rely on me, and rest secure,

        *A common name for lapdogs.

I'll serve you to the utmost of my Pow'r;
As I'm a Dog of Honor, Sir: – but this
I only take the Freedom to advise,
That you'd a little lay your Roughness by,
And learn to practise Complaisance, like me.

  For that let me alone: I'll have a care,
And top my part, I warrant, to a hair:
There's not a Courtier of them all shall vie
For Fawning and for Suppleness with me.

  And thus resolv'd at last, the Travellers
Towards the House together shape their course:
The Dog, who Breeding well did understand,
In walking gives his Ghest the upper hand:
And as they walk along, they all the while
With Mirth and pleasant Raillery beguile
The tedious Time and Way, till Day drew near,
And Light came on; by which did soon appear
The Mastiff's Neck to view all worn and bare.

  This when his Camrade spi'd, *What means* (said he)
This Circle bare, which round your Neck I see?
If I may be so bold; – Sir, you must know,
That I at first was rough, and fierce, like you,
Of Nature curs'd, and often apt to bite
Strangers, and else, who ever came in sight:
For this I was tied up, and underwent
The Whip sometimes, and such light Chastisement:
Till I at length by Discipline grew tame,
Gentle, and tractable, as now I am:
'Twas by this short and slight severity
I gain'd these Marks and Badges, which you see:
But what are they? Allons Monsieur! *let's go.*
Not one step farther: Sir, excuse me now.
Much joy t'ye of your envied, bless'd Estate:
I will not buy Preferment at that rate:
  A God's name, take your golden Chains. For me:
  Faith, I'd not be a King, not to be free:
  Sir Dog, your humble Servant, so Godbw'y.

JOHN OLDHAM

From *A Satyr Against Man*

Were I (who to my cost already am
One of those strange prodigious Creatures *Man*)
A Spirit free to choose for my own share,
What Case of Flesh and Blood, I pleas'd to weare,)
I'd be a *Dog*, a *Monkey*, or a *Bear*;
Or any thing but that vain *Animal*,
Who is so proud of being rational.
The senses are too gross, and he'll contrive
A Sixth, to contradict the other Five;
And before certain instinct, will preferr
Reason, which Fifty times for one does err.
Reason, an *Ignis fatuus* in the Mind,
Which leaving light of *Nature*, sense, behind;
Pathless and dang'rous wandring ways it takes,
Through error's Fenny-*Boggs*, and Thorny *Brakes*;
Whilst the misguided follower climbs with pain,
Mountains of Whimseys, heap'd in his own *Brain*:
Stumbling from thought to thought, falls head-long
    down,
Into doubt's boundless Sea, where like to drown,
Books bear him up awhile, and makes him try,
To swim with Bladders of *Philosophy*;
In hopes stil t'oretake th'escaping light,)
The *Vapour* dances in his dazled sight,)
Till spent, it leaves him to eternal Night.)
Then Old Age, and experience, hand in hand,
Lead him to death, and make him understand,
After a search so painful, and so long,
That all his Life he has been in the wrong:
Hudled in dirt, the reas'ning *Engine* lyes,
Who was so proud, so witty, and so wise.
Pride drew him in, as *Cheats* their *Bubbles* catch,
And makes him venture, to be made a *Wretch*.

His wisdom did his happiness destroy,
Aiming to know that *World* he shou'd enjoy;
And *Wit* was his vain frivolous pretence,
Of pleasing others, at his own expence.

JOHN WILMOT,
EARL OF ROCHESTER

The Doctor and his Patients

There was a prudent grave Physician,
Careful of Patients as you'd wish one;
Much good he did with Purge and Glister,
And well he knew to raise a Blister;
Many he cur'd, and more he wou'd,
By Vomit, Flux, and letting Blood;
But still his Patients came again,
And most of their old Ills complain;
The Drunkards drank, and spoild their Liver: ⎫
Beaux ply'd the Smock as much as ever, ⎬
And got the high Veneral Feaver: ⎭
The Glutton cram'd at Noon and Supper,
And doubled both his Paunch and Crupper.
One Day he call'd 'em all together,
And one by one, he askt 'em whether
It were not better by good Diet,
To keep their Blood and Humours quiet;
With Tost and Ale to cool their Brains,
Than nightly Fire 'em with *Champains*;
To sup sometimes on Water-grewel,
Than drink themselves into a Duel;
To change their lewd, for sober Life,
And rotten Whore, for sounder Wife?
They all agreed that his Advice ⎫
Was honest, wholsom, grave and wise; ⎬
But not one Man, wou'd quit his Vice; ⎭

For after all his vain Attacks,
They rose and din'd well at *Pontack*'s:

THE MORAL

The Wise may preach, and Satyrists rail,
Custom and Nature will prevail.

SIR CHARLES SEDLEY

The Two Friends

Freeman and *Wild*, two young hot Gallants,
Fam'd through the Town for swindging Talents,
At making or at acting Love,
And Beaus too over and above;
Like *Friends* had a fine Buxom Woman,
(Like *Friends* indeed, you'll say) in common.
Now one of these two Sparks attack'd her,
So furiously, so like a Hector,
He got a Girl, who to a Tittle,
Her Mother's Picture was in little:
When both *Jack Freeman* and *Ned Wild*
Would own the Fair, the chopping Child;
Both own the Babe (and who would not!)
Sweet as the Sin by which 'twas Got;
Ned, that he's sure he Got her Cries,
She has his Dimple and his Eyes:
That she was his, *Jack Freeman* Swore,   )
That she resembled him all o're,   }
The Devil was not more like a *Moor*:   )
But when at length the Girl began
To grow capacious of a Man,
Changing their Minds, each Spark chose rather
To be the Sinner than the Father:
Says *Wild* to *Freeman*, *Jack*, this Lass
Is thy own Flesh and Blood; she has

The very Leer of Lewd *Jack Freeman*,
Adzwounds that Sham won't pass on me, Man,
(Cries *Freeman* to his Brother *Wild*)
Mine is the Lass, and thine the Child.
Says *Wild* to *Freeman* thou'lt be Damn'd,
Ay, ay, *Ned*, but I won't be shamm'd.

JOHN DENNIS

Grecian Kindness

The utmost Grace the *Greeks* could shew,
  When to the *Trojans* they grew kind,
Was with their Arms to let 'em go,
  And leave their lingring Wives behind.
They beat the Men, and burnt the Town,
Then all the Baggage was their own.

There the kind Deity of Wine
  Kiss'd the soft wanton God of Love;
This clapt his Wings, that press'd his Vine,
  And their best Pow'rs united move:
While each brave *Greek* embrac'd his Punk,
Lull'd her alseep, and then grew drunk.

JOHN WILMOT, EARL OF ROCHESTER

Song

Drink about till the Day find us,
  These are Pleasures that will last;
Let no foolish Passion blind us,
  Joys of Love they fly too fast.

Maids are long e're we can win'um,
  And our Passions waste the while,
In a Beer-glass we'll begin'um,
  Let some Beau take th'other Toil.

Yet we will have store of good Wenches,
   Though we venture fluxing for't,
Upon Couches, Chairs, and Benches,
   To out-do them at the Sport.

Joyning thus both Mirth and Beauty,
   To make up our full Delight:
In Wine and Love we pay our Duty
   To each friendly coming Night.

SIR CHARLES SEDLEY

Anacreontick

Fill a Boul of lusty Wine,
Briskest Daughter of the Vine;
Fill't untill it Sea-like flow,
That my cheek may once more glow.
I am fifty Winters old,
Bloud then stagnates and grows cold,
And when Youthfull heat decays,
We must help it by these ways.
Wine breeds Mirth, and Mirth imparts
Heat and Courage to our hearts,
Which in old men else are lead,
And not warm'd would soon be dead.

   Now I'm sprightly, fill agen,
Stop not though they mount to ten;
Though I stagger do not spare,
'Tis to rock and still my Ear;
Though I stammer 'tis no matter,
I should doe the same with water;
When I belch, I am but trying
How much better 'tis than sighing;
If a tear spring in mine eye,
'Tis for joy not grief I cry:

This is living without thinking,
These are the effects of drinking.

  Fill a main, (Boy) fill a main,
Whilst I drink I feel no pain;
Gout or Palsie I have none,
Hang the Chollick and the Stone;
I methinks grow young again,
New bloud springs in ev'ry vein,
And supply it (Sirrah) still,
Whilst I drink you sure may fill:
If I nod, Boy, rouse me up
With a bigger fuller Cup;
But when that, Boy, will not doe,
Faith e'en let me then goe to,
For 'tis better far to lie
Down to sleep than down to dye.

CHARLES COTTON

To Julius

Thou swear'st thou'lt drink no more; kind Heaven send
Me such a Cook or Coach-man, but no Friend.

SIR CHARLES SEDLEY

From *Bacchanalia:*
Or a Description of a Drunken Club

But by this time Tongues 'gan to rest;
The Talking game was at the best.
A sleepy Scene beginneth to appear.
    Bright Reason's ray,
By damp of Wine, within this Hemisphere,
Was quench'd before: and now dim sense, to stay
    Must not expect, long after Her;

So when, Night's fairest Lanthorn, *Cynthia* bright
Is set; each little mist, or thin-spread Cloud
      Sufficient is to shroud
The pink-ey'd Stars, and make a pitchy Night.
    Old *Morpheus* comes, with Leaden Key,
    His drowsie Office to perform:
    Though some there are, that do affirm,
    'Twas *Bacchus* did it; and that He
Had Legal Right, to lock up each man's Brain:
      Since every Room
      His own Goods did contain,
And was his proper Wine-Cellar become.

Some down into their Seats do shrink,
    As snuffs in Sockets sink;
Some throw themselves upon the Bed,
Some at Feet, and some at Head,
    Some Cross, some Slope-wise, as they can;
Like Hogs in straw, or Herrings in a pan.
Some on the Floor do make their humble Bed,
     (Proper effect of Wine!)
     So over-laden Vine,
    Prop failing, bowes its bunchy Head,
To kiss the Ground, from whence 'twas nourished.
One, stouter than the rest, maintain'd the Field,
     And scorn'd to yield.
A *Roman* Emperour, standing vow'd to die,
    And so, quoth he, will I;
Till nodding, as he stood, the Churlish Wall
Repuls'd his Head, and made him, reeling fall;
     So with a jot,
    Embrac'd the common lot,
The last, but yet the greatest, Trophy, of them all.

    So slept they sound; but whilst they slept,
    Nature, which all this while, had kept
     Her last reserve of strength,

In Stomach's mouth, where *Helmont** saith,
The Soul its chiefest Mansion hath,
      Began at length
    To kick, and frisk, and stoutly strove
    To throw the Liquid Rider off.
For now her Case, like Marriners, was grown,
In leaky Ship, she must or pump, or drown.
Or whether that the Wine, which, till this time,
Was wont to dwell in Cellar's cooler Clime,
      Now put in Stomach's boiling-pot,
Found its new Habitation too hot?
    What e're it was, the Floods gusht out
      From ev'ry spout,
With such a force; they made a fulsome fray.
    One who athwart his Neighbour lay,
Did right into his Pocket disembogue;
For which the other would have call'd him Rogue,
But that his forestall'd mouth (brawls to prevent)
Replenisht was with the same Element.
    I'th' next Man's face Another spues,
Who doth, with nimble Repartee, retort
    His own, and His Assailant's juice,
    And so returns him double for't.
    One with a Horizontal mouth,
    Discharges up into the Air,
Which falls again in Perpendicular:
    Much like those Clouds, in Sea that's South,
    Which in a Lump, descend, and quite
O're-whelm the Ship, on which they chance to light:
The Floor with such a Deluge was o'reflown,
As would infallibly have ran
Quite through, and to its native Cellar gone,
As Rivers Circulate to th'Ocean:
Had it not been incrassate with a scum,
Which did, for company, from Stomach come.

* Johann Baptist van Helmont (1577–1644), Belgian chemist and medical writer.

Nor was this all: The surly Element,
    With Orall Channels not content,
Reverberates; and downward finds a Vent.
    Which my Nice Muse to tell forebears,
And begs, for what is past, the pardon of your Ears.

CHARLES DARBY

Upon Nothing

Nothing thou Elder Brother ev'n to shade,
Thou hadst a Being e're the World was made,
And (well fixt) art alone of ending not afraid.

E're time and place were, time and place were not
When Primitive Nothing something strait begot,
Then all proceeded from the great united – What?

Something, the gen'ral Attribute of all,
Sever'd from thee, its sole Original,
Into thy boundless self, must undistinguish'd fall.

Yet something did thy mighty Pow'r command,
And from thy fruitful emptiness's hand,
Snatcht Men, Beasts, Birds, Fire, Water, Aire, and Land.

Matter, the wicked'st Offspring of thy Race,
By forme assisted, flew from thy embrace,
And Rebel Light obscur'd thy reverend dusky Face.

With form and Matter, time and place did join,
Body, thy Foe, with these did Leagues combine,
To spoil thy peaceful Realm, and ruin all thy Line.

But Turn-Coat Time assists the Foe in vain,
And brib'd by thee, destroys their short-liv'd Reign,
And to thy hungry Womb, drives back thy Slaves again.

Tho Mysteries are barr'd from Laick-Eyes,*
And the Divine alone with Warrant pryes
Into thy Bosome, where thy truth in private lyes,

Yet this of thee the wise may freely say,
Thou from the Virtuous, nothing dost delay,
And to be part of thee, the Wicked wisely pray.

Great Negative, how vainly wou'd the Wise,
Enquire, define, distinguish, teach, devise,
Didst thou not stand to point their blind Philosophies!

Is or is not, the Two great ends of Fate,
And true, or false, the Subject of debate,
That perfect, or destroy, the vast designs of State,

When they have rack'd the Politician's Breast,
Within thy Bosome, most securely rest,
And when reduc'd to thee, are least unsafe, and best.

But Nothing, why does something still permit,
That Sacred Monarchs shou'd at Councel sit,
With Persons highly thought, at best, for Nothing fit,

Whil'st weighty Something modestly abstains,
From Princes' Coffers, and from States-Men's Brains,
And Nothing there, like stately Something reigns?

Nothing who dwellst with Fools, in grave disguise,
From whom they Reverend shapes and forms devise,
Lawn-sleeves, and Furrs, and Gowns, when they like thee
   look wise.

French Truth, *Dutch* Prowess, *British* Policy,
Hybernian Learning, *Scotch* Civility,
Spaniards' dispatch, *Danes'* Wit, are mainly seen in thee.

*i.e. The eyes of laymen.

THE LIBERTINES

The great Man's gratitude to his best Friend,
Kings' Promises, Whores' Vows, towards thee they bend,
Flow swiftly into thee, and in thee ever end.

JOHN WILMOT, EARL OF ROCHESTER

Moralists and Visionaries

The Creation of Man
from *Paradise Lost*, Book 7

There wanted yet the Master work, the end
Of all yet don; a Creature who not prone
And Brute as other Creatures, but endu'd
With Sanctitie of Reason, might erect
His Stature, and upright with Front serene
Govern the rest, self-knowing, and from thence
Magnanimous to correspond with Heav'n,
But grateful to acknowledge whence his good
Descends, thither with heart and voice and eyes
Directed in Devotion, to adore
And worship God Supream, who made him chief
Of all his works: therefore the Omnipotent
Eternal Father (For where is not hee
Present) thus to his Son audibly spake.
    Let us make now Man in our image, Man
In our similitude, and let them rule
Over the Fish and Fowle of Sea and Aire,
Beast of the Field, and over all the Earth,
And every creeping thing that creeps the ground.
This said, he formd thee, *Adam*, thee O Man
Dust of the ground, and in thy nostrils breath'd
The breath of Life; in his own Image hee
Created thee, in the Image of God
Express, and thou becam'st a living Soul.
Male he created thee, but thy consort
Femal for Race; then bless'd Mankinde, and said,
Be fruitful, multiplie, and fill the Earth,
Subdue it, and throughout Dominion hold
Over Fish of the Sea, and Fowle of the Aire,
And every living thing that moves on the Earth.

                                        JOHN MILTON

The Salutation

These little Limmes,
 These Eys and Hands which here I find,
These rosie Cheeks wherwith my Life begins,
    Where have ye been? Behind
What Curtain were ye from me hid so long!
Where was? in what Abyss, my Speaking Tongue?

    When silent I
 So many thousand thousand yeers,
Beneath the Dust did in a Chaos lie,
    How could I Smiles or Tears,
Or Lips or Hands or Eys or Ears perceiv?
Welcome ye Treasures which I now receiv.

    I that so long
 Was Nothing from Eternitie,
Did little think such Joys as Ear or Tongue,
    To Celebrat or See:
Such Sounds to hear, such Hands to feel, such Feet,
Beneath the Skies, on such a Ground to meet.

    New Burnisht Joys!
 Which yellow Gold and Pearl excell!
Such Sacred Treasures are the Lims in Boys,
    In which a Soul doth Dwell;
Their Organized Joynts, and Azure veins
More Wealth include, than all the World contains.

    From Dust I rise,
 And out of Nothing now awake,
These Brighter Regions which salute mine Eys,
    A Gift from GOD I take.
The Earth, the Seas, the Light, the Day, the Skies,
The Sun and Stars are mine; if those I prize.

Long time before
I in my Mother's Womb was born,
A GOD preparing did this Glorious Store,
    The World for me adorne.
Into this Eden so Divine and fair,
So Wide and Bright, I com his Son and Heir.

    A Stranger here
Strange Things doth meet, strange Glories See;
Strange Treasures lodg'd in this fair World appear,
    Strange all, and New to me.
But that they mine should be, who nothing was,
That Strangest is of all, yet brought to pass.

THOMAS TRAHERNE

The Vision

Flight is but the Preparative: The Sight
    Is Deep and Infinit;
Ah me! tis all the Glory, Love, Light, Space,
    Joy, Beauty and Varietie
That doth adorn the Godhead's Dwelling Place
    Tis all that Ey can see:
Even Trades them selvs seen in Celestial Light,
    And Cares and Sins and Woes are Bright.

Order the Beauty even of Beauty is,
    It is the Rule of Bliss,
The very Life and Form and Caus of Pleasure;
    Which if we do not understand,
Ten thousand Heaps of vain confused Treasure
    Will but oppress the Land.
In Blessedness it self we that shall miss
    Being Blind which is the Caus of Bliss.

First then behold the World as thine, and well
      Upon the Object Dwell.
See all the Beauty of the Spacious Case,
  Lift up thy pleasd and ravisht Eys,
Admire the Glory of the Heavnly place,
      And all its Blessings prize.
That Sight well seen thy Spirit shall prepare,
  The first makes all the other Rare.

Men's Woes shall be but foyls unto thy Bliss,
      Thou once Enjoying this:
Trades shall adorn and Beautify the Earth,
  Their Ignorance shall make thee Bright,
Were not their Griefs Democritus his Mirth?
      Their Faults shall keep thee right.
All shall be thine, becaus they all Conspire,
  To feed and make thy Glory higher.

To see a Glorious Fountain and an End
      To see all Creatures tend
To thy Advancement, and so sweetly close
  In thy Repose: To see them shine
In Use in Worth in Service, and even Foes
      Among the rest made thine.
To see all these unite at once in Thee
  Is to behold Felicitie.

To see the Fountain is a Blessed Thing,
      It is to see the King
Of Glory face to face: But yet the End,
  The Glorious Wondrous End is more;
And yet the fountain there we Comprehend,
      The Spring we there adore.
For in the End the Fountain best is Shewn,
  As by Effects the Caus is Known.

From One, to One, in one to see All Things
      To see the King of Kings
At once in two; to see his Endless Treasures

Made all mine own, my self the End
Of all his Labors! Tis the Life of Pleasures!
To see my self His friend!
Who all things finds conjoynd in Him alone,
Sees and Enjoys the Holy one.

THOMAS TRAHERNE

Description of Chaos
from *Prince Arthur*

Almighty Vigour strove through all the Void,
And such prolifick Influence employ'd,
That ancient, barren Night did pregnant grow,
And quicken'd with the World in Embrio.
The struggling Seeds of unshap'd Matter ly,
Contending in her Womb for Victory.
No Order, Form, or Parts distinct and clear,
Did in the Crude Conception, yet appear.
Thick Darkness did the unripe Light Embrace,
That faintly glanc'd on Chaos' shady Face.
The unfledg'd Fire has no bright Wings to rise,
But scarce distinguish'd, with the Water lies.
Its sprightly, ruddy Youth not yet attain'd,
The glitt'ring Seeds, Mother of Fire, remain'd
Like golden Sands, thick scatter'd on the Shore,
Of the wild Deep, and shone in burning Oar.
In glowing Heaps the Stars lay dusky bright,
Rude and unpolish'd Balls of unwrought Light.
The Sphears pil'd up about their Poles were Furl'd,
Design'd the Swadling Bands of th'Infant World.
The Sky dispers'd, lay in Etherial Oar,
And azure Veins betray'd th'Empyreal Store.
The watry Treasures in th'unfashion'd Birth,
Lay in the rough Embraces of the Earth;
But at the great Command will Thaw, and throw
The Dross off, and like melted Metals flow.

Besides vast numbers of loose Atoms stray,
And in the restless Deep of Chaos play.
In dark Encounters they for Empire strive,
And gain what Chance, and wild Confusion give,
Which joyntly here possess the Sov'raign Sway,
Pleas'd with those Subjects most, that least Obey.
Order, a banish'd Rebel, flies the Place,
And Strife and Uproar fill the noisy Space.
Tumult and Misrule please at Chaos' Court,
And everlasting Wars his Throne Support.
Troops arm'd with Heat have here a Battel won,
But Moist and Cold the Victor soon dethrone.
Here heavier Seeds rush on in numerous Swarms,
And crush their Lighter Foes, with pond'rous Arms.
The Lighter strait Command with equal Pride,
And on wild Whirlwinds in mad Triumph ride.
None long submits to a Superior Power,
Each yields, and in his turn is Conquerour.
If some grown mild from fierce Contention cease,
And with calm Neighbours court a separate Peace;
If Truce they make, and in kind Leagues combine,
Their short Embraces some rude Shocks disjoyn.

SIR RICHARD BLACKMORE

Description of Chaos
from *Paradise Lost*, Book 2

Before thir eyes in sudden view appear
The secrets of the hoarie deep, a dark
Illimitable Ocean without bound,
Without dimension, where length, breadth, and highth,
And time and place are lost; where eldest Night
And *Chaos*, Ancestors of Nature, hold
Eternal *Anarchie*, amidst the noise
Of endless warrs, and by confusion stand.
For hot, cold, moist, and dry, four Champions fierce
Strive here for Maistrie, and to Battel bring

74

Thir embryon Atoms; they around the flag
Of each his faction, in thir several Clanns,
Light-arm'd or heavy, sharp, smooth, swift or slow,
Swarm populous, unnumber'd as the Sands
Of *Barca* or *Cyrene*'s* torrid soil,
Levied to side with warring Winds, and poise
Thir lighter wings. To whom these most adhere,
Hee rules a moment; *Chaos* Umpire sits,
And by decision more imbroiles the fray
By which he Reigns: next him high Arbiter
Chance governs all. Into this wilde Abyss,
The Womb of nature and perhaps her Grave,
Of neither Sea, nor Shore, nor Air, nor Fire,
But all these in thir pregnant causes mixt
Confus'dly, and which thus must ever fight,
Unless th'Almighty Maker them ordain
His dark materials to create more Worlds,
Into this wilde Abyss the warie fiend
Stood on the brink of Hell and look'd a while,
Pondering his Voyage; for no narrow frith
He had to cross. Nor was his eare less peal'd
With noises loud and ruinous (to compare
Great things with small) than when *Bellona*† storms,
With all her battering Engines bent to rase
Som Capital City, or less than if this frame
Of Heav'n were falling, and these Elements
In mutinie had from her Axle torn
The stedfast Earth. At last his Sail-broad Vannes
He spreads for flight, and in the surging smoak
Uplifted spurns the ground, thence many a League
As in a cloudy Chair ascending rides
Audacious, but that seat soon failing, meets
A vast vacuitie: all unawares
Fluttring his pennons vain plumb down he drops
Ten thousand fadom deep, and to this hour

*Neighbouring states situated on the Mediterranean coast between
Egypt and Carthage.
†Roman goddess of War.

Down had been falling, had not by ill chance
The strong rebuff of som tumultuous cloud
Instinct with Fire and Nitre hurried him
As many miles aloft: that furie stay'd,
Quencht in a Boggie *Syrtis*,* neither Sea,
Nor good dry Land: nigh founderd on he fares,
Treading the crude consistence, half on foot,
Half flying; behoves him now both Oare and Saile.
As when a Gryfon through the Wilderness
With winged course ore Hill or moarie Dale,
Pursues the *Arimaspian*,† who by stelth
Had from his wakeful custody purloind
The guarded Gold: So eagerly the fiend
Ore bog or steep, through strait, rough, dense, or rare,
With head, hands, wings, or feet pursues his way,
And swims or sinks, or wades, or creeps, or flyes ...

JOHN MILTON

Three Songs from
The Pilgrim's Progress

I

Who would true Valour see,
Let him come hither;
One here will Constant be,
Come Wind, come Weather.
There's no *Discouragement*,
Shall make him once *Relent*,
His first avow'd *Intent*,
To be a Pilgrim.

*Quicksand. From the ancient name of two dangerous gulfs on the
southern shore of the Mediterranean (mod. Gulf of Qabes and Gulf of
Sidra).

†The griffins, half lion and half eagle, possessed hoards of gold
which the Arimaspi, a one-eyed race living in the extreme North of the
habitable world, were continually trying to steal.

Who so beset him round,
With dismal *Storys*,
Do but themselves Confound;
His Strength the *more is*.
No *Lyon* can him fright,
He'l with a *Gyant* Fight,
But he will have a right,
To be a Pilgrim.

Hobgoblin, nor foul *Fiend*,
Can *daunt* his Spirit:
He knows, he *at the end*,
Shall Life Inherit.
Then Fancies fly away,
He'l fear not what men say,
He'l labor Night and Day,
To be a Pilgrim.

II

The Shepherd's Boy's Song

He that is down, needs fear no fall,
He that is low, no Pride:
He that is humble, ever shall
Have God to be his Guide.

I am content with what I have,
Little be it, or much:
And, Lord, contentment still I crave,
Because thou savest such.

Fulness to such a burden is
That go on Pilgrimage:
Here little, and hereafter Bliss,
Is best from Age to Age.

III

What Danger is the Pilgrim in?
How many are his Foes?
How many ways there are to Sin?
No living Mortal knows.

Some of the Ditch, shy are, yet can
Lie tumbling in the Myre.
Some tho they shun the Frying-pan,
Do leap into the Fire.

JOHN BUNYAN

The Reply

Since you desire of me to know
Who's the Wise man, I'll tell you who.
Not he whose rich and fertile mind
Is by the Culture of the Arts refin'd,
Who has the Chaos of disorder'd thought
By Reason's Light to Form and method brought;
Who with a clear and piercing sight
Can see through nicetys as dark as night.
You err, if you think this is He,
Tho seated on the top of the *Porphyrian* tree.*

Nor is it He to whom kind Heaven
A secret *Cabala* has given
T'unriddle the mysterious Text
Of Nature, with dark Comments more perplext,
Or to decypher her clean-writ and fair
But most confounding puzling character;
That can through all her windings trace
This slippery wanderer, and unveil her face,
Her inmost Mechanism view,
Anatomize each part, and see her through and through.

*A diagram devised by the philosopher Porphyrius (A.D. 233–*c.* 301)
to represent the logical structure of the Aristotelian definition of man.

Nor he that does the Science know,
Our only Certainty below,
That can from Problems dark and nice
Deduce Truths worthy of a Sacrifice.
Nor he that can confess the stars, and see
What's writ in the black leaves of Destiny;
That knows their laws, and how the Sun
His dayly and his annual stage does run,
As if he did to them dispense
Their Motions, and there sate supream Intelligence.

Nor is it he (altho he boast
Of wisdom, and seem wise to most)
Yet 'tis not he, whose busy pate
Can dive into the deep intrigues of State;
That can the great Leviathan controul,
Menage and rule't, as if he were its soul.
The wisest King thus gifted was
And yet did not in these true Wisdom place.
Who then is by the Wise man meant?
He that can want all this, and yet can be content.

JOHN NORRIS

Blisse

All Blisse
Consists in this,
To do as Adam did:
And not to know those Superficial Toys
Which in the Garden once were hid.
Those little new Invented Things,
Cups, Saddles, Crowns are Childish Joys
So Ribbans are and Rings,
Which all our Happiness destroys.

Nor God
In his Abode
Nor Saints nor little Boys
Nor Angels made them: only foolish Men,
 Grown mad with Custom on those Toys
 Which more increas their Wants do dote,
 And when they Older are do then
  Those Bables chiefly note
 With Greedier Eys, more Boys tho Men.

THOMAS TRAHERNE

From *Religio Laici*

Dim, as the borrow'd beams of Moon and Stars
To *lonely*, *weary*, *wandring* Travellers,
Is *Reason* to the *Soul*: And as on high,
Those rowling Fires *discover* but the Sky
Not light us *here*; So *Reason*'s glimmering Ray
Was lent, not to *assure* our *doubtfull* way,
But *guide* us upward to a *better Day*.
And as those nightly Tapers disappear
When Day's bright Lord ascends our Hemisphere;
So pale grows *Reason* at *Religion*'s sight;
So *dyes*, and so *dissolves* in *Supernatural Light*.
Some few, whose Lamp shone brighter, have been
   led
From Cause to Cause, to *Nature*'s secret head;
And found that *one first principle* must be:
But *what*, or *who*, that UNIVERSAL HE;
Whether some *Soul* incompassing this Ball
Unmade, unmov'd; yet *making, moving All*;
Or various *Atom*'s interfering Dance
Leapt into *Form* (the Noble work of Chance)
Or this great *All* was from *Eternity*;
Not ev'n the *Stagirite** himself could see;
And *Epicurus Guess*'d as well as He:

*Aristotle, so called from his birthplace, Stageira.

As *blindly grop*'d they for a *future State*;
As *rashly Judg*'d of *Providence* and *Fate*:
But least of all could their Endeavours find
What most concern'd the good of Human kind:
For *Happiness* was never to be found;
But vanish'd from 'em, like Enchanted ground.
One thought *Content* the Good to be enjoy'd:
This, every little *Accident* destroy'd:
The *wiser Madmen* did for *Vertue* toyl:
A Thorny, or at best a barren Soil:
In *Pleasure* some their glutton Souls would steep; ⎫
But found their Line too short, the Well too deep; ⎬
And leaky Vessels which no *Bliss* cou'd keep. ⎭
Thus, *anxious Thoughts* in *endless Circles* roul,
Without a *Centre* where to fix the *Soul*:
In this wilde Maze their vain Endeavours end.
How can the *less* the *Greater* comprehend?
Or *finite Reason* reach *Infinity*?
For what cou'd *Fathom GOD* were *more* than *He*.

JOHN DRYDEN

From *The Philosopher's Disquisition directed to the Dying Christian*

Tell me, why Heav'n at first did suffer Sin?
  Letting Seed grow which it had never sown?
Why, when the Soule's first Fever did begin,
  Was it not cur'd, which now a Plague is grown?

Why did not Heav'n's prevention Sin restraine?
  Or is not Pow'r's permission a consent?
Which is in Kings as much as to ordaine;
  And ills ordain'd are free from punishment.

And since no Crime could be e're Lawes were fram'd;
    Lawes dearly taught us how to know offence;
Had Lawes not been, we never had been blam'd;
    For not to know we sin, is innocence.

Sin's Childhood was not starv'd, but rather more
    Than finely fed; so sweet were pleasures made
That nourisht it: for sweet is lust of Pow'r,
    And sweeter, Beauty, which hath power betray'd.

Sin, which at fullest growth is childish still,
    Would but for pleasure's company decay;
As sickly Children thrive that have their will;
    But quickly languish being kept from play.

Since only pleasure breeds sin's appetite;
    Which still by pleasant objects is infus'd;
Since 'tis provok'd to what it doth commit;
    And ills provokt may plead to be excus'd;

Why should our Sins, which not a moment last,
    (For, to Eternity compar'd, extent
Of Life, is, e're we name it, stopt and past)
    Receive a doome of endless punishment?

If Soules to Hell's vast Prison never come
    Committed for their Crimes, but destin'd be,
Like Bondmen born, whose prison is their home,
    And long e're they were bound could not be free;

Then hard is Destinie's dark Law, whose Text
    We are forbid to read, yet must obey;
And reason with her useless eyes is vext,
    Which strive to guide her where they see no way.

Doth it our Reason's mutinies appease,
    To say, the Potter may his own Clay mould
To ev'ry use, or in what shape he please,
    At first not councell'd, nor at last controul'd?

Pow'r's hand can neither easie be nor strict
  To lifeless Clay, which ease nor torment knows;
And where it cannot favour nor afflict,
  It neither Justice nor Injustice shows.

But Soules have life, and life eternal too;
  Therefore if doom'd before they can offend,
It seems to shew what Heavenly power can do,
  But does not in that deed that Pow'r commend.

That we are destin'd after Death to more
  Than Reason thinks due punishment for Sins;
Seemes possible, because in life, before
  We know to sin, our punishment begins.

Why else do Infants with incessant cries
  Complaine of secret harme as soon as born?
Or why are they, in Cities' destinies,
  So oft by Warr from ravisht Mothers torne?

Doth not belief of being destin'd draw
  Our Reason to Presumption or dispaire?
If Destiny be not, like human Law,
  To be repeal'd, what is the use of Prayer?

Why even to all was Prayer enjoyn'd? since those
  Whom God (whose will ne'r alters) did elect
Are sure of Heaven; and when we Pray it shows
  That we his certainty of will suspect.

Those who to lasting darkness destin'd were,
  Though soon as born they pray, yet pray too late:
Avoidless ills we to no purpose feare;
  And none, when fear is past, will Supplicate.

SIR WILLIAM DAVENANT

From *To the Duke of* Buckingham, *a Man of a great Mind, reduc'd to a little Fortune*

He is not Great who gives to others Law,
But He whose Patience can his Passions awe;
Who best his worst State still can undergo,
And Constancy in Change of Fortunes shew;
Who, in his great Adversities, can find
Sure Happiness in an unshaken Mind.
Such still art Thou, and such thy happy State,
Above the Injuries of grinding Fate:
Secure of Soul, thou can'st all Fortune brave,
Scorning to be false Expectation's Slave.
No flatt'ring Hopes can thy firm Peace defeat,
Hopes, that like Shadows, when pursu'd, retreat!
To Thee external Accidents are Sport,
Who fear'st not Fate, and do'st disdain to court.
Thou then art like a God, who owes to None
His Happiness but to Himself alone.

WILLIAM WYCHERLEY

To the Honourable Charles Montague, *Esq.*

Howe'r, 'tis well, that whilst Mankind,
    Thro' Fate's Fantastick Mazes errs,
He can imagin'd Pleasures find,
    To combat against real Cares.

Fancies and Notions we pursue,
    Which ne'er had Being but in thought;
And like the doting Artist woo,
    The Image we our selves have wrought.

Against Experience we believe,
  And argue against Demonstration;
Pleas'd that we can our selves deceive,
  And set our Judgment by our Passion.

The hoary Fool who many Days,
  Has strugled with continued Sorrow,
Renews his Hope, and blindly lays
  The desp'rate Bett upon to Morrow.

To Morrow comes, 'tis Noon, 'tis Night,
  The Day like all the former fled;
Yet on he runs to seek Delight
  To Morrow, till to Night he's dead.

Our Hopes like tow'ring Falcons aim
  At Objects in an Airy height,
But all the Pleasure of the Game,
  Is afar off to view the Flight.

The worthless Prey but only shows,
  The Joy consisted in the Strife;
What-e're we take, as soon we lose,
  In *Homer*'s Riddle, and in Life.

So whilst in Fev'rish Sleeps we think
  We taste what waking we desire;
The Dream is better than the Drink,
  Which only feeds the sickly Fire.

To the Mind's Eye things well appear,
  At distance through an Artful Glass;
Bring but the flattering Objects near,
  They're all a senseless gloomy Mass.

Seeing aright, we see our Woes,
 Then what avails it to have Eyes?
From Ignorance our Comfort flows,
 The only wretched are the Wise.

We wearied should lie down in Death,
 This Cheat of Life would take no more;
If you thought Fame but Stinking Breath,
 And *Phillis* but a perjur'd Whore.

MATTHEW PRIOR

Plain Dealing's Downfall

Long time plain dealing in the Hauty Town,
Wandring about, though in thread-bare Gown,
At last unanimously was cry'd down.

When almost starv'd, she to the Countrey fled,
In hopes, though meanly she shou'd there be fed,
And tumble Nightly on a Pea-straw Bed.

But Knav'ry knowing her intent, took post,
And Rumour'd her approach through every Coast,
Vowing his Ruin that shou'd be her host.

Frighted at this, each *Rustick* shut his door,
Bid her be gone, and trouble him no more,
For he that entertain'd her must be poor.

At this grief seiz'd her, grief too great to tell,
When weeping, sighing, fainting, down she fell,
Whilst Knavery Laughing, Rung her passing Bell.

JOHN WILMOT, EARL OF ROCHESTER

Of the last Verses in the Book

When we for Age could neither read nor write,
The Subject made us able to indite.
The Soul with Nobler Resolutions deckt,
The Body stooping, does Herself erect:
No Mortal Parts are requisite to raise
Her, that Unbody'd can her Maker praise.

The Seas are quiet, when the Winds give o're;
So calm are we, when Passions are no more:
For then we know how vain it was to boast
Of fleeting Things, so certain to be lost.
Clouds of Affection from our younger Eyes
Conceal that emptiness, which Age descries.

The Soul's dark Cottage, batter'd and decay'd,
Lets in new Light thrô chinks that time has made
Stronger by weakness, wiser Men become
As they draw near to their Eternal home:
Leaving the Old, both Worlds at once they view,
That stand upon the Threshold of the New.

Miratur Limen Olympi.
Virgil

EDMUND WALLER*

*The punctuation of the last stanza is that of the earliest printed version in the fifth edition of Waller's *Poems* (1686). Modern editors have preferred to add a full stop at the end of the second line.

The Chroniclers

From *A Poem upon the Death of His late Highnesse the Lord Protector*

I saw him dead, a leaden slumber lyes
And mortall sleep over those wakefull eys:
Those gentle Rayes under the lidds were fled
Which through his lookes that piercing sweetnesse shed:
That port which so Majestique was and strong,
Loose and depriv'd of vigour stretch'd along:
All wither'd, all discolour'd, pale and wan,
How much another thing, no more that man?
Oh human glory vaine, Oh death, Oh wings,
Oh worthlesse world, Oh transitory things!

   Yet dwelt that greatnesse in his shape decay'd
That still though dead greater than death he layd.
And in his alter'd face you something faigne
That threatens death he yet will live againe.

   Not much unlike the sacred Oake which shoots
To heav'n its branches and through earth its roots:
Whose spacious boughs are hung with Trophees round
And honour'd wreaths have oft the Victour crown'd.
When angry Jove darts lightning through the Aire
At mortalls' sins, nor his own plant will spare
(It groanes and bruses all below that stood
So many yeares the shelter of the wood)
The tree ere while foreshorten'd to our view
When faln shews taller yet than as it grew.

   So shall his praise to after times increase
When truth shall be allow'd and faction cease,
And his own shadows with him fall. The Eye
Detracts from objects than it selfe more high:
But when death takes them from that envy'd seate
Seing how little we confesse how greate.

   Thee many ages hence in martiall verse
Shall th'English souldier ere he charge rehearse:
Singing of thee inflame themselvs to fight

And with the name of Cromwell armyes fright.
As long as rivers to the seas shall runne,
As long as Cynthia shall relieve the sunne,
While staggs shall fly unto the forests thick,
While sheep delight the grassy downs to pick,
As long as future time succeeds the past,
Always thy honour, praise and name shall last.
   Thou in a pitch how farre beyond the sphere
Of human glory towr'st, and raigning there
Despoyld of mortall robes, in seas of blisse
Plunging dost bathe, and tread the bright Abysse:
There thy greate soule yet once a world dos see
Spacious enough and pure enough for thee.
How soon thou Moses hast and Joshua found
And David for the sword, and harpe renown'd?
How streight canst to each happy Mansion goe?
(Farr better known above than here below)
And in those joyes dost spend the endlesse day
Which in expressing we our selves betray.
   For we since thou art gone with heavy doome
Wander like ghosts about thy loved tombe:
And lost in tears have neither sight nor minde
To guide us upward through this Region blinde:
Since thou art gone who best that way could'st teach
Onely our sighs perhaps may thither reach.

ANDREW MARVELL

News from Colchester

Or, a Proper new Ballad of certain Carnal passages
betwixt a Quaker *and a* Colt,
at Horsly *near* Colchester *in Essex*

To the Tune of, Tom of Bedlam

All in the Land of *Essex*,
Near *Colchester* the Zealous,
    On the side of a bank,
    Was play'd such a Prank,
As would make a Stone-horse jealous.

Help *Woodcock*, *Fox* and *Nailor*,
For Brother *Green*'s a Stallion,
    Now alas what hope
    Of converting the Pope,
When a Quaker turns *Italian*?

Even to our whole profession
A scandal 'twill be counted,
    When 'tis talkt with disdain
    Amongst the Profane,
How brother *Green* was mounted.

And in the Good time of Christmas,
Which though our Saints have damn'd all,*
    Yet when did they hear
    That a damn'd Cavalier
Ere play'd such a Christmas gambal?

* The puritans had tried to suppress the popular festivities associated
with Christmas.

Had thy flesh, O *Green*, been pamper'd
With any Cates unhallow'd,
    Hadst thou sweetned thy Gums
    With Pottage of Plums,
Or prophane minc'd Pie hadst swallow'd,

Roll'd up in wanton Swine's-flesh,
The Fiend might have crept into thee;
    Then fullness of gut
    Might have caus'd thee to rut,
And the Devil have so rid through thee.

But alas he had been feasted
With a Spiritual Collation,
    By our frugal Mayor,
    Who can dine on a Prayer,
And sup on an Exhortation.

'Twas meer impulse of Spirit,
Though he us'd the weapon carnal:
    Filly Foal, quoth he,
    My Bride thou shalt be:
And how this is lawful, learn all.

For if no respect of Persons
Be due 'mongst the Sons of *Adam*,
    In a large extent,
    Thereby may be meant
That a *Mare*'s as good as a *Madam*.

Then without more Ceremony,
Not Bonnet vail'd, nor kist her,
    But took her by force,
    For better for worse,
And us'd her like a Sister.

Now when in such a Saddle
A Saint will needs be riding,
    Though we dare not say
    'Tis a falling away,
May there not be some back-sliding?

No surely, quoth *James Naylor*,*
'Twas but an insurrection
    Of the Carnal part,
    For a Quaker in heart
Can never lose perfection.

For (as our Masters teach us)   *The Jesuites.*
The intent being well directed,
    Though the Devil trepan
    The Adamical man,
The Saint stands un-infected.

But alas a Pagan Jury
Ne're judges what's intended,
    Then say what we can,
    Brother *Green*'s outward man
I fear will be suspended.

And our Adopted Sister
Will find no better quarter,
    But when him we inroul
    For a Saint, Filly Foal
Shall pass her self for a Martyr.

Rome that Spiritual *Sodom*,
No longer is thy debter,
    O *Colchester*, now
    Who's *Sodom* but thou,
Even according to the Letter?

SIR JOHN DENHAM

*Quaker extremist (1617?–60), found guilty of 'horrid blasphemy'
in 1656.

From *Jter Boreale*

I, he, who whileom sate and sung in Cage,
My King's and Country's Ruines, by the rage
Of a rebellious Rout: Who weeping saw
Three goodly Kingdoms (drunk with fury) draw
And sheath their Swords (like three enraged Brothers)
In one another's sides, ripping their Mother's
Belly, and tearing out her bleeding heart;
Then jealous that their Father fain would part
Their bloody Fray, and let them fight no more,
Fell foul on him, and slew him at his dore.
I that have only dar'd to whisper Verses,
And drop a tear (by stealth) on loyal Herses,
I that enraged at the *Times* and *Rump,*
Had gnaw'd my Goose-quill to the very stump,
And flung that in the fire, no more to write
But to sit down poor *Britain*'s *Heraclyte*;*
Now sing the tryumphs of the Men of War,
The glorious rayes of the bright Northern Star,
Created for the nonce by Heaven, to bring
The Wisemen of three Nations to their King:
MONCK! the great *Monck*!† That syllable out-shines
Plantagenet's bright name, or *Constantine*'s.
'Twas at his Rising that *Our Day* begun,
Be He the *Morning Star* to *Charles* our *Sun*:
He took Rebellion rampant, by the Throat,
And made the Canting *Quaker* change his Note;
His Hand it was that wrote (we saw no more)
Exit Tyrannus over *Lambert*'s‡ dore:

*i.e. Heraclitus, the weeping philosopher of antiquity.
† George Monck (1608–70), commander of the army of Scotland
and subsequently first Duke of Albermarle, was the most important
single agent in bringing about the Restoration. His forces reached
London in February 1660.
‡ Major-General John Lambert (1619–83) had unsuccessfully tried to
oppose Monck's march on London.

Like to some subtile Lightning, so his words
Dissolved in their Scabbards Rebels' swords:
He with success the soveraign skill hath found,
To dress the Weapon, and so heal the Wound.
   George, and his Boyes (as Spirits do, they say)
   Only by Walking scare our Foes away.

ROBERT WILD

On the Fair Weather just at the Coronation, it having rained immediately before and after

So clear a season, and so snatch'd from storms,
Shews Heav'n delights to see what Man performs.
Well knew the Sun, if such a day were dim,
It would have been an injury to him:
For then a Cloud had from his eye conceal'd
The noblest sight that ever he beheld.
He therefore check'd th'invading Rains we fear'd,
And in a bright *Parenthesis* appear'd.
So that we knew not which look'd most content,
The King, the People, or the Firmament.
But the Solemnity once fully past,
The storm return'd with an impetuous hast.
And Heav'n and Earth each other to out-do,
Vied both in Cannons and in Fire-works too.
So *Israel* past through the divided floud,
While in obedient heaps the Ocean stood:
But the same Sea (the *Hebrews* once on shore)
Return'd in torrents where it was before.

ORINDA
(*Katherine Philips*)

The Cavalier

We have ventur'd our estates,
    And our liberties and lives,
For our Master and his mates,
And been toss'd by cruel fates,
   Where the rebellious Devil drives,
   So that not one of ten survives.
     We have laid all at stake
     For his Majesty's sake,
     We have fought, we have paid,
     We've been sold and betray'd,
And tumbled from nation to nation:
     But now those are thrown down
     That usurped the Crown,
     Our hopes were that we
     All rewarded should be,
But we're paid with a Proclamation.

Now the times are turn'd about,
    And the Rebels race is run:
That many headed beast, the Rout,
Who did turn the Father out
   When they saw they were undon,
   Were for bringing in the Son.
     That phanatical crue
     Which made us all rue,
     Have got so much wealth,
     By their plunder and stealth,
That they creep into profit and power:
     And so come what will,
     They'll be uppermost still;
     And we that are low,
     Shall still be kept so
While those domineer and devour.

Yet we will be loyal still,
   And serve without reward or hire,
To be redeem'd from so much ill,
May stay our stomacks, though not fill;
   And if our patience do not tire,
   We may in time have our desire.

ALEXANDER BROME

The Retirement

Pindarique Ode made in the time of the Great Sickness 1665

In the milde close of an hot Summers day,
   When a cool Breeze had fann'd the air,
   And Heaven's face lookt smooth and fair;
   Lovely as sleeping Infants be,
   That in their slumbers smiling ly,
     Dandled on the Mother's knee,
       You hear no cry,
     No harsh, nor inharmonious voice,
But all is innocence without a noise:
When every sweet, which the Sun's greedy ray
   So lately from us drew,
Began to trickle down again in dew;
   Weary, and faint, and full of thought,
   Tho for what cause I knew not well,
   What I ail'd, I could not tell,
I sate me down at an ag'd Poplar's root,
Whose chiding leaves excepted and my breast,
All the impertinently-busi'd-world enclin'd to rest.

   I list'ned heedfully around,
   But not a whisper there was found.
   The murmuring Brook hard by,
     As heavy, and as dull as I,

Seem'd drowsily along to creep;
  It ran with undiscovered pace,
And if a pibble stopt the lazy race,
'Twas but as if it started in its sleep.
Eccho her self, that ever lent an ear
    To any piteous moan;
    Wont to grone, with them that grone,
    Eccho her self, was speechless here.
  Thrice did I sigh, Thrice miserably cry,
  Ai me! the *Nymph* ai me! would not reply,
Or churlish, or she was asleep for company.

   I thought on every pensive thing,
    That might my passion strongly move,
    That might the sweetest sadness bring;
Oft did I think on death, and oft on Love,
The triumphs of the *little God*, and that same *ghastly King.*
    The ghastly King, what has he done?
    How his pale Territories spread!
Strait scantlings now of consecrated ground
    His swelling Empire cannot bound,
But every day new *Colonies* of dead
Enhance his Conquests, and advance his Throne.
The mighty *City* sav'd from storms of war,
    Exempted from the Crimson floud,
  When all the Land o'reflow'd with blood,
Stoops yet once more to a new Conqueror:
    The *City* which so many Rivals bred,
Sackcloth is on her loyns, and ashes on her head.

When will the frowning heav'n begin to smile;
    Those pitchy clouds be overblown,
    That hide the mighty Town,
    That I may see the mighty pyle?
When will the angry Angel cease to slay;
    And turn his brandisht sword away
    From that illustrous *Golgotha*,

London, the great *Aceldama*?*
When will that stately *Landscape* open lie,
The mist withdrawn that intercepts my ey?
    That heap of *Pyramids* appear,
Which now, too much like those of *Egypt* are:
    Eternal Monuments of Pride and Sin,
Magnificent and tall without, but Dead men's bones
    within.

THOMAS FLATMAN

From *Annus Mirabilis*

The warlike Prince† had sever'd from the rest
    Two giant ships, the pride of all the Main;
Which, with his one, so vigorously he press'd,
    And flew so home they could not rise again.

Already batter'd, by his Lee they lay,
    In vain upon the passing winds they call:
The passing winds through their torn canvass play,
    And flagging sails on heartless Sailors fall.

Their open'd sides receive a gloomy light,
    Dreadful as day let in to shades below:
Without, grim death rides bare-fac'd in their sight,
    And urges ent'ring billows as they flow.

When one dire shot, the last they could supply,
    Close by the board the Prince's Main-mast bore:
All three now, helpless, by each other lie,
    And this offends not, and those fear no more.

*The 'field of blood' purchased with the thirty pieces of silver returned by Judas.
† Prince Rupert. An incident from the Four Days Battle, June 1666.

So have I seen some fearful Hare maintain
    A Course, till tir'd before the Dog she lay:
Who, stretch'd behind her, pants upon the plain,
    Past pow'r to kill as she to get away.

With his loll'd tongue he faintly licks his prey,
    His warm breath blows her flix up as she lies:
She, trembling, creeps upon the ground away,
    And looks back to him with beseeching eyes.

JOHN DRYDEN

London mourning in Ashes;

OR, *Lamentable Narrative lively expressing the Ruine
of that Royal City by fire which began in* Pudding-
lane *on* September *the second,* 1666. *at one of the
clock in the morning being* Sunday, *and continuing until*
Thursday *night following, being the sixth day, with the
great care the King, and the Duke of York took in their
own Persons, day and night to quench it.*

The Tune, *In sad and ashy weeds.*

Of Fire, Fire, Fire I sing,
    that have more cause to cry,
In the Great Chamber of the King
    (a City mounted High);
Old *London* that,
Hath stood in State,
    above six hundred years,
In six days space,
Woe and alas!
    is burn'd and drown'd in tears.

The second of *September* in
    the middle time of night,

In *Pudding-lane* it did begin,
 to burn and blaze out right;
Where all that gaz'd,
Were so amaz'd,
 at such a furious flame,
They knew not how,
Or what to do
 that might expel the same.

It swallow'd *Fishstreet hil*, and straight
 it lick'd up *Lombard-street*,
Down *Canon-street* in blazing State
 it flew with flaming feet;
Down to the *Thames*
   Whose shrinking streams,
    began to ebb away;
   As thinking that,
   The power of Fate
    had brought the latter day.

Eurus the God of *Eastern* Gales
 was *Vulcan*'s Bellows now,
And did so fill the flagrant sayls,
 that High-built Churches bow;
The Leads they bear,
Drop'd many a Tear,
 to see their Fabricks burn;
The sins of Men,
Made Churches then,
 in Dust and Ashes mourn.

The second part to the same Tune.

With hand and feet, in every street,
 they pack up Goods and fly,
Pitch, Tarr, and Oyl, increase the spoyl
 old *Fishstreet* 'gins to frye;

The Fire doth range,
Up to the *Change*,
   and every King commands,
But in despight,
Of all its might,
   the stout old Founder stands.*

Out of the Shops the Goods are tane,
   and hal'd from every shelf,
(As in a Shipwrack) every man
   doth seek to save himself;
The Fire so hot,
A strength hath got,
   No water can prevail;
An hundred Tun
Were it powr'd on,
   would prove but like a Pail.

The Crackling flames do fume and roar,
   as Billows do retyre,
The City (though upon the shoar)
   doth seem a sea of fire;
Where Steeple Spires,
Shew in the Fires,
   like Vessels sinking down.
The open fields,
More safety yields,
   and thither fly the Town.

Up to the head of aged *Pauls*
   the flame doth fluttering flye,
Above a hundred thousand souls
   upon the ground do lye;
Sick souls and lame,
All flie the flame,
   women with Child we know,

*Sir Thomas Gresham, whose statue in the Royal Exchange
survived when those of the kings of England were destroyed.

Are forc'd to run,
The fire to shun,
  have not a day to goe.

Cradles were rock'd in every field,
  and Food was all their cry,
Till the King's bowels bread did yield
  and sent them a supply;
A Father He,
Of his Countrey,
  Himself did sweetly shew,
Both day and night,
With all His might,
  He sought to ease our woe.

The King Himself in Person there,
  was, and the Duke of *York*,
And likewise many a Noble Peer,
  assisted in the Work;
To quell the ire,
Of this Wild fire,
  whose Army was so high,
And did invade,
So that it made,
  ten hundred thousand fly.

From *Sunday* morn, till *Thursday* at night,
  it roar'd about the Town,
There was no way to quell its might
  but to pull Houses down;
And so they did,
As they were bid
  By *Charles*, His Great Command;
The Duke of *York*,
Some say did work,
  with Bucket in his hand.

At *Temple Church* and *Holborn-bridge*,
   and *Pyecorner* 'tis stench'd,
The Water did the Fire besiege,
   At *Aldersgate* it quench'd;
At *Criplegate*
(Though very late)
   And eke at *Coleman-street*,
At *Basing-hall*
The Fire did fall,
   we all were joy'd to see't.

Bishopsgate-street to *Cornhill* end,
   And *Leaden-hall*'s secure,
It to the *Postern* did extend,
   Fanchurch doth still endure;
Clothworkers-Hall,
Did (ruin'd) fall,
   yet stop'd the fire's haste;
Mark-lane, *Tower-dock*,
Did stand the shock,
   And all is quench'd at last.

Many of *French* and *Dutch* were stop'd
   and also are confin'd,
'Tis said that they their Fire-balls drop'd
   and this Plot was design'd,
By Them and Those
That are our Foes,
   yet some think nothing so;
But that our God,
With His flaming Rod,
   for Sin sends all this woe.

Although the Fire be fully quench'd
   yet if our sins remain,
And that in them we stil are drench'd,
   the Fire will rage again;

Or what is worse,
A heavier Curse,
    in Famine will appear;
Where shall we tread,
When want of Bread,
    and Hunger draweth near.

If this do not reform our lives,
    A worse thing will succeed,
Our kindred, children, and our wives,
    will dye for want of Bread;
When Famine comes,
'Tis not our Drums,
    Our Ships our Horse or Foot,
That can defend,
But if we mend,
    we never shall come to't.

Pepys Collection

The Rebirth of London
from *Annus Mirabilis*

Me-thinks already, from this Chymick flame,
    I see a City of more precious mold:
Rich as the Town which gives the *Indies* name,
    With Silver pav'd, and all divine with Gold.

Already, labouring with a mighty fate,
    She shakes the rubbish from her mounting brow,
And seems to have renew'd her Charter's date,
    Which Heav'n will to the death of time allow.

More great than human, now, and more *August*,
    New deifi'd she from her fires does rise:
Her widening streets on new foundations trust,
    And, opening, into larger parts she flies.

Before, she like some Shepherdess did show,
    Who sate to bathe her by a River's side:
Not answering to her fame, but rude and low,
    Nor taught the beauteous Arts of Modern pride.

Now, like a Maiden Queen, she will behold,
    From her high Turrets, hourly Sutors come:
The East with Incense, and the West with Gold,
    Will stand, like Suppliants, to receive her doom.

The silver *Thames*, her own domestick Floud,
    Shall bear her Vessels, like a sweeping Train;
And often wind (as of his Mistress proud)
    With longing eyes to meet her face again.

The wealthy *Tagus*, and the wealthier *Rhine*,
    The glory of their Towns no more shall boast:
And *Sein*, that would with *Belgian* Rivers joyn,*
    Shall find her lustre stain'd, and Traffick lost.

The vent'rous Merchant, who design'd more far,
    And touches on our hospitable shore:
Charm'd with the splendour of this Northern Star,
    Shall here unlade him, and depart no more.

Our pow'rful Navy shall no longer meet,
    The wealth of *France* or *Holland* to invade:
The beauty of this Town, without a Fleet,
    From all the world shall vindicate her Trade.

And, while this fam'd Emporium we prepare,
    The *British* Ocean shall such triumphs boast,
That those who now disdain our Trade to share,
    Shall rob like Pyrats on our wealthy Coast.

Already we have conquer'd half the War,
    And the less dang'rous part is left behind:
Our trouble now is but to make them dare,
    And not so great to vanquish as to find.

*An allusion to the French invasion of the Netherlands.

Thus to the Eastern wealth through storms we go;
   But now, the Cape once doubled, fear no more:
A constant Trade-wind will securely blow,
   And gently lay us on the Spicy shore.

JOHN DRYDEN

The Dutch in the Thames
from The Last Instructions to a Painter

Ruyter the while, that had our Ocean curb'd,
Sail'd now among our Rivers undisturb'd:
Survey'd their chrystall streams, and Banks so green,
And Beauties ere this never naked seen.
Through the vain Sedge, the bashfull Nymphs he ey'd:
Bosomes, and all which from themselves they hide.
The Sun much brighter, and the Skyes more cleare
He finds, the Aire, and all things, sweeter here.
The sudden change, and such a tempting Sight
Swells his old Veins with fresh Blood, fresh Delight:
Like am'rous Victors he begins to shave,
And his new Face looks in the *English* wave;
His sporting Navy all about him swim,
And witnesse their complacence in their Trimme.
Their streaming Silks play through the weather faire
And with inveigling colors court the Aire;
While the red Flaggs breath on their Top-masts high,
Terror and War, but want an Enemy.
Among the Shrowds the Seamen sit and sing,
And wanton Boyes on evry Rope do cling.
Old *Neptune* springs the Tides, and water lent:
(The *Gods* themselves do help the provident.)
And, where the deep keel on the shallow cleav's,
With *Trident*'s leaver, and great shoulder heav's.
Æolus* their sailes inspires with *Eastern* wind,
Puffs them along, and breaths upon them kind.

* The god, or more strictly guardian, of the winds. See *Odyssey*, X, 1–75.

With pearly Shell the *Tritons* all the while
Sound the Sea-march, and guide to *Sheppy Isle*.

    So have I seen, in *Aprill*'s *Bud*, arise
A Fleet of clouds sailing along the skyes:
The liquid Region with their squadrons fill'd,
Their airy Sterns the Sun behind do's guild;
And gentle gales them steere, and Heaven drives.
When, all on sudden, their calm bosom rives
With Thund'r and Lightning from each armed Clowd:
Shepheards themselvs in vain in bushes shrowd.
Such up the Stream the *Belgick* Navy glides,
And at *Sheernesse* unloads its stormy sides.
Sprag there, though practis'd in the Sea-command,
With panting Heart lay like a Fish on Land:
And quickly judg'd the Fort was not *tenable*,
Which if a House yet were not *tenantable*.
No man can sit there safe, the Canon powrs
Thorow the Walls untight, and Bullet showrs:
The neighb'rhood ill, and an unwholsome Seat.
So at the first Salute resolvs Retreat,
And swore that he would never more dwell there
Untill the *City* put it in repaire.
So he in front, his Garrison in reare,
March streight to *Chatham*, to increase the feare.

    There our sick Ships unrigg'd in Summer lay,
Like molting Fowle, a weak and easy Prey;
For whose strong bulk Earth scarce could Timber finde,
The Ocean water, or the Heavens wind:
Those Oaken Gyants of the ancient race,
That rul'd all Seas, and did our Chanell grace.
The conscious Stag, so once the Forrest's dread,
Flyes to the Wood, and hides his armlesse Head.
Ruyter forthwith a Squadron do's untack:
They saile securely through the River's track.
An *English* Pilot too (O shame, O Sin!),
Cheated of Pay, was he that show'd them in.

Our wretched Ships within their Fate attend,
And all our hopes now on fraile Chain depend:
Engine so slight to guard us from the Sea,
It fitter seem'd to captivate a Flea.
A *Skipper* rude shocks it without respect;
Filling his Sailes more force to recollect.
Th'*English* from Shore the Iron deaf invoke
For its last aid: Hold Chain or we are broke!
But with her sailing weight, the *Holland* keele
Snapping the brittle links, do's thorow reele;
And to the rest the open'd passage shew.
Monke from the bank the dismall Sight do's view.
Our feather'd Gallants, which came down that day
To be spectators safe of the new Play,
Leave him alone when first they hear the Gun;
(*Cornb'ry* the fleetest) and to *London* run.
Our Seamen, whom no Danger's shape could fright,
Unpaid refuse to mount our Ships for spight:
Or to their fellows swim on board the *Dutch*,
Which show the tempting metall in their clutch.
Oft had he sent of *Duncome* and of *Legg**

Canon and Powder but in vain to beg:
And *Upnor*-Castle's ill-defended Wall,
Now needfull, do's for ammunition call.
He finds, wheres'ere he Succor might expect,
Confusion, Folly, Treach'ry, Feare, Neglect.
But when the *Royall Charles* (what rage, what grief!)
He saw seis'd, and could give her no releif!
That sacred Keele, which had, as he, restor'd
His exil'd Soveraign on its happy board,
And thence the Brittish Admirall became;
Crown'd for that merit with their Master's Name:
That Pleasure-boat of War, in whose dear Side
Secure so oft he had this Foe defy'd:
Now a cheap spoyle, and the mean Victor's slave

*Sir John Duncombe, one of the commissioners for the office of Master of the Ordnance, and Lieutenant-General William Legge, Governor and Treasurer of the Ordnance.

Taught the *Dutch* Colors from its Top to wave;
Of former gloryes the reproachfull thought
With present shame compar'd, his Mind distraught.
Such from *Euphrates* bank, a Tygresse fell,
After the robber, for her Whelps doth Yell:
But sees inrag'd the River flow between.
Frustrate Revenge, and Love, by losse more keen,
At her own Breast, her uselesse claws do's arme:
She tears her self since him she can not harme.

ANDREW MARVELL

A Lampoon

Good people draw neare,
   If a Ballad you'l heare
Which will teach you the right way of thriving.
   Nere trouble your Heads
   With your Bookes and your Beads
Now the World's rul'd by cheating, and swiving.

If you prattle, or prate
   For Myter, or State,
It will never avayle you a Button.
   Hee, that talkes of the Church,
   Will bee left in the lurch
Without e're a tatter to putt on.

Old fatt Gutts* himselfe
   With his tripes and his pelfe,
And a purse as full as his paunch is,
   Will confesse that his Nanny
   Fob-doudled our Jamy,
And his Kingdome came by his Haunches.

*Edward Hyde, Earl of Clarendon. His daughter, Ann, was the
first wife of James, Duke of York, later James II.

Our Arlington Harry,
The prime Secretary,
Was first to the Smocke a Secretist;
He was Squire of the frocke,
And being true to the Smocke,
Now admitted to manage the State is.

And Dapper his Clarke,*
Being true to the marke,
Is boeth his Scribe, and his setter:
Now Joseph, wee heare,
Shall bee made a peere:
Lord and Lackey begin with a letter.

Our Comptroller Clifford
Was forct to stand stiff for't,
To make his way to the Table.
Hee'd a freind att a shift,
That gave him a lift.
Tom foole may thanke God for's Bauble.

'Tis well for the Babbs,†
That the pimpes, and the Drabs
Are now in high way of promotion,
Else Villers, and May
Had beene out of play:
But poore Denham went off with a potion.

Then there's Castlemaine,‡
That prerogative Queane:
If I had such a bitch, I would spay her:
Shee swives, like a stoate,
Goes to 't hand and foote,
Levell-Coyle with a prince, and a player.

                                    Bodl. MS Don. b 8.

*Sir Joseph Williamson.
  †Baptist May (1629–98), keeper of the privy purse to Charles II.
  ‡Barbara Palmer (née Villiers), Countess of Castlemaine and later
Duchess of Cleveland (1641–1709).

A Ballad call'd the Hay-Markett Hectors*

I sing a Woofull Ditty
Of a Wound that long will smart-a
Given (the more's the Pitty)
In the Realme of Magna Charta:
Youth! youth! thou'dst better be slaine by thy Foes
Than live to be hang'd for cutting a Nose.

Our good King Charles the Second
Too flipant of Treasure and moysture,
Stoop'd from the Queene infecond
To a Wench of Orange and Oyster.
Consulting his Cazzo,† he found it expedient
To engender Don Johns, on Nell the Comedian.

The leacherous vaine Glory
Of being Lim'd with Majestie
Mounts up to such a Story
This Bichington Travesty
That to equall her Lover, the Baggage must dare
To be Hellen the Second, and cause of a Warr.

And he our Amorous Jove
Whilst she lay dry-bob'd under
To repair the defects of his Love
Must send her his Lightning and Thunder,
And for one Night prostitutes to her Comands
His Mounmouth, Life-Guard, Obrian and Sands.‡

*Sir John Coventry, a member of parliament who had alluded slightingly in the House to the king's actress-mistresses, was seized in the Haymarket on 21 December 1670, by a troop of Horse-guards and his nose slit to the bone.

†i.e. penis (*Ital.*)

‡Sir Thomas Sandys and Captain Charles Obrien, the leaders of the assault on Coventry.

And now all the Feares of the French
    And pressing need of Navy
        Are dwindl'd into a Salt Wench*
    And Amo, Amas, Amavi.
Nay he'll venture his Subsidy soe she may Cloven see,
In Female Revenge, the Nose of Coventry.

       Oh yee Hay Markett Hectors
    How came yee thus Charm'd
        To be the Dissectors
    Of one poore Nose unarm'd?
Unfit to weare Sword or follow a Trumpet
That wou'd Brandish your Knives at the word of a
        Strumpet!

       But was't not ungratefull
    In Monmouth, Ap Sidney, Ap Carlo,†
        To contrive an Act soe hatefull
    O Prince of Wales by Barlow!‡
Since the kind World had dispenc'd with his Mother
Might not he well have spar'd, the Nose of John Brother?

       Beware all yee Parlim'nteers
    How each of his voyce disposes:
        Bab May in the Commons, Charles Rex in the
        Peeres
Sit telling your Fates on your Noses,
And Decree at the mention of every Slutt,
Whose Nose shall continue, and whose shall be cutt.

       If the Sister of Rose
    Be a Whore soe anoynted
        That the Parliment's Nose
    Must for her be disjoynted

---

*As in 'salt bitch', i.e. a bitch in heat.
 †Monmouth, although acknowledged by Charles, was widely
rumoured to be the son of Colonel Robert Sidney.
 ‡Lucy Barlow (née Walters), Monmouth's mother.

Shou'd you but name the Prerogative Whore,*
How the Bulletts wou'd whistle, the Cannons wou'd
Roare!

attrib. ANDREW MARVELL

Upon *Blood's attempt to Steale the Crown* (1671)

When daring Blood, his rents to have regain'd,
Upon the English Diadem distrain'd,
He chose the Cassock, surcingle, and Gown
(No mask so fit for one that robbs a Crown):
But his Lay-pity underneath prevayl'd
And while he spares the Keeper's life, he fail'd.
With the Priest's Vestments had he but put on
A Bishop's cruelty, the Crown was gone.

ANDREW MARVELL

From *Satyr II*
('Upon the Jesuits')

When the first Traitor *Cain* (too good to be
Thought Patron of this black *Fraternity*)
His bloudy Tragedy of old design'd,
One death alone quench'd his revengful mind,
Content with but a quarter of Mankind:
Had he been *Jesuit*, had he but put on
Their savage cruelty, the rest had gone:
His hand had sent old *Adam* after too,
And forc'd the Godhead to create anew.

JOHN OLDHAM

*The Duchess of Portsmouth

Loyola's Instructions to his Followers
from *Loyola's Will*
(*Satyr upon the Jesuits III*)

First, and the chiefest thing by me enjoyn'd,
The Solemn'st tie, that must your Order bind:
Let each without demur, or scruple pay
A strict Obedience to the *Roman* Sway:
To the unerring Chair all Homage Swear,
Altho' a Punk, a Witch, a Fiend sit there:
Who e're is to the Sacred Mitre rear'd,
Believe all Vertues with the place conferr'd:
Think him establish'd there by Heaven, tho' he ⎫
Has Altars rob'd for Bribes the choice to buy, ⎬
Or pawn'd his Soul to Hell for Simony: ⎭
Tho' he be Atheist, Heathen, *Turk*, or *Jew*,
Blaspheamer, Sacriligious, Perjured too:
Tho' Pander, Bawd, Pimp, Pathick, Buggerer,
What e're Old *Sodom*'s Nest of Lechers were:
Tho' Tyrant, Traitor, Pois'oner, Parricide,
Magician, Monster, all that's bad beside:
Fouler than Infamy; the very Lees,
The Sink, the Jakes, the Common-shore of Vice:
Strait count him Holy, Vertuous, Good, Devout,
Chast, Gentle, Meek, a Saint, a God, what not?
  Make Fate hang on his Lips, nor Heaven have
Pow'r to Predestinate without his leave:
None be admitted there, but who he please,
Who buys from him the Patent for the Place.
Hold these amongst the highest rank of Saints,
Whom e're he to that Honour shall advance,
Tho' here the Refuse of the Jail and Stews,
Whom Hell it self would scarce for lumber chuse:
But count all Reprobate, and Damn'd, and worse,
Whom he, when Gout, or Tissick rage, shall curse:
Whom he in anger Excommunicates

For *Fryday* Meale and abrogating Sprats,
Or in just Indignation spurnes to Hell
For jeering holy Toe and Pantofle.
    What e're he sayes esteem for Holy Writ,
And text Apocryphal if he think fit:
Let arrant Legends, worst of Tales and Lies,
Falser than *Capgrave*'s and *Voragine*'s,*
Than *Quixot*, *Rablais*, *Amadis de Gaul*,
If signed with Sacred Lead, and Fisher's Seal, }
Be thought Authentick and Canonical.
Again, if he ordain't in his Decrees,
Let very Gospel for meer Fable pass:
 Let Right be Wrong, Black White, and Vertue Vice,
No Sun, no Moon, nor no Antipodes:
Forswear your Reason, Conscience, and your Creed,
Your very Sense, and *Euclid*, if he bid.

JOHN OLDHAM

On Rome's Pardons

If *Rome* can pardon Sins, as *Romans* hold,
And if those *Pardons* can be bought and sold,
It were no Sin, t'adore and worship *Gold*.

If they can purchase *Pardons* with a Sum,
For Sins they may commit in time to come,
And for Sins past, 'tis very well for *Rome*.

At this rate they are happy'st that have most;
They'll purchase *Heav'n* at their own proper cost,
Alas! the Poor! all that are so are lost.

* John Capgrave (1393–1464) and Jacobus a Voragine (1230–98),
compilers of collections of church legends and saints' lives.

Whence came this knack, or when did it begin?
What *Author* have they, or who brought it in?
Did *Christ* e're keep a *Custom-house* for Sin?

Some subtle *Devil*, without more ado,
Did certainly this sly invention brew,
To gull 'em of their *Souls*, and *Money* too.

attrib. JOHN WILMOT, EARL OF ROCHESTER

From *Absalom and Achitophel*

From hence began that Plot; the Nation's Curse,
Bad in it self, but represented worse.
Rais'd in extremes, and in extremes decry'd;
With Oaths affirm'd, with dying Vows deny'd.
Not weigh'd, or winnow'd by the Multitude;
But swallow'd in the Mass, unchew'd and Crude.
Some Truth there was, but dash'd and brew'd with
    Lyes;
To please the Fools, and puzzle all the Wise.
Succeeding times did equal folly call,
Believing nothing, or believing all.

JOHN DRYDEN

From *The Affections of my Soul, after Judgment given against me in a Court of Justice, upon the Evidence of False Witnesses*

O Father of Mercy,
Behold thy Child, who hath been a Prodigal;
Who, having wasted all his Goods,
And spent his time in Vanity,
Drawn by thy Grace and Love,
Is now returning to thy house,

And humbly begs for Pardon at thy hands.
    Alas!
I have lived as without reason,
Since first I had the use of reason;
I have done nothing of my self but evil,
From the time that I first knew what Good was;
I have sinned against Heaven, and against thee,
I deserve not the Title of thy Son,
Or to have admittance into thy house.
And though I am wholly Innocent
Of the Crime for which I am sentenced now to
    Dye,
Yet from thy hands I have deserved a Death to All
    Eternity.
But thou hast made me know,
That thou canst not cease to be a Father,
For my having often ceased to comport my self as
    thy child.
Thou canst not lose thy Goodness,
By my having often forgotten my Gratitude;
Thou canst not forget to be a Father of Mercy,
By my having become a Child of Misery.

    O my Father,
O Thou the best of all Fathers,
Have pity on the most wretched of all thy
    Children . . .

            RICHARD LANGHORN*

*Langhorn, a Roman Catholic, was executed at Tyburn in July
1679 for complicity in the fictitious 'Popish Plot'.

The Careless Good Fellow
Written, March 9 1680

A Pox of this fooling and plotting of late,
What a pother and stir has it kept in the State?
Let the Rabble run mad with Suspicions and Fears,
Let them scuffle and jar, till they go by the ears:
    Their Grievances never shall trouble my pate,
    So I can enjoy my dear Bottle at quiet.

What Coxcombs were those, who would barter their ease
And their Necks for a Toy, a thin Wafer and Mass?
At old *Tyburn* they never had needed to swing,
Had they been but true Subjects to Drink, and their
    King;
    A Friend, and a Bottle is all my design;
    He has no room for Treason, that's top-full of Wine.

I mind not the Members and makers of Laws,
Let them sit or Prorogue, as his Majesty please:
Let them damn us to Woollen,* I'll never repine
At my Lodging, when dead, so alive I have Wine:
    Yet oft in my Drink I can hardly forbear
    To curse them for making my Claret so dear.

I mind not grave Asses, who idly debate
About Right and Succession, the trifles of State;
We've a good King already: and he deserves laughter
That will trouble his head with who shall come after:
    Come, here's to his Health, and I wish he may be
    As free from all Care, and all Trouble, as we.

What care I how Leagues with the *Hollander* go?
Or Intrigues betwixt *Sidney*, and Monsieur *D'Avaux*?
What concerns it my Drinking, if *Casel* be sold,

*There was an unpopular and much-abused law that shrouds should
be made of English wool instead of the traditional linen.

If the Conqueror take it by Storming, or Gold?
    Good *Bordeaux* alone is the place that I mind,
    And when the Fleet's coming, I pray for a Wind.

The Bully of *France*, that aspires to Renown
By dull cutting of Throats, and vent'ring his own;
Let him fight and be damn'd, and make Matches, and
    Treat,
To afford the News-mongers and Coffee-house Chat:
    He's but a brave wretch, while I am more free,
    More safe, and a thousand times happier than He.

Come He, or the Pope, or the Devil to boot,
Or come Faggot and Stake; I care not a Groat;
Never think that in *Smithfield* I Porters will heat:
No, I swear, Mr. *Fox*,* pray excuse me for that.
    I'll drink in defiance of Gibbet and Halter,
    This is the Profession, that never will alter.

JOHN OLDHAM

A Panegyrick upon Oates†

Silvestrem tenui musam meditemur avena

Of all the *Grain* our Nation yields
In Orchards, Gardens, or in Fields,
There is a *Grain*, (which tho 'tis common)
Its *Worth* till now, was known to no man.
Not *Ceres'* Sicle 'ere did *Crop*,
A *Grain* with *Ears* of greater hope;
For why? some say, the Earth n'ere bore

---

* John Fox (1516–87) whose *Book of Martyrs* recorded the sufferings of the victims of the Marian persecution.

† A satire on Titus Oates (1649–1705) whose largely invented revelations had touched off the 'Popish Plot' panic and sent a number of innocent Catholics to the gallows.

In any Clime, such *Seed* before.

   Yet this *Grain* has (as all must own)
To *Grooms* and *Ostlers* well bin *known*;
And often has, without disdain,
In *Musty Barn* and *Manger layn*;
As if it had bin only good
To be for *Birds* and *Beasts* the Food:
But now by new inspired force
It keeps alive both *Man* and *Horse*.
Speak then, my Muse, for now we guess,
What *Grain* it is, thou wouldst express.
It is not Barley, Rye, or Wheat,
That can pretend to such a Feat;
'Tis *Oates, bare Oates*, which is become⎫
The *Health* of *England, Bane* of *Rome*, ⎬
And *Wonder* of all *Christendom*. ⎭
And therefore *Oates* has well deserv'd,⎫
From *Musty Barn* to be *prefer'd*, ⎬
And now in *Royal Court preserv'd*; ⎭
That, like *Hesperian Fruit, Oates* may
Be *watch'd* and *Garded* night and Day;*
Which is but just Retaliation
For having *Guarded* a whole Nation.

   Hence every lofty Plant which stands
'Twixt *Barwick Wals* and *Dover Sands*,
The *Oake* it self, which well we stile
The Pride and safe-guard of our Isle,
Must *Wave* and *Strike* its lofty Head,
And now Salute an *Oaten Reed*:
For surely *Oates* deserves to be
Exalted far 'bove any *Tree*.

   Th'*Egyptians* once (tho' it seems odd)
Did worship *Onyons* for a *God*;
And poor *peel'd Garlick* was with them
Esteem'd beyond the greatest *Gemm*.

---

*The golden apples of the Hesperides or 'daughters of evening'
were guarded by a fierce dragon named Ladon. Herculues stole them as
his eleventh labour.

What would they've done, had they, think ye,⎞
Had such a *Blade* of *Oates* as we? ⎟
Oates of such known *Divinity*! ⎠
Since then by *Oates* such *good* we find,
Let *Oates* at least now be *enshrin'd*,
Or in some sacred *Press* enclos'd
Be only kept to be *expos'd*;
And all fond *Reliques* else, shall be
Deem'd *Objects* of *Idolatry*.
Popelings may tell us, how they saw
Their *Garnet's Picture* on a *Straw*;*
'Twas a *great* miracle we know
To see him *drawn* in *little* so,
But on an *Oaten Stalk*, there is
A greater *miracle* than this,
A *Visage*, which with *lively Grace*
Does Twenty *Garnets* now *Out-face*,
And like *Twig* of *Dodona's Grove*†
E'en *speaks* as if *inspir'd* by *Jove*.
Nay, to add to the Wonder more,
Declares *unheard-of* Things before,
And Thousand *mysteries* does unfold,
As *plain* as *Oracles* of old;
By which we *steer* affaires of State,
And *stave* off *Britain's* sullen Fate.

Let's then, in honour of the name
Of *Oates* enact some *Solemn Game*,
Where *Oaten Pipe* shall us inspire
Beyond the *Charms* of *Orpheus' Lyre*;
Stones, *Stocks* and every *Senceless thing*⎞
To *Oates* shall *dance*, to *Oates* shall *sing*, ⎟
Whilst *Woods amaz'd* to th'*Ecchos* ring.⎠
And as (that Heroes' names may not

*One of several miracles attributed to Henry Garnet, a Jesuit executed in 1606 for complicity in the Gunpowder Plot.

†Priests at the shrine of Zeus at Dodona received their oracles from the rustling branches of a sacred oak.

When they are rotten, be forgot)
We *hang Atchievements** o're their Dust
(A debt to their great merits just):
So if *Deserts* of *Oates* we prize,
Let *Oates* still *hang* before our eyes;
Thereby to raise our Contemplation,
Oates being to this *Happy* Nation
The *Mystic Embleme* of *Salvation.*

RICHARD DUKE (?)

The State of the Nation (1680)

The Rabble hate, the Gentry feare
And wise men want support;
A riseing Country threatens there
And here a starving Court.

Not for the Nation but the faire
Our Treasury provides;
Bulkly's Godolphin's only care
As Middleton is Hide's.†

Rowly‡ too late will understand
What now he shuns to find:
That nothing's quiet in the Land
Except his careless mind.

---

*Escutcheons granted in memory of some signal feat. The more common form is 'Hatchments'.

†Sidney Godolphin and Laurence Hyde, subsequently Earl of Rochester, were Lords of the Treasury and among Charles's most trusted advisers in the early 1680's. Godolphin was credited with amorous designs on Sophia Bulkeley, wife of the Master of the King's Household. Hyde was reportedly an admirer of a court beauty, Mrs Jane Middleton.

‡Charles II. A reduction of the Latin *Carolus.*

England is now 'twixt thee and York
The Fable of the Frogg.
He is the fierce devouring Stork
And thou the Lumpish Logg.

BM. MS. Add 34362.

My Opinion

After thinking this Fortnight of Whig and of Tory,
This to me is the long and the short of the Story:
They are all Fools and Knaves; and they keep up this
    pother,
On both sides, designing to cheat one another.

Poor *Rowley* (whose Maxims of State are a riddle)
Has plac'd himself much like the Pin in the middle:*
Let which corner so ever be tumbled down first,
'Tis ten Thousand to one, but he comes by the worst.

'Twixt Brother and Bastard (those Dukes of Renown)†
He'l make a wise shift to get rid of his Crown.
Had he half common Sense (were it ne'r so uncivil)
He'd have had 'em long since tipt down to the Devil.

The first is a Prince well fashion'd, well featur'd,
No Bigot to speak of, not false, nor ill natur'd:
The other for Government can't be unfit,
He's so little a Fop, and so plaguy a Wit.

Had I this soft Son, and this dangerous Brother,
I'd hang up the one, then I'd piss upon t'other.
I'd make this the long and the Short of the Story;
The Fools might be Whigs, none but Knaves should be
    Torye.

CHARLES SACKVILLE, EARL OF DORSET

*A reference to the game of ninepins.
†The Dukes of York and Monmouth.

From *The Medal*

Almighty Crowd, thou shorten'st all dispute;
Pow'r is thy Essence; Wit thy Attribute!
Nor Faith nor Reason make thee at a stay,
Thou leapst o'r all eternal truths, in thy *Pindarique* way!
Athens, no doubt, did righteously decide,
When *Phocion** and when *Socrates* were try'd:
As righteously they did those dooms repent;
Still they were wise, what ever way they went.
Crowds err not, though to both extremes they run;
To kill the Father, and recall the Son.
Some think the Fools were most, as times went then;
But now the World's o'r stock'd with prudent men.
The common Cry is ev'n Religion's Test;
The *Turk*'s is, at *Constantinople*, best;
Idols in *India*, Popery at *Rome*;
And our own Worship onely true at home.
And true, but for the time, 'tis hard to know
How long we please it shall continue so.
This side to day, and that to morrow burns;
So all are God-a'mighties in their turns.
A Tempting Doctrine, plausible and new:
What Fools our Fathers were, if this be true!
Who, to destroy the seeds of Civil War,
Inherent right in Monarchs did declare:
And, that a lawfull Pow'r might never cease,
Secur'd Succession, to secure our Peace.
Thus, Property and Sovereign Sway, at last
In equal Balances were justly cast:
But this new *Jehu* spurs the hot mouth'd horse;
Instructs the Beast to know his native force;
To take the Bit between his teeth and fly
To the next headlong Steep of Anarchy.
Too happy *England*, if our good we knew;

*An Athenian statesman, unjustly put to death for treason in
318 B.C.

Wou'd we possess the freedom we pursue!
The lavish Government can give no more:
Yet we repine; and plenty makes us poor.
God try'd us once; our Rebel-fathers fought;
He glutted 'em with all the pow'r they sought:
Till, master'd by their own usurping Brave,
The free-born Subject sunk into a Slave.
We loath our Manna, and we long for Quails;
Ah, what is man, when his own wish prevails!
How rash, how swift to plunge himself in ill;
Proud of his Pow'r, and boundless in his Will!
That Kings can doe no wrong we must believe:
None can they doe, and must they all receive?
Help Heaven! or sadly we shall see an hour,
When neither wrong nor right are in their pow'r!
Already they have lost their best defence,
The benefit of Laws, which they dispence.
No justice to their righteous Cause allow'd;
But baffled by an Arbitrary Crowd.
And Medalls grav'd, their Conquest to record,
The Stamp and Coyn of their adopted Lord.*

JOHN DRYDEN

On *Algernon Sidney*†

Algernon Sidney fills this tomb
An Atheist by disclaiming Rome,
A Rebell bold for striving still
To keep the Laws above the will
And hindering those would tread them down
To leave no limit to a crown:

---

*The medal struck by the followers of Shaftesbury to celebrate his acquittal in November 1681. He had been charged with high treason.

†Sidney was executed in 1683 for alleged complicity in the Rye House plot and having maintained Republican principles in an unpublished political treatise.

Crimes damn'd by Church and Government!
But oh! where must his soul be sent?
Of heaven it must quite dispair
If that the Pope be Turnkey there,
And Hell it ne're can entertain
For there is all tyrannick Raign,
And Purgatory is such pretence
It ne're deceived a man of sence.
Where goes it then? why where it ought to go,
Where neither Pope nor Devill has to do.

Bodl. MS. Douce 357.

A Ballad to the Tune of Bateman

You Gallants all, that love good Wine,
  For shame your Lives amend;
With Strangers go to Church, or Dine,
  But drink with an old Friend.

For with him tipling all the Night,
  You kiss, hugg, and embrace;
Whereas a Stranger, at first sight,
  May kill you on the Place.

There was a rich old Usurer,
  A gallant Son he had;
Who slew an ancient Barrister,
  Like a true mettled Lad.

All in that very House, where Saint
  Holds Devil by the Nose;
These Drunkards met to Roar and Rant,
  But quarrell'd in the close.

The Glass flew chearfully about,
  And drunken Chat went on;
Which Troops had fail'd, and which were stout,
  When *Namur* wou'd be won.

A learned Lawyer,* at the last,
   No Tory, as I'm told,
Began to talk of Tyrants past,
   In Words both sharp and bold.

He toucht a little on our Times,
   Defin'd the Power of Kings,
What were their Vertues, what their Crimes,
   And many dangerous Things.

A Stranger that sat silent by,
   And scarce knew what he meant,
O'recome with Wine and Loyalty,
   Did thus his Passion vent:

I cannot bear the least ill Word,
   That lessens any King;
And the bold Man shall feel my Sword;
   At that their Friends stept in.

The Quarrel seem'd a while compos'd,
   And many Healths there past,
But one to Blood was ill dispos'd,
   As it appear'd at last.

The Counsellor was walking Home,
   Sober, as he was wont,
The young Man after him did come,
   With Sword, that was not blunt.

A Blow there past, which no Man saw,
   From Cane of Lawyer bold;
The young Man did his Weapon draw,
   And left the Lawyer cold.

* John Hoyle, a close friend of Aphra Behn and, according to one
contemporary, 'an Atheist, a Sodomite professed, a corrupter of
youth, and a Blasphemer of Christ'. He was stabbed to death by George
Pitts early on Friday 27 May 1692.

Which Cane held up, in his Defence,
 Was judg'd a Weapon drawn:
What needs there farther Evidence,
 Th'Assault was very plain.

At *Hixes*'s Hall, by Jury grave,
 It was Man-slaughter found.
O what wou'd it have cost to have
 A Pardon from the Crown?

Then learn, my honest Country-men,
 To take yourselves the Pence;
Wisely prevent the Courtier's Gain,
 And save us that Expence.

Ye Gallants all, take heed how you
 Come to untimely Ends;
Justice has bid the World adieu,
 And dead Men have no Friends.

SIR CHARLES SEDLEY

On K.W.3^d*

As I walk'd by my self
And talk'd to my self,
My self said unto me,
Look to thy self,
Take care of thy self,
For nobody cares for Thee.

I answer'd my self,
And said to my self,
In the self-same Repartee,
Look to thy self
Or not look to thy self,
The self-same thing will be.

BM. MS. Harl 7317.

*King William III.

Reasons of Love

The Creation of Woman

from *Paradise Lost*, Book 7

Hee ended, or I heard no more, for now
My earthly by his Heav'nly overpowerd,
Which it had long stood under, streind to the highth
In that celestial Colloquie sublime,
As with an object that excels the sense,
Dazl'd and spent, sunk down, and sought repair
Of sleep, which instantly fell on me, call'd
By Nature as in aide, and clos'd mine eyes.
Mine eyes he clos'd, but op'n left the Cell
Of Fancie my internal sight, by which
Abstract as in a transe methought I saw,
Though sleeping, where I lay, and saw the shape
Still glorious before whom awake I stood;
Who stooping op'nd my left side, and took
From thence a Rib, with cordial spirits warme,
And Life-blood streaming fresh; wide was the wound,
But suddenly with flesh fill'd up and heal'd:
The Rib he formd and fashond with his hands;
Under his forming hands a Creature grew,
Manlike, but different sex, so lovly faire,
That what seemd fair in all the World, seemd now
Mean, or in her summd up, in her contain
And in her looks, which from that time infus'd
Sweetness into my heart, unfelt before,
And into all things from her Aire inspir'd
The spirit of love and amorous delight.
She disappeerd, and left me dark, I wak'd
To find her, or for ever to deplore
Her loss, and other pleasures all abjure:
When out of hope, behold her, not farr off,
Such as I saw her in my dream, adornd
With what all Earth or Heaven could bestow
To make her amiable: On she came,

Led by her Heav'nly Maker, though unseen,
And guided by his voice, nor uninformd
Of nuptial Sanctitie and marriage Rites:
Grace was in all her steps, Heav'n in her Eye,
In every gesture dignitie and love.

JOHN MILTON

Song from *Tyrannick Love*

Ah how sweet it is to love,
Ah how gay is young desire!
And what pleasing pains we prove
When we first approach Love's fire!
    Pains of Love be sweeter far
    Than all other pleasures are.

Sighs which are from Lovers blown,
Do but gently heave the Heart:
Ev'n the tears they shed alone
Cure, like trickling Balm, their smart.
    Lovers when they lose their breath,
    Bleed away in easie death.

Love and Time with reverence use,
Treat 'em like a parting friend:
Nor the golden gifts refuse
Which in youth sincere they send:
    For each year their price is more,
    And they less simple than before.

Love, like Spring-tides full and high,
Swells in every youthful vein:
But each Tide does less supply,
Till they quite shrink in again:
    If a flow in Age appear,
    'Tis but rain, and runs not clear.

JOHN DRYDEN

Song

'Twas a dispute 'twixt heav'n and Earth
   Which had produc't the Nobler birth;
For Heav'n Appear'd Cynthya with all her Trayne
     Till you came forth
     More glorious and more Worth,
Than shee with all those trembling imps of Light
    With which this Envious Queene of night
      Had Proudly deck't her Conquer'd selfe in Vaine.

I must have perish't in that first surprize
   Had I beheld your Eyes:
Love Like Appollo when he would inspire
   Some holy brest, laide all his gloryes by.
Els the god cloath'd in his heavnly fire
Would have possest too powerfully
   And making of his Preist a sacrifize
   Had soe return'd unhallow'd to the Skyes.

JOHN WILMOT, EARL OF ROCHESTER

To Cloris

Cloris, I cannot say your Eyes
Did my unwary Heart surprize;
Nor will I swear it was your Face,
Your Shape, or any nameless Grace:
For you are so intirely Fair,
To love a Part, Injustice were;
No drowning Man can know which Drop
Of Water his last Breath did stop;
So when the Stars in Heaven appear,
And joyn to make the Night look clear;
The Light we no one's Bounty call,
But the obliging Gift of all.

He that does Lips or Hands adore,
Deserves them only, and no more;
But I love All, and every Part,
And nothing less can ease my Heart.
Cupid, that Lover weakly strikes,
Who can express what 'tis he likes.

SIR CHARLES SEDLEY

A Song

Methinks the Poor Town has been troubled too long
With *Phillis* and *Cloris* in every Song;
By fools, who at once can both love and despair,
And will never leave calling them cruel and fair;
Which justly provokes me, in Rhime, to express
The truth that I know of bonny *Black Bess*.

This *Bess* of my Heart, this *Bess* of my Soul,
Has a Skin white as milk, and Hair black as Cole;
She's plump, yet with ease you may span round her waste,
But her round swelling thighs can scarce be embrast:
Her Belly is soft, not a word of the rest,
But I know what I think when I drink to the Best.

The Ploughman and Squire, the Erranter Clown,
At home she subdu'd in her Paragon Gown;
But now she adornes the Boxes and Pit,
And the proudest town Gallants are forc'd to submit;
All hearts fall a leaping wherever she comes,
And beat day and night, like my Lord *Craven*'s* Drums.

I dare not permit her to come to *Whitehall*,
For she'd out-shine the Ladies, Paint, Jewels, and all;
If a Lord should but whisper his love in the Croud,

*William, Earl of Craven (1606–97), the friend and champion of
Elizabeth of Bohemia, was Colonel of the Coldstream Guards.

She'd sell him a Bargain,* and laugh out aloud;
Then the *Queen* overhearing what *Betty* did say,
Would send Mr *Roper* to take her away.

But to these that have had my dear *Bess* in their arms,
She's gentle, and knows how to soften her charms;
And to every beauty can add a new Grace,
Having learn'd how to lisp, and to trip in her Pace;
And with Head on one side, and a Languishing Eye,
To kill us by looking, as if she would Dye.

CHARLES SACKVILLE, EARL OF DORSET

Song

Phillis, Men say that all my Vows
    Are to thy Fortune paid;
Alas, my Heart he little knows
    Who thinks my Love a Trade.

Were I, of all these Woods, the Lord,
    One Berry from thy Hand
More real Pleasure would afford,
    Than all my large Command.

My humble Love has learnt to live,
    On what the nicest Maid,
Without a conscious Blush, may give
    Beneath the Myrtle-shade.

SIR CHARLES SEDLEY

*'Make a fool of him.' The literal sense may also be intended.

The Slight

I did but crave that I might kiss,
   If not her lip, at least her hand,
The coolest Lover's frequent bliss,
    And rude is she that will withstand
       That inoffensive libertie;
Shee (would you think it?) in a fume
    Turn'd her about and left the room,
    Not she, she vow'd, not she.

Well *Chariessa* then said I,
   If it must thus for ever be,
I can renounce my slavery,
    And since you will not, can be free:
       Many a time she made me dye,
Yet (would you think't?) I lov'd the more,
    But I'le not tak't as heretofore,
    Not I, I'le vow, not I.

THOMAS FLATMAN

Three Songs

I

My dear Mistress has a Heart
   Soft as those kind looks she gave me;
When with Love's resistless Art,
   And her Eyes she did enslave me.
But her Constancy's so weak,
   She's so wild, and apt to wander;
That my jealous Heart wou'd break,
   Should we live one day asunder.

Melting Joys about her move,
Killing Pleasures, wounding Blisses;
  She can dress her Eyes in Love,
And her Lips can arm with Kisses.
  Angels listen when she speaks,
She's my delight, all Mankind's wonder:
  But my jealous Heart would break,
Should we live one day asunder.

II

While on those lovely looks I gaze,
  To see a Wretch pursuing,
In Raptures of a blest amaze,
  His pleasing happy ruine;
'Tis not for pitty, that I move,
  His Fate is too aspiring,
Whose Heart, broke with a Load of love,
  Dyes wishing and admiring.

But if this Murder you'd forgo,
  Your Slave from Death removing,
Let me your Art of Charming know,
  Or learn you mine of Loving.
But whether Life, or Death betide,
  In love, 'tis equal measure.
The Victor lives with empty pride,
  The Vanquisht dye with pleasure.

III

Love *and* Life, *a Song*

All my past Life is mine no more,
  The flying hours are gone;
Like transitory Dreams giv'n o're,
Whose Images are kept in store,
  By Memory alone.

What ever is to come is not,
   How can it then be mine?
The present Moment's all my Lot,
And that as fast as it is got,
   Phillis, is wholly thine.

Then talk not of inconstancy,
   False Hearts, and broken Vows.
If I by Miracle can be,
This live-long Minute true to thee,
   'Tis all that Heav'n allows.

JOHN WILMOT, EARL OF ROCHESTER

To Cloe

Prethee *Cloe*, not so fast,
Let's not run and Wed in hast;
We've a thousand things to do,
You must fly, and I persue;
You must frown, and I must sigh;
I intreat, and you deny.
Stay – If I am never crost,
Half the Pleasure will be lost;
Be, or seem to be severe,
Give me reason to Despair;
Fondness will my Wishes cloy,
Make me careless of the Joy.
Lovers may of course complain
Of their trouble and their pain;
But if Pain and Trouble cease,
Love without it will not please.

JOHN OLDMIXON

To Cloris

Cloris, I justly am betray'd,
By a Design my self had laid;
Like an old Rook, whom in his Cheat,
A run of Fortune does defeat.
I thought at first with a small Sum
Of Love, thy Heap to overcome;
Presuming on thy want of Art,
Thy gentle and unpractis'd Heart;
But naked Beauty can prevail,
Like open force, when all things fail.
Instead of that thou hast all mine,
And I have not one Stake of thine;
And, like all Winners, dost discover
A Willingness to give me over.
And though I beg, thou wilt not now;
'Twere better thou should'st do so too;
For I so far in debt shall run,
Even thee I shall be forc'd to shun.
My Hand, alas, is no more mine,
Else it had long ago been thine;
My Heart I give thee, and we call
No Man unjust that parts with all.

SIR CHARLES SEDLEY

A Song

Absent from thee I languish still,
    Then ask me not, when I return;
The straying Fool 'twill plainly kill,
    To wish all Day, all Night to Mourn.

Dear, from thine Arms then let me flie,
    That my Fantastick mind may prove,
The Torments it deserves to try,
    That tears my fixt Heart from my Love.

When wearied with a world of Woe,
    To thy safe Bosom I retire
Where Love and Peace and Truth does flow,
    May I contented there expire.

Lest once more wandring from that Heav'n
    I fall on some base heart unblest;
Faithless to thee, false, unforgiv'n,
    And lose my Everlasting rest.

JOHN WILMOT, EARL OF ROCHESTER

The Kind Mistress*

Long days of absence, Dear, I could endure,
If thy divided heart were mine secure,
But each minute I find myself without thee,
Methinks I find my Rival's arms about thee.

But she perhaps her interest can improve,
By all the studied arts of wealth and love;
Whilst I, alas! poor kind and harmless Creature,
Plung'd in true patience, trust me it shews good nature.

In her fair hand lay silver and rich gold,
But what I must not name let my hand hold:
Give her rich robes, and jewels without measure,
Do but allow me every night the pleasure.

*In one version of this ballad, the speaker is identified as Nell Gwyn.
The rival, in this case, would be the Duchess of Portsmouth.

I dye to think that hapless I should lose,
Those sweet imbraces no one can refuse,
Yet dare I not for shame my flames discover,
I dread the name of, Poor Forsaken Lover.

If she have wit and beauty, charms of love,
Some think I have the same, and those will move;
If she can smile, and kiss, and cling about you,
All these I'll do before I'll go without you.

O let not all my Rivals laugh and say,
I am become a silly Cast-away;
Though all are bound to pay you wealth and honour,
It all comes short of what you lay upon her.

I'll force my soul, and summon all my charms,
E'er any she shall lye within your arms,
Except I found decays in every feature,
Or that old age had spoil'd the works of Nature.

Oh! oh! my Dear, where art, where art thou now?
Hear my sweet call, and hearken to my vow,
What tho' you love her, yet you ought to leave her,
I vow my heart shall be thine own for ever.

I'll act such things, I'll laugh, and dance, and sing,
I'll hug and kiss, and love like any thing;
Then change me not, till I can do no longer,
I'll use a means to make my spirits stronger.

But if she must have interest in your heart,
Dear Love, let it be but the weaker part;
Or if she once enjoys a greater blessing,
You know my thoughts without the words expressing.

Should I be left by you, and quite forlorn,
All other objects my proud heart would scorn;
But if you still persist and will not mind me,
I'll mourn to death and leave her here behind me.

When Death hath done its worst, and I am cold,
'Twill force a sigh when you such clay behold;
Alas! too late you'll with your Friends lament me,
But when I was alive you'd not content me.

Roxburghe Collection, *British Museum*

Song from *The Rivals*

My lodging it is on the Cold ground,
    and very hard is my fare,
But that which troubles me most, is
    the unkindness of my dear;
Yet still I cry, O turn Love,
    and I prethee Love turn to me,
For thou art the Man that I long for,
    and alack what remedy.

I'l Crown thee with a Garland of straw then,
    and I'le Marry thee with a Rush ring,
My frozen hopes shall thaw then,
    and merrily we will Sing:
O turn to me my dear Love,
    and prethee love turn to me,
For thou art the Man that alone canst
    procure my Liberty.

But if thou wilt harden thy heart still,
    and be deaf to my pittyful moan,
Then I must endure the smart still,
    and tumble in straw alone;
Yet still I cry, O turn Love,
    and I prethee Love turn to me,
For thou art the Man that alone art
    the cause of my misery.

SIR WILLIAM DAVENANT

The Mistress

An Age in her Embraces past,
    Would seem a Winter's day;
Where Life and Light, with envious hast,
    Are torn and snatch'd away.

But, oh how slowly Minutes rowl,
    When absent from her Eyes,
That feed my Love, which is my Soul,
    It languishes and dyes.

For then no more a Soul but shade,
    It mournfully does move;
And haunts my Breast, by absence made
    The living Tomb of Love.

You Wiser men despise me not,
    Whose Love-sick Fancy raves
On Shades of Souls, and Heaven knows what;
    Short Ages live in Graves.

When e're those wounding Eyes, so full
    Of Sweetness, you did see;
Had you not been profoundly dull,
    You had gone mad like me.

Nor Censure us you who perceive
    My best belov'd and me,
Sigh and lament, complain and grieve,
    You think we disagree.

Alas! 'tis Sacred Jealousie,
    Love rais'd to an Extream;
The only Proof 'twixt her and me,
    We love, and do not dream.

Fantastick Fancies fondly move,
    And in frail Joys believe,
Taking false Pleasure for true Love;
    But Pain can ne're deceive.

Kind Jealous Doubts, tormenting Fears,
    And Anxious Cares, when past;
Prove our Hearts' Treasure fixt and dear,
    And make us blest at last.

JOHN WILMOT, EARL OF ROCHESTER

The Parting

Too happy had I been indeed, if Fate
Had made it lasting, as she made it great;
But 'twas the Plot of unkind Destiny,
To lift me to, then snatch me from my Joy:
She rais'd my Hopes, and brought them just in view,
And then in spight the pleasing Scene withdrew.
So *He* of old the *promis'd Land* survey'd,*
Which he might only see, but never tread:
So Heav'n was by that damned *Caitiff*† seen, ⎫
He saw't, but with a mighty Gulf between,   ⎬
He saw't to be more wretched, and despair agen:⎭
Not Souls of dying Sinners, when they go,
Assur'd of endless Miseries below,
Their Bodies more unwillingly desert,
Than I from you, and all my Joys did part.
As some young Merchant, whom his Sire unkind
Resigns to every faithless Wave and Wind;
If the kind Mistriss of his Vows appear,
And come to bless his Voyage with a Prayer,
Such Sighs he vents as may the Gale increase,
Such Floods of Tears as may the Billows raise:
And when at length the launching Vessel flies,

*Moses.   †Dives.

148

And severs first his Lips, and then his Eyes;
Long he looks back to see what he adores,
And, while he may, views the beloved Shores.
Such just concerns I at your Parting had,
With such sad Eyes your turning Face survey'd:
Reviewing, they pursu'd you out of sight,
Then sought to trace you by left Tracks of Light:
And when they could not Looks to you convey,　⎞
Tow'rds the lov'd Place they took delight to stray,　⎬
And aim'd uncertain Glances still that way.　⎠

JOHN OLDHAM

To *Mrs*. M[ary] A[wbrey] *upon Absence*

'Tis now since I began to die
    Four months, yet still I gasping live;
Wrapp'd up in sorrow do I lie,
    Hoping, yet doubting, a Reprieve.
Adam from Paradise expell'd
Just such a wretched Being held.

'Tis not thy Love I fear to lose,
    That will in spight of absence hold;
But 'tis the benefit and use
    Is lost, as in imprison'd Gold:
Which though the Sum be ne're so great,
Enriches nothing but conceit.

What angry Star then governs me
    That I must feel a double smart,
Prisoner to fate as well as thee;
    Kept from thy face, link'd to thy heart?
Because my Love all love excells,
Must my grief have no Parallels?

149

Sapless and dead as Winter here
　I now remain, and all I see
Copies of my wild state appear,
　But I am their Epitome.
Love me no more, for I am grown
Too dead and dull for thee to own.

ORINDA
(*Katherine Philips*)

The Tempest

Standing upon the margent of the Main,
　Whilst the high boiling Tide came tumbling in,
I felt my fluctuating thoughts maintain
　As great an Ocean, and as rude, within;
　　As full of Waves, of Depths, and broken Grounds,
　　As that which daily laves her chalky bounds.

Soon could my sad Imagination find
　A Parallel to this half World of Floud,
An Ocean by my walls of Earth confin'd,
　And Rivers in the Chanels of my Bloud:
　　Discovering man, unhappy man, to be
　　Of this great Frame Heaven's Epitome.

There pregnant *Argosies* with full Sails ride,
　To shoot the Gulphs of Sorrow and Despair,
Of which the Love no Pilot has to guide,
　But to her Sea-born Mother steers by Pray'r,
　　When, oh! the Hope her Anchor lost, undone,
　　Rolls at the mercy of the Regent Moon.

'Tis my ador'd *Diana*, then must be
　The Guid'ress to this beaten Bark of mine,
'Tis she must calm and smooth this troubled Sea,

And waft my hope over the vaulting Brine:
Call home thy venture *Dian* then at last,
And be as merciful as thou art chaste.

CHARLES COTTON

Song

Love still has somthing of the Sea,
    From whence his Mother rose;
No time his Slaves from Doubt can free,
    Nor give their Thoughts repose.

They are becalm'd in clearest Days,
    And in rough Weather tost;
They wither under cold Delays,
    Or are in Tempests lost.

One while, they seem to touch the Port,
    Then straight into the Main,
Some angry Wind in cruel sport
    The Vessel drives again.

At first Disdain and Pride they fear,
    Which if they chance to 'scape,
Rivals and Falshood soon appear
    In a more dreadful shape.

By such Degrees to Joy they come,
    And are so long withstood,
So slowly they receive the Sum,
    It hardly does them good.

'Tis cruel to prolong a Pain,
    And to defer a Joy;
Believe me, gentle *Celemene*,
    Offends the winged Boy.

An hundred thousand Oaths your Fears
   Perhaps would not remove;
And if I gaz'd a thousand Years
   I could no deeper love.

SIR CHARLES SEDLEY

Song

Smooth was the Water, calm the Air,
   The Evening-Sun deprest,
Lawyers dismist the noisie Bar,
   The Labourer at rest,

When *Strephon*, with his charming Fair,
   Cross'd the proud River *Thames*,
And to a Garden did repair,
   To quench their mutual Flames.

The crafty Waiter soon espy'd
   Youth sparkling in her Eyes;
He brought no Ham, nor Neats-tongues dry'd,
   But Cream and Strawberries.

The amorous *Strephon* ask'd the Maid,
   What's whiter than this Cream?
She blush'd, and could not tell, she said:
   Thy Teeth, my pretty Lamb.

What's redder than these Berries are?
   I know not, she reply'd:
Those Lips, which I'll no longer spare,
   The burning Shepherd cry'd,
     And strait began to hug her:
      This Kiss, my Dear,
      Is sweeter far
Than Strawberries, Cream and Sugar.

SIR CHARLES SEDLEY

Rondelay

Chloe found *Amyntas* lying
  All in Tears, upon the Plain;
Sighing to himself, and crying,
  Wretched I, to love in vain!
Kiss me, Dear, before my dying;
  Kiss me once, and ease my pain!

Sighing to himself, and crying
  Wretched I, to love in vain:
Ever scorning and denying
  To reward your faithful Swain:
Kiss me, Dear, before my dying;
  Kiss me once, and ease my pain!

Ever scorning, and denying
  To reward your faithful Swain;
Chloe, laughing at his crying,
  Told him that he lov'd in vain:
Kiss me, Dear, before my dying;
  Kiss me once, and ease my pain!

Chloe, laughing at his crying,
  Told him that he lov'd in vain;
But repenting, and complying,
  When he kiss'd, she kiss'd again:
Kiss'd him up, before his dying;
  Kiss'd him up, and eas'd his pain.

JOHN DRYDEN

An Amorous Dialogue between John and his Mistris

Being a compleat and true Relation of some
merry passages between the Mistris and her Apprentice,
who pleased her so well, that she rewarded him with
fifty broad pieces for his pains.

Here by this Dialogue you may discern,
While old Cats nibble Cheese the young ones learn.

To the Tune of, *Packington's pound*, or,
What should a young woman, &c., or, *Captain Digby.*

Come *John* sit thee down I have somewhat to say,
In my mind I have kept it this many a day,
Your Master you know is a Fool and a Sot,
And minds nothing else but the Pipe and the Pot:
Till twelve or till one he will never come home,
And then he's so drunk that he lies like a Mome:
    Such usage as this would make any one mad,
    But a Woman will have it if 'tis to be had.

'Tis true forsooth Mistris, the case is but hard,
That a woman should be of her pleasure debar'd:
But 'tis the sad fate of a thousand beside,
Or else the whole City is fouly beli'd:
There is not a man among twenty that thrives,
Not ten or fifteen that do lie with their Wives,
    Yet still you had better be merry than sad,
    And take it where ever it is to be had.

But John, 'tis a difficult matter to find,
A man that is trusty and constantly kind:
An Inns-of-Court Gallant he cringes and bows,
He's presently known by his Oaths and his Vows,

And though both his cloaths and his speeches be gay,
Yet he loves you but onely a night and away:
  Such usage as this would make any one mad,
  Yet a Woman will have it, if 'tis to be had.

What think you of one that belongs to the Court,
They say they are youthful, and given to sport:
He'l present you with bracelets, and jewels, and Rings,
With stones that are precious, and twenty fine things:
Or if you are not for the Court nor the Town,
What think you forsooth of a man with a Gown?
  You must have a gallant, a good or a bad,
  And take it where ever it is to be had.

The Second Part, to the same Tune

No John, I confess that not any of these,
Had ever the power my fancy to please;
I like no such blades for a trick that I know,
For as soon as they've trod they are given to crow;
Plain dealing is best, and I like a man well,
That when he has kiss'd will be hang'd e're he'l tell:
  My meaning is honest, and thou art the Lad,
  Then give it and take it where 'tis to be had.

Alas! my dear mistris, it never can be,
That you can affect such a fellow as me:
Yet heaven forbid, once I am but your man,
I should ever refuse to do all that I can;
But then if my master should know what we've done
We both shou'd be blown up as sure as a Gun:
  For after our joys, he would make us as sad,
  For taking it where it ought not to be had.

But how shou'd he know it thou scrupulous Elf,
Do'st think I'me so silly to tell him my self?
If we are but so wise our own counsel to keep,
We may laugh and lye down while the sot is asleep:

Some hundreds I know in the city that use
To give to their men what their masters refuse:
   The man is the master, the Prentice the Dad,
   For women must take it where 'tis to be had.

Some Prentices use it, forsooth, I allow,
But I am a Novice and cannot tell how:
However, I hope that I shall not be blam'd,
For to tell you the truth I am somwhat asham'd;
I know how to carry your Bible to Church,
But to play with my mistris I'me left in the lurch:
   Yet if you can shew me the way good or bad,
   I'le promise you all that there is to be had.

You quickly may learn it, my *Johnny*, for . . . . Thus,
Before you proceed we begin with a buss;
And then you must clasp me about with your arm,
Nay, fear me not *Johnny* I'le do thee no harm:
Now I sigh, now I tremble, now backwards I lye,
And now dear *Johnny*, ah now I must dye:
   Oh! who can resist such a mettle-some Lad,
   And refuse such a pleasure when 'tis to be had.

Alas, pretty mistris the pleasure is such,
We never can give one another too much:
If this be the business, the way is so plain,
I think I can easily find it again:
'Twas *Thus* we began; and . . . . *Thus* we lye down,
And *thus* . . . . Oh *thus*! that we fell in a swoun:
   Such sport to refuse who was ever so mad,
   I'le take it where ever it is to be had.

Now *Johnny* you talk like an ignorant mome,
You can have such pleasure no where but at home,
Here's fifty broad pieces for what you have done,
But see that you never a gadding do run;

For no new imployment then trouble your brains,
For here when you work you'l be paid for your pains:
  But shou'd you deceive me no woman's so sad,
  To lose all the pleasure that once she has had.

A mistris so noble I never will leave,
'Twere a sin and a shame such a friend to deceive;
For my Master's shop no more will I care,
'Tis pleasanter handling my mistriss's ware:
A fig for Indentures for now I am made,
Free of a Gentiler and pleasanter trade:
  I know when I'me well, I was never so mad,
  To forsake a good thing when 'tis to be had.

                    Roxburghe Collection, *British Museum*

From the Latin

Enflam'd with Love and led by blind desires,
  The man persues, the blushfull Maid retires.
He hopes for pleasures, but shee feares the Paine,
  His Love but Ignorance is, her feares more vaine.
When e're he tast's those Joys so pris'd before
  He'l love no longer and she'le feare no more.

CHARLES SACKVILLE, EARL OF DORSET

Song from *Theodosius*

Now, now the Fight's done, and the great God of War
  Lies sleeping in shades, and unravels his care;
Love laughs at his rest, and the Soldiers' allarms;
  He Drums and he Trumpets, and struts in his Arms;
He rides on his Lance, and the Bushes he bangs,
  And his broad bloody Sword on the Willow-tree hangs.

Love smiles when he feels the sharp point of his Dart,
   And he wings it to hit the grim God in the heart,
Who leaves his Steel Bed, and Bolsters of Brass,
   For Pillows of Roses, and Couches of Grass.
His Courser of Lightning is now grown so slow,
   That a *Cupid* ith'Saddle sits bending his Bow.

Love, *Love* is the cry; *Love* and *Kisses* go round,
   Till *Phillis* and *Damon* lie clasp'd on the ground.
The Shepheard too quick does her pleasure destroy,
   'Tis abortive, she cries, and he murders my Joy:
But he rallies again by the force of her Charms,
   And Kisses, Embraces, and dies in her Arms.

NATHANIEL LEE

Song from *An Evening's Love, or the Mock Astrologer*

Damon   *Celimena*, of my heart,
          None shall e're bereave you:
          If, with your good leave, I may
          Quarrel with you once a day,
          I will never leave you.

Celimena Passion's but an empty name
          Where respect is wanting:
          Damon you mistake your ayme;
          Hang your heart, and burn your flame,
          If you must be ranting.

Damon   Love as dull and muddy is,
          As decaying liquor:
          Anger sets it on the lees,
          And refines it by degrees,
          Till it workes it quicker.

Celimena   Love by quarrels to beget
               Wisely you endeavour;
               With a grave Physician's wit
               Who to cure an Ague fit
               Put me in a Feavor.

Damon   Anger rouzes love to fight,
               And his only bayt is,
               'Tis the spurre to dull delight,
               And is but an eager bite,
               When desire at height is.

Celimena   If such drops of heat can fall
               In our wooing weather;
               If such drops of heat can fall,
               We shall have the Devil and all
               When we come together.

                              JOHN DRYDEN

The Advice

Wou'd you in Love succeed, be Brisk, be Gay,
Cast all dull Thoughts and serious Looks away;
Think not with down cast Eyes, and mournful Air,
To move to pity, the Relentless Fair,
Or draw from her bright Eyes a Christal Tear.
This Method Foreign is to your Affair,
Too formal for the Frolick you prepare:
Thus, when you think she yields to Love's advance,
You'll find 'tis no Consent, but Complaisance.
Whilst he who boldly rifles all her Charms,
Kisses and Ravishes her in his Arms,
Seizes the favour, stays not for a Grant,
Alarms her Blood, and makes her sigh and pant;
Gives her no time to speak, or think't a Crime,
Enjoys his Wish, and well imploys his time.

        CHARLES SACKVILLE, EARL OF DORSET

Ode

Was ever man of Nature's framing
　　So given o'er to roving,
Who have been twenty years a taming
By ways that are not worth the naming,
　　And now must die of loving?

Hell take me if she been't so winning
　　That now I love her mainly,
And though in jeast at the beginning,
Yet now I'd wond'rous fain be sinning,
　　And so have told her plainly.

At which she cries I doe not love her,
　　And tells me of her Honor;
Then have I no way to disprove her,
And my true passion to discover,
　　But streight to fall upon her.

Which done, forsooth, she talks of wedding,
　　But what will that avail her?
For though I am old Dog at Bedding,
I'm yet a man of so much reading,
　　That there I sure shall fail her.

No, hang me if I ever marry,
　　Till Womankind grow stancher:
I do delight delights to vary,
And love not in one Hulk to tarry,
　　But only Trim and Launch her.

CHARLES COTTON

Song from *The Spanish Fryar*

Farwell ungratefull Traytor,
　Farwell my perjur'd Swain,
Let never injur'd Creature
　Believe a Man again.
The Pleasure of Possessing
Surpasses all Expressing,
But 'tis too short a Blessing,
　And Love too long a Pain.

'Tis easie to deceive us
　In pity of your Pain,
But when we love you leave us
　To rail at you in vain.
Before we have descry'd it
There is no Bliss beside it,
But she that once has try'd it
　Will never love again.

The Passion you pretended
　Was onely to obtain,
But when the Charm is ended
　The Charmer you disdain.
Your Love by ours we measure
Till we have lost our Treasure,
But Dying is a Pleasure,
　When Living is a Pain.

JOHN DRYDEN

Song

Phillis, let's shun the common Fate,
And let our Love ne'r turn to Hate;
I'll dote no longer than I can,

Without being call'd a faithless Man.
When we begin to want Discourse,
And Kindness seems to tast of Force,
As freely as we met, we'll part,
Each one possest of their own Heart.
Thus whilst rash Fools themselves undo;
We'll Game, and give off Savers too;
So equally the Match we'll make,
Both shall be glad to draw the Stake.
A Smile of thine shall make my Bliss,
I will enjoy thee in a Kiss;
If from this Height our Kindness fall,
We'll bravely scorn to Love at all:
If thy Affection first decay,
I will the Blame on Nature lay.
Alas, what Cordial can remove
The hasty Fate of dying Love?
Thus we will all the World excel
In Loving, and in Parting well.

SIR CHARLES SEDLEY

To a Lady in a Letter

Such perfect Bliss, fair *Cloris*, we
    In our Enjoyment prove:
'Tis pity restless Jealousie
    Should mingle with our Love.

Let us, since Wit has taught us how,
    Raise Pleasure to the Top:
You Rival Bottle must allow,
    I'le suffer Rival Fop.

Think not in this that I design
    A Treason 'gainst Love's Charms,
When following the God of Wine
    I leave my *Cloris'* Arms.

Since you have that, for all your haste,
  At which I'le ne're repine,
Will take its Liquor off as fast,
  As I can take off mine.

There's not a brisk insipid Spark,
  That flutters in the Town:
But with your wanton Eyes you mark
  Him out to be your own.

Nor do you think it worth your care
  How empty, and how dull,
The heads of your Admirers are,
  So that their Cods be full.

All this you freely may confess,
  Yet we ne're disagree:
For did you love your Pleasure less,
  You were no Match for me.

Whilst I, my Pleasure to pursue,
  Whole nights am taking in
The lusty Juice of Grapes, take you
  The Juice of lusty Men.

JOHN WILMOT, EARL OF ROCHESTER

Song from *Sir Antony Love,*
or the Rambling Lady
(1690)

Pursuing Beauty, Men descry
  The distant Shore, and long to prove
(Still richer in Variety)
  The Treasures of the Land of Love.

We Women, like weak *Indians*, stand
    Inviting, from our Golden Coast,
The wandring Rovers to our Land:
    But she, who Trades with 'em, is lost.

With humble Vows they first begin,
    Stealing, unseen, into the Heart;
But by Possession setled in,
    They quickly act another part.

For Beads and Baubles, we resign,
    In Ignorance, our shining Store,
Discover Nature's richest Mine,
    And yet the Tyrants will have more.

Be wise, be wise, and do not try,
    How he can Court, or you be Won:
For Love is but Discovery,
    When that is made, the Pleasure's done.

THOMAS SOUTHERNE

No true Love between Man *and* Woman

No, no – 'tis not Love – You may talk till Dooms day,
    If you tell me 'tis more than meer Satisfaction;
I'll never believe a Tittle you say,
    Tho' *Baxter* and *Oates* were the Heads of your
      Faction.*

The Poets therefore were a number of Owls,
    To make such a stir with a Baby-face God;
While they set poor *Priapus* to scare the wild Fowls,†
    That rules with a far more Scepter-like Rod.

*Richard Baxter (1615–91), Presbyterian divine, and Titus Oates
(1649–1705), perjurer.
†One of Horace's *Satires* (I. viii.) is narrated by a wooden statue of
Priapus which had been placed in a garden to keep the birds away.

'Tis true, he may sometimes be blindly put to't;
    But the Bow and the Arrows are surely his due;
For when that his Arrows are ready to shoot,
    They make the more pleasing wound of the two.

'Twas he was the Father of all the Graces;
    For he's the beginning and end of our wooing;
Your Smiles, and your Ogles, and alluring Grimaces;
    They all do but end in Feeling and Doing.

When a Man to a Woman comes crèeping and cringing,
    And spends his high Raptures on her Nose and her
        Eyes;
'Tis *Priapus* inspires the Talkative Engine,
    And all for the sake of her lilly white Thighs.

Your Vows and Protests, your Oaths all and some,
    Ask *Solon*, *Lycurgus*,* both Learned and Smart;
They'll tell you the place from whence they all come,
    Is half a Yard almost below the Heart.

There's nothing but Vertue the Object of Love;
    Not Beauty nor Colour Love minds in the least:
They're only the Idols of Pleasure, by *Jove*,
    Where th'Altar's Desire, *Priapus* High Priest.

Your Lips, and your Eyes, with their Diamonds and Coral,
    Are only like Capers and Samphire in Pickle;
For talk what you please, 'tis her Men adore all,
    That has the best Fiddle *Priapus* to tickle.

Now if she be rich, 'tis the Portion he'd have,
    Or a Coach and fine Cloaths, that her Love do
        encourage;
But alass! if either do either deceive,
    Love presently cools like a Mess of Beef Porridge.

   *Two famous sages of the ancient world, the first an Athenian, the second a Spartan.

Then if this be your Love, the Devil take Love,
    Where Self-Satisfaction is all the design:
But let me have that which all Men approve,
    An Angel in Purse, and a Glass of good Wine.

From Chorus Poetarum (1694)

Song

Love a Woman! y'are an Ass,
'Tis a most inspid Passion,
To choose out for your happiness
The silliest part of God's Creation.

Let the Porter, and the Groome,
Things design'd for dirty Slaves,
Drudge in fair *Aurelia*'s Womb,
To get supplies for Age and Graves.

Farewel Woman, I intend,
Henceforth, ev'ry Night to sit,
With my lewd well-natur'd Friend,
Drinking, to engender Wit.

Then give me Health, Wealth, Mirth, and Wine,
And if busie Love intrenches,
There's a sweet soft Page of mine,
Does the trick worth Forty Wenches.

JOHN WILMOT, EARL OF ROCHESTER

The Women's Complaint to Venus
1698

How happy were good English Faces
    Till Mounsieur from France
    Taught Pego* a Dance
To the tune of old Sodom's Embraces.

But now we are quite out of Fashion:
    Poor Whores may be Nuns
    Since Men turn their Guns
And vent on each other their passion.

In the Raign of good *Charles* the Second
    Full many a Jade
    A Lady was made
And the Issue Right Noble was reckon'd:

But now we find to our Sorrow
    We are overrun
    By Sparks of the Bum
And peers of the Land of Gommorah.

The Beaus too, whom most we rely'd on
    At Night make a punk
    Of him that's first drunk
Tho' unfit for the Sport as *John Dryden.*

The Souldiers, whom next we put trust in,
    No widdow can tame
    Or virgin reclaim
But at the wrong Place will be thrusting.

*'The penis of a man or beast.' (Grose.)

Fair *Venus*, Thou Goddess of Beauty,
　　Receive our Complaint
　　Make Rigby* Recant
And the Souldiers henceforth do their duty.

Bodl. MS. Rawl. Poet. 152

Caelia

Mistress of all my Senses can invite,
Free as the Air, and unconfin'd as Light;
Queen of a thousand Slaves that fawn and bow,
And with submissive Fear, my Pow'r allow,
Shou'd I exchange this noble State of Life,
To gain the vile detested Name of Wife:
Shou'd I my native Liberty betray,
Call him my Lord, who at my Footstool lay?
No: Thanks kind Heav'n that has my Soul employ'd,
With my great Sex's useful Virtue, Pride,
That gen'rous Pride, that noble just Disdain,
That scorns the Slave that wou'd presume to Reign.
Let the raw am'rous Scribler of the Times
Call me his *Cælia* in insipid Rhimes;
I hate and scorn you all, proud, that I am
T'revenge my Sex's Injuries on Man.
Compar'd to all the Plagues in Marriage dwell,
It were Preferment to lead Apes in Hell.

RICHARD DUKE

*Edward Rigby, a naval captain, was convicted in December 1698 of 'an attempt of sodomy', and sentenced to a fine of £1,000, a year's imprisonment and to stand three times in the pillory.

REASONS OF LOVE

The Batchelor's Song

Like a Dog with a bottle, fast ti'd to his tail,
Like Vermin in a trap, or a Thief in a Jail,
Or like a *Tory* in a Bog,
Or an Ape with a Clog:
Such is the man, who when he might go free,
Does his liberty loose,
For a Matrimony noose,
And sels himself into Captivity.
The Dog he do's howl, when his bottle do's jog,
The Vermin, the Theif, and the *Tory* in vain
Of the trap, of the Jail, of the Quagmire complain.
But welfare poor *Pug*! for he playes with his Clog;
And tho' he would be rid on't rather than his life,
Yet he lugg's it, and he hug's it, as a man does his wife.

The Second Part

How happy a thing were a wedding
And a bedding,
If a man might purchase a wife
For a twelve month, and a day;
But to live with her all a man's life,
For ever and for ay,
'Till she grow as grey as a Cat,
Good faith, Mr Parson, I thank you for that.

THOMAS FLATMAN

Constancy

Fear not, my Dear, a Flame can never dye,
That is once kindled by so bright an Eye;
View but thy self, and measure thence my Love,
Think what a Passion such a Form must move;
For though thy Beauty first allur'd my Sight,

R.V.—8   169

Now I consider it but as the Light
That led me to the Treasury of thy Mind,
Whose inward Vertue in that Feature shin'd.
That Knot be confident will ever last,
Which Fancy ty'd, and Reason has made fast;
So fast that time, although it may disarm
Thy lovely Face, my Faith can never harm;
And Age deluded, when it comes, will find
My Love removed, and to thy Soul assign'd.

SIR CHARLES SEDLEY

Song

See! *Hymen* comes; How his Torch blazes!
    Looser Loves, how dim they burn;
No Pleasures equal chaste Embraces,
    When we Love for Love return.

When Fortune makes the Match he rages,
    And forsakes th'unequal Pair;
But when Love two Hearts engages,
    The kind God is ever there.

Regard not then high Blood, nor Riches;
    You that would his Blessings have,
Let untaught Love guide all your Wishes,
    Hymen shou'd be *Cupid*'s Slave.

Young Virgins, that yet bear your Passions,
    Coldly as the Flint its Fire,
Offer to *Hymen* your Devotions,
    He will warm you with Desire.

Young Men, no more neglect your Duty,
    To the God of Nuptial Vows:
Pay your long Arrears to Beauty,
    As his chaster Law allows.

SIR CHARLES SEDLEY

A Wife

Since thou'rt condemn'd to wed a thing,
　　And that same thing must be a she;
And that same she to thee must cling
　　For term of life of her and thee;
　　I'll tell thee what this thing shall bee.

I would not have her virtuous,
　　For such a wife I ne'er did see;
And 'tis a madness to suppose
　　What never was, nor e're shall bee;
　　To seem so is enough to thee.

Do not desire she should be wise,
　　Yet let her have a waggish wit;
No circumventing subtilties,
　　But pretty slights to please and hit,
　　And make us laugh at her, or it.

Nor must thou have one very just,
　　Lest she repay thee in thy kind;
And yet she must be true to trust;
　　Or if to sport she has a mind,
　　Let her be sure to keep thee blind.

One part of valour let her have;
　　Not to return but suffer ill,
To her own passion be no slave
　　But to thy laws obedient still,
　　And unto thine submit her will.

Be thou content she have a tongue,
　　That's active so it be not lowd;
And so she be straight-limb'd and young,
　　Though not with beauty much endow'd,
　　No matter, so she be but proud.

Tir'd she should be, not satisfi'd,
  But alwaies tempting thee for more,
So cunningly she been't espy'd.
  Let her act all parts like a whore,
  So she been't one, I'ld ask no more.

But above all things, let her be
  Short liv'd and rich, no strong-dock'd *Jone*,
That dares to live till 53,
  Find this wife, if thou must have one;
  But there's no wife so good as none.

ALEXANDER BROME

Song

To friend and to foe,
To all that I know,
That to Marriage Estate do prepare,
  Remember your days
  In several ways,
Are troubled with sorrow and care.

For he that doth look
In the married man's book,
And read but his *Items* all over,
  Shall finde them to come,
  At length to a Sum,
Shall empty Purse, Pocket, and Coffer.

In the pastimes of love,
When their labors do prove,
And the Fruit beginneth to kick,
  For this, and for that,
  And I know not for what,
The woman must have, or be sick.

There's *Item* set down,
For a Loose-bodied Gown,
In her longing you must not deceive her;
For a Bodkin, a Ring,
Or the other fine thing,
For a Whisk, a Scarf, or a Beaver.

Deliver'd and well,
Who is't cannot tell,
Thus while the Childe lies at the Nipple,
There's *Item* for wine,
And Gossips so fine,
And Sugar to sweeten their Tipple.

There's *Item* I hope,
For Water and Sope,
There's *Item* for Fire and Candle,
For better for worse,
There's *Item* for Nurse,
The Babe to dress and to dandle.

When swadled in lap,
There's *Item* for Pap,
And *Item* for Pot, Pan, and Ladle;
A Corral with Bells,
Which custom compells,
And *Item* ten Groats for a Cradle;

With twenty odd Knacks,
Which the little one lacks,
And thus doth thy pleasure bewray thee:
But this is the sport,
In Countrey and Court,
Then let not these pastimes betray thee.

From *The New Academy of Complements* (1669)

Sonnet

Chloris, whilst thou and I were free,
Wedded to nought but Liberty,
How sweetly happy did we live,
How free to promise, free to give?

Then, Monarchs of our selves, we might
Love here, or there, to change delight,
And ty'd to none, with all dispence,
Paying each Love its recompence.

But in that happy freedom, we
Were so improvidently free,
    To give away our liberties;

And now in fruitless sorrow pine
At what we are, what might have bin,
    Had thou, or I, or both been wise.

CHARLES COTTON

Love's Bravo
Song

Why should we murmur, why repine,
    Phillis at thy fate, or mine?
Like Pris'ners, why do we those fetters shake,
    Which neither thou, nor I can break?
There is a better way to baffle fate,
    If Mortals would but mind it,
    And 'tis not hard to find it:
Who would be happy, must be desperate;
    He must despise those Stars that fright
    Only Fools that dread the night;

174

Time and chance he must out-brave,
He that crouches is their Slave.
Thus the wise *Pagans* ill at ease,
Bravely chastiz'd their surly *Deities*.

THOMAS FLATMAN

Song from *Marriage A-la-Mode*

Why should a foolish Marriage Vow
    Which long ago was made,
Oblige us to each other now
    When Passion is decay'd?
We lov'd, and we lov'd, as long as we cou'd,
    Till our Love was lov'd out in us both:
But our Marriage is dead, when the Pleasure is
        fled:
    'Twas Pleasure first made it an Oath.

If I have Pleasures for a Friend,
    And farther love in store,
What wrong has he whose joys did end,
    And who cou'd give no more?
'Tis a madness that he should be jealous of me,
    Or that I shou'd bar him of another:
For all we can gain, is to give our selves pain,
    When neither can hinder the other.

JOHN DRYDEN

Song from *Love in a Wood*

A spouse I do hate,
For either she's false or she's jealous;
But give us a Mate,
Who nothing will ask us or tell us.

She stands on no terms,
Nor chaffers by way of Indenture,
Her love for your Farms;
But takes her kind man at a venture.

If all prove not right,
Without an Act, Process, or Warning,
From Wife for a night,
You may be divorc'd in the morning.

When Parents are Slaves,
Their Bratts cannot be any other;
Great Wits and great Braves,
Have always a Punk to their Mother.

WILLIAM WYCHERLEY

Forbidden Fruit

Pish! 'tis an idle fond excuse,
And *Love*, enrag'd by this abuse,
Is deaf to any longer truce.

My *Zeal*, to Lust you still impute,
And when I justifie my suit,
You tell me: *'Tis Forbidden Fruit*.

What though your Face be Apple-round,
And with a Rosy colour Crown'd?
Yet, Sweet, it is no Apple found.

Nor have you ought resembling more
That fatal Fruit the Tree once bore,
But that indeed your Heart's a core.*

'Tis true, the bliss that I would tast,
Is something lower than the wast,
And in your Garden's Centre plact.

A Tree of Life too, I confess,
Though but Arbuscular in dress,
Yet not forbidden ne'retheless.

It is a tempting golden tree,
Which all Men must desire that see,
Though it concern'd Eternity.

Then, since those blessings are thine own,
Not subject to Contrition,
Then, *Fairest, Sweetest*, grant me one.

Thy *Dragon*, wrapt in drowsiness,
Ne're thinks whose bed thy beauties bless,
Nor dreams of his *Hesperides*.

CHARLES COTTON

From *Hudibras*

Marriage is but a Beast, some say,
That *carries double in foul way*,
And therefore 'tis not to be admir'd,

*A bilingual pun.

It should so suddenly be tyr'd:
A bargain, at a venture made,
Between two Part'ners in a *Trade*,
(For what's infer'd by *T'have and t'hold*,
But something past away and sold?)
That as it makes but one, of two,
Reduces all things else, as low:
And at the best is but a *Mart*
Between the one, and th'other part,
That on the Marriage-day is paid,
Or, hour of Death, the Bet it laid:
And all the rest of *Bett'r or worse*
Both are but losers, out of Purse.
For when upon their ungot Heirs
Th'intail themselves, and all that's theirs,
What blinder Bargain e're was driven,
Or Wager laid at *six and seven*?
To pass themselves away, and turn
Their Children's Tenants, e're th'are born?
Beg one another *Idiot*,*
To *Guardians* e're they are begot;
Or ever shall, perhaps, by th'one,
Who's bound to vouch 'em for his own,
Though got b'*Implicite Generation*,†
And *General Club* of all the Nation;
For which she's fortify'd no less
Than all the Island, with four *Seas*:
Exacts the Tribute of her Dow'r
In ready Insolence, and Pow'r;
And makes him pass away, to *Have*

---

*Guardianships of insane persons, which brought with them the
right to manage property, were in the gift of the king and were eagerly
sought after both by relatives and courtiers.

†According to one early sense of the adjective, mixed or multiple
generation (i.e. generation by more than one father). It is possible,
however, that Butler is referring to the common law assumption that
as long as husband and wife both reside in Great Britain, he is the
implied father of all her children.

And *Hold*, to her, himself, her slave,
More wretched than an *Ancient Villain*,
Condemn'd to *Drudgery* and *Tilling*,
While all he does upon the By,
She is not bound to justifie;
Nor at her proper cost, and charge
Maintain the Feats, he does at large.
Such hideous Sots, were *those obedient*
Old Vassals, to their *Ladies Regent*;
To give the Cheats, the *Eldest hand*
In *Foul Play*, by the Laws o'th Land,
For which so many a *legal Cuckold*
Has been run down in Courts, and truckled.

A Law that most unjustly yokes,
All *Johns* of *Stiles*, to *Joans* of *Nokes*,
Without distinction of degree,
Condition, Age, or Quality,
Admits no *Pow'r* of *Revocation*,
Nor *valuable Consideration*,
Nor *Writ* of *Error*, nor *Reverse*,
Of *Judgement* past, *For better, or worse*;
Will not allow the Priviledges
That Beggers challenge under Hedges,
Who when th'are griev'd can make dead Horses
Their Spiritual Judges of Divorces;
While nothing else, but *Rem in Re*,
Can set the proudest Wretches free.
A slavery, beyond induring,
But that 'tis of their own procuring.
As Spiders never seek the Fly,
But leave him, of himself, t'apply:
So Men are by themselves betray'd
To quit the freedom they injoy'd,
And run their Necks into a Noose,
They'ld break 'em after, to break loose.
As some, whom *Death would not depart*,
Have done the Feat themselves, by Art.

Like *Indian Widdows* gone to Bed
In *Flaming Curtains*, to the Dead,
And Men as often dangled for't,
And yet will never leave the Sport.

SAMUEL BUTLER

Song

Phillis, be gentler I advise,
    Make up for time mispent,
When Beauty on its Death-Bed lyes,
    'Tis high time to repent.

Such is the Malice of your Fate,
    That makes you old so soon,
Your pleasure ever comes too late,
    How early e're begun.

Think what a wretched thing is she,
    Whose Stars contrive in spight,
The Morning of her love shou'd be,
    Her fading Beauties' Night.

Then if to make your ruin more,
    You'll peevishly be coy,
Dye with the scandal of a Whore,
    And never know the joy.

JOHN WILMOT, EARL OF ROCHESTER

Verses by Mr Prior

Whilst Beauty, Youth, and gay Delight
In all thy Looks and Gestures shine,
Thou hast, my Dear, undoubted Right
To rule this destin'd Heart of mine.
My Reason bends to what your Eyes ordain,
For I was born to Love, and you to Reign.

But, would you meanly then rely
On Power you know I must obey,
It is but legal Tyranny
To do an Ill because you may:
Why must I thee as Atheists Heav'n adore,
Not see thy Mercy, and but dread thy Pow'r?

Take Care, my Dear, Youth flies apace;
Time equally with Love is blind:
Soon must these Glories of thy Face
The Fate of vulgar Beauties find:
The thousand Loves that arm thy potent Eye
Must drop their Quivers, flag their Wings, and dye.

Then thou wilt sigh, when in each Frown
One hateful Wrinkle more appears,
And putting peevish Humors on
Seems but the sad effect of Years;
Ev'n Kindness, then, too weak a Charm will prove
To reinflame the Ashes of my Love.

Forc'd Compliments, and formal Bows,
Will shew thee just above Neglect;
The heat with which thy Lover glows
Will settle into cold Respect:
A talking dull *Platonic* I shall turn,
Learn to be Civil, when I cease to burn.

Then shun that Ill, and know, my Dear,
Kindness and Constancy will prove
The only Pillars fit to bear
So vast a Weight as that of Love:
If thou wouldst wish to make my Flames endure,
Thine must be very fierce and very pure.

Haste, *Celia*, haste, whilst Love invites,
Obey the gentle Godhead's Voice;
Fill ev'ry Sense with soft Delights,

And give thy Soul a loose to Joys;
Let millions of repeated Blisses prove
That thou art Kindness all, and I all Love.

Be mine, and only mine, take care
Thy Words, thy Looks, thy Dreams to guide
To me alone, nor come so far
As liking any Youth beside;
What Men e're Court thee, flie them, and believe
They're Serpents all, and thou the tempted *Eve*.

So will I Court thy dearest Truth,
When Beauty ceases to engage,
And, thinking on thy pleasing Youth,
I'le love thee on in spite of Age:
So Time itself our Transports shall improve,
And still we'le wake to Joys, and live to love.

MATTHEW PRIOR

The Fire of Love in Youthful Blood

The Fire of Love in youthful Blood,
    Like what is kindled in Brushwood
  But for a Moment burns,
Yet in that Moment makes a mighty Noise:
It crackles, and to Vapour turns,
    And soon it self destroys.

But when crept into aged Veins,
  It slowly burns, and long remains,
    And with a sullen Heat,
Like Fire in Logs, it glows and warms 'em long;
  And tho' the Flame be not so great,
    Yet is the Heat as strong.

CHARLES SACKVILLE, EARL OF DORSET

Fading Beauty

Take Time, my Dear, e're Time takes wing;
Beauty knows no second Spring:
Marble Pillars, Tombs of Brass,
Time breaks down, much more this Glass;
Then e're that Tyrant Time bespeak it,
Let's drink healths in't first, then break it.
  At Twenty five in Women's eyes
  Beauty does fade, at Thirty dyes.

A New Collection of Poems (1674)

A Song of a young Lady to her Ancient Lover

Ancient Person, for whom I,
All the flattering Youth defy;
Long be it e're thou grow Old,
Aking, shaking, crazy, cold.
But still continue as thou art,
Antient Person of my Heart.

On thy withered Lips and dry,
Which like barren Furrows lye;
Brooding Kisses I will pour,
Shall thy youthful Heart restore.
Such kind Show'rs in Autumn fall,
And a second Spring recall:
Nor from thee will ever part,
Antient Person of my Heart.

Thy Nobler part, which but to name
In our Sex wou'd be counted shame,
By Ages' frozen grasp possest,

From their Ice shall be releast:
And, sooth'd by my reviving hand,
In former Warmth and Vigor stand.
All a Lover's wish can reach,
For thy Joy my Love shall teach:
And for thy Pleasure shall improve,
All that Art can add to Love.
Yet still I love thee without Art,
Antient Person of my Heart.

JOHN WILMOT, EARL OF ROCHESTER

One Writeing Against his Prick

Base mettell hanger by your Master's Thigh!
Eternall shame to all Prick's heraldry,
Hide thy despised head and doe not dare
To Peepe, no not soe much as take the aire
But through a Button hole, but pine and dye
Confin'd within the Codpeice Monestry.
The Little Childish Boy that hardly knowes
The way through which his Urine flowes
Toucht by my Mistris her Magnetick hand
His Little needle presently will stand.
Did shee not raise thy drooping head on high
As it lay Nodding on her wanton thigh?
Did shee not clap her leggs aboute my back
Her Port hole open? Damn'd Prick what is't
      you lack?
Henceforth stand stiff and gaine your creditt lost
Or I'le nere draw thee, but against a Post.

Harvard MS Eng. 636F

The Old Man's Complaint:
By Mr Wells

Ah, pity Love where e'r it grows!
See how in me it overflows,
In dripping Eyes and dropping Nose.

So strange a thing is seldom seen;
My Age is dull, my Love is keen;
Above I'm grey, but elswhere green.

Aloof, perhaps I court and prate;
But something near I would be at,
Tho' I'm so old I scarce know what.

The Maid's Answer

For Shame your Green-wood Fires then smother,
You drop at one End, burn at t'other,
You'd have a Wife to spoil a Mother.

I pity much your Eyes o'rflowing;
But sure the World must needs be going,
When Rheums and Rottenness run a woeing.

Then let Age make you cease your chat;
And since you have forgot what's what;
Old Rats love Cheese, go construe that.

From *Miscellany Poems upon Several Occasions* (1692)

Advice to the Old Beaux

Scrape no more your harmless Chins,
   Old Beaux, in hope to please;
You shou'd repent your former Sins,
   Not study their Increase;
Young awkard Fops, may shock our Sight,
But you offend by Day and Night.

In vain the Coachman turns about,
   And whips the dappl'd Greys;
When the old Ogler looks out,
   We turn away our Face.
True Love and Youth will ever charm,
But both affected, cannot warm.

Summer-fruits we highly prise,
   They kindly cool the Blood;
But Winter-berries we despise,
   And leave 'em in the Wood;
On the Bush they may look well,
But gather'd, lose both taste and smell.

That you languish, that you dye,
   Alas, is but too true;
Yet tax not us with Cruelty,
   Who daily pity you.
Nature henceforth alone accuse,
In vain we grant, if she refuse.

SIR CHARLES SEDLEY

And forgive us our Trespasses

How prone we are to Sin, how sweet were made
The pleasures, our resistless hearts invade!
Of all my Crimes, the breach of all thy Laws,
Love, soft bewitching Love! has been the cause;
Of all the Paths that Vanity has trod,
That sure will soonest be forgiven of God;
If things on Earth may be to Heaven resembled,
It must be love, pure, constant, undissembled:
But if to Sin by chance the Charmer press,
Forgive, O Lord, forgive our Trespasses.

APHRA BEHN

The Translators

An Ode of Anacreon, *Paraphras'd*
The Cup

Make me a Bowl, a mighty Bowl,
Large, as my capacious Soul,
Vast, as my thirst is; let it have
Depth enough to be my Grave;
I mean the Grave of all my Care,
For I intend to bury't there;
Let it of Silver fashion'd be,
Worthy of Wine, worthy of me,
Worthy to adorn the Spheres,
As that bright Cup amongst the Stars:
That Cup which Heaven deign'd a place
Next the Sun, its greatest Grace.
Kind Cup! that to the Stars did go,
To light poor Drunkards here below:
Let mine be so, and give me light,
That I may drink, and revel by't:
Yet draw no shapes of Armour there,
No Casque, nor Shield, nor Sword, nor Spear,
Nor Wars of *Thebes*, nor Wars of *Troy*,
Nor any other martial Toy:
For what do I vain Armour prize,
Who mind not such rough Exercise,
But gentler Sieges, softer Wars,
Fights, that cause no Wounds or Scars?
I'll have no Battles on my Plate,
Lest sight of them should Brawls create,
Lest that provoke to Quarrels too,
Which Wine it self enough can do.
Draw me no Constellations there,
No Ram, nor Bull, nor Dog, nor Bear,
Nor any of that monstrous fry
Of Animals, which stock the sky:

For what are Stars to my Design, ⎱
Stars, which I, when drunk, out-shine, ⎰
Out-shone by every drop of Wine?
I lack no Pole Star on the Brink,
To guide in the wide Sea of Drink,
But would for ever there be tost;
And wish no Haven, seek no Coast.
Yet, gentle Artist, if thou'lt try
Thy Skill, then draw me (let me see)
Draw me first a spreading Vine,
Make its Arms the Bowl entwine,
With kind embraces, such as I
Twist about my loving she.
Let its Boughs o're-spread above
Scenes of Drinking, Scenes of Love:
Draw next the Patron of that Tree,
Draw *Bacchus* and soft *Cupid* by;
Draw them both in toping Shapes,
Their Temples crown'd with cluster'd Grapes:
Make them lean against the Cup,
As 'twere to keep their Figures up:
And when their reeling Forms I view,
I'll think them drunk, and be so too:
   The Gods shall my examples be,
   The Gods, thus drunk in Effigy.

JOHN OLDHAM

Upon his Drinking a Bowl

Vulcan contrive me such a Cup,
   As *Nestor* us'd of old;
Shew all thy skill to trim it up,
   Damask it round with Gold.

Make it so large that fill'd with Sack,
   Up to the swelling brim;
Vast Toasts, on the delicious Lake,
   Like Ships at Sea may swim.

Engrave not Battail on his Cheek,
    With War, I've nought to do;
I'm none of those that took *Mastrich*,
    Nor *Yarmouth* Leager knew.*

Let it no name of Planets tell,
    Fixt Stars or Constellations;
For I am no Sir *Sydrophell*,†
    Nor none of his Relations.

But carve thereon a spreading Vine,
    Then add Two lovely Boys;
Their Limbs in Amorous folds intwine,
    The Type of future joys.

Cupid and *Bacchus* my Saints are,
    May drink and Love still reign,
With Wine I wash away my cares,
    And then to Cunt again.

JOHN WILMOT, EARL OF ROCHESTER

The Cause of Thunder‡
from *Lucretius*, Book VI

But now to chase these *Phantoms* out of sight
By the plain *Magick* of *true Reason*'s light,
Tho I have sung a *Thousand things* before,

*The military camp at Yarmouth. Maastricht was captured by an Anglo-French force in June 1673.
†The astrologer in Samuel Butler's *Hudibras* (see *Portraits and Histories*).
‡The scientific sections of the *De rerum natura* of Lucretius (c. 99 to c. 55 B.C.) are based on the teachings of the Greek atomists Democritus and Leucippus as transmitted by Epicurus.

The Subject My *labouring Muse* must sing a *Thousand* more,
How *Thunder, Storm,* and how *swift Lightning*
    flies,
Singeing with *fiery* wings the *wounded* Skies;
Lest, *Superstitious,* you observe the flame,
If those quick Fires from *lucky quarters* came,
Or with sad *Omen* fell, and how they burn
Thro *closest* Stones, and wast, and then return.
And you my *sweetest Muse,* come lead me on,
I'me eager, and tis time that I was gone;
Come lead me on, and show the *Path* to gain
The *Race* and *Glory* too, and *crown* my Pain.

    First then, the *dreadful Thunder* roars aloud,
When *fighting* Winds drive *heavy Cloud* on
Of Thunder   Cloud:
For where the *Heaven* is *clear,* the Sky *serene,*
No dreadful *Thunder's* heard, no *Lightning* seen;
But where the *Clouds* are thick, there *Thunders*
    rise,
The furious Infant's born, and speaks, and dies.
Now *Clouds* are not so thick, so close
    combin'd
As *Stones,* nor yet so *thin,* and so refin'd
As rising *Mists,* or subtle *Smoak,* or *Wind;*
For then the *upper* Clouds, like weighty Stone,
Would fall abruptly, and come tumbling
    down;
Or else *disperse* like *Smoak,* and ne're enclose
The hanging drops of Rain, nor Hail, nor
    Snows:
They give the *Crack,* as o're a Theater
Vast *Curtains* spread are *ruffled* in the Air,
Or torn (for *such a sound* is often known
From Thunder's crack) they give a *mighty*
    groan;
Or as *spread* Cloaths, or Sheets of *Paper* flie
Before the *Wind,* and rattle o're the Sky.
    But Clouds meet not *directly* still, but slide,

And rudely grate each other's *injur'd* side;
And hence that *buzzing* Noise we often hear,
That with *harsh Murmurs* fills the lower Air;
Continues long, but with a *softer* sound,
At length it *gathers strength*, and breaks the
    bound.
But more, the *Thunder* arm'd with *pointed*
    flame,
May seem to *shake* the World, and break the
    frame;
When e're a *fierce*, a *strong*, and *furious* Wind,
In *narrow*, *thick*, and *hollow* Clouds confin'd,
Breaks thro the *Prison* with a *mighty* Noise,
And shouts at *Liberty* with dreadful voice:
Nor is this strange, when *one poor breath* of Air,
That starts from *broken Bladders*, sounds so far.
  But more, tis *Reason* too that Noise should
    rise,
When *violent* Storms rage o're the *lower* Skies;
For *thousand* Clouds appear, *rough*, *close*,
    combin'd,
And *thick*, and able to *resist* the Wind:
Thus *Noise* must rise; as when the *Woods* they
    wound
The *injur'd* Boughs sigh forth a *mournful* sound:
These Winds do *cut* the *Clouds*, and passing
    thro,
With murmuring Sounds fill all the Air below:
For that the Winds may *break* the Clouds, and
    flie
Thro all *resistance* in the lower Sky,
Tis easie to discover, since they *break*,
And twist *our* Trees; yet *here* their *force* is *weak*.
  Besides, vast waves of Clouds seem roll'd
    above,
And in confus'd, and tumbling order move;
These meeting *strike*, and break, and loudly
    roar,

As *Billows* dashing on the *trembling* shore.
   Or else *hot Thunder* falls on Rain, or Snow,
And dies, or *hisses* as it passes thro:
As when we quench a *glowing* Mass, the fires
Flie off with *noise*, with noise the Heat expires.
   But if the Cloud is *dry*, and *Thunder* fall,
A *crackling Blaze* doth rise, and spread o're all;
As when *fierce Fires*, prest on by Winds, do
    seize
Our *Laurel* Groves, and wast the *Virgin* Trees,
The Leaves all crackle: *She that fled the chase
Of* Phoebus' *Love, still flies the Flame's
    embrace.**

THOMAS CREECH

Lucretius
The Fourth Book

Concerning the Nature of Love

Thus therefore, he who feels the Fiery dart
Of strong desire transfix his amorous heart,
Whether some beauteous Boy's alluring face,
Or lovelyer Maid with unresisted Grace,
From her each part the winged arrow sends,
From whence he first was struck, he thither tends;
Restless he roams, impatient to be freed,
And eager to inject the sprightly seed.
For fierce desire does all his mind employ,
And ardent Love assures approaching joy.
Such is the nature of that pleasing smart,
Whose burning drops distil upon the heart,
The Feaver of the Soul shot from the fair,
And the cold Ague of succeeding care.

---

*Daphne, fleeing from Phoebus, was changed into a laurel tree. See
Ovid, *Metamorphoses*, i, 452–567.

If absent, her Idea still appears;
And her sweet name is chiming in your ears:
But strive those pleasing fantomes to remove,
And shun th'Aerial images of Love
That feed the flame: When one molests thy mind
Discharge thy loyns on all the leaky kind;
For that's a wiser way than to restrain
Within thy swelling nerves, that hoard of pain.
For every hour some deadlier symptom shows,
And by delay the gath'ring venom grows,
When kindly applications are not us'd;
The Scorpion, Love, must on the wound be bruis'd:
On that one object 'tis not safe to stay,
But force the tide of thought some other way:
The squander'd Spirits prodigally throw,
And in the common Glebe of Nature sow.
Nor wants he all the bliss, that Lovers feign,
Who takes the pleasure, and avoids the pain;
For purer joys in purer health abound,
And less affect the sickly than the sound.
When Love its utmost vigour does imploy,
Ev'n then, 'tis but a restless wandring joy:
Nor knows the Lover, in that wild excess,
With hands or eyes, what first he wou'd possess:
But strains at all; and fast'ning where he strains,
Too closely presses with his frantique pains:
With biteing kisses hurts the twining fair,
Which shews his joyes imperfect, unsincere:
For stung with inward rage, he flings around,
And strives t'avenge the smart on that which gave the
    wound.
But love those eager bitings does restrain,
And mingling pleasure mollifies the pain.
For ardent hope still flatters anxious grief,
And sends him to his Foe to seek relief:
Which yet the nature of the thing denies;
For Love, and Love alone of all our joyes
By full possession does but fan the fire,

The more we still enjoy, the more we still desire.
Nature for meat and drink provides a space;
And when receiv'd they fill their certain place;
Hence thirst and hunger may be satisfi'd,
But this repletion is to Love deny'd:
Form, feature, colour, whatsoe're delight
Provokes the Lover's endless appetite,
These fill no space, nor can we thence remove
With lips, or hands, or all our instruments of love:
In our deluded grasp we nothing find,
But thin aerial shapes, that fleet before the mind.
As he who in a dream with drought is curst,
And finds no real drink to quench his thirst,
Runs to imagin'd Lakes his heat to steep,
And vainly swills and labours in his sleep;
So Love with fantomes cheats our longing eyes,
Which hourly seeing never satisfies;
Our hands pull nothing from the parts they strain,
But wander o're the lovely limbs in vain:
Nor when the Youthful pair more closely joyn,
When hands in hands they lock, and thighs in thighs they
    twine,
Just in the raging foam of full desire,
When both press on, both murmur, both expire,
They gripe, they squeeze, their humid tongues they dart,
As each wou'd force their way to t'other's heart:
In vain; they only cruze about the coast,
For bodies cannot pierce, nor be in bodies lost:
As sure they strive to be, when both engage,
In that tumultuous momentary rage,
So 'tangled in the Nets of Love they lie,
Till Man dissolves in that excess of joy.
Then, when the gather'd bag has burst its way,
And ebbing tydes the slacken'd nervs betray,
A pause ensues; and Nature nods a while,
Till with recruited rage new Spirits boil;
And then the same vain violence returns,
With flames renew'd th'erected furnace burns.

Agen they in each other wou'd be lost,
But still by adamantine bars are crost;
All wayes they try, successeless all they prove,
To cure the secret sore of lingring love.

JOHN DRYDEN

Horace Lib. I. Ode 9

Behold yon Mountain's hoary height
  Made higher with new Mounts of Snow;
Again behold the Winter's weight
  Oppress the lab'ring Woods below:
And streams with Icy fetters bound,
Benum'd and crampt to solid ground.

With well heap'd Logs dissolve the cold,
  And feed the genial hearth with fires;
Produce the Wine, that makes us bold,
  And sprightly Wit and Love inspires:
For what hereafter shall betide,
God, if 'tis worth his care, provide.

Let him alone with what he made,
  To toss and turn the World below;
At his command the storms invade;
  The winds by his Commission blow;
Till with a Nod he bids 'em cease,
And then the Calm returns, and all is peace.

To-morrow and her works defie,
  Lay hold upon the present hour,
And snatch the pleasures passing by,
  To put them out of Fortune's pow'r:
Nor love, nor love's delights disdain,
What e're thou get'st today is gain.

Secure those golden early joyes,
    That Youth unsowr'd with sorrow bears,
E're with'ring time the taste destroyes,
    With sickness and unweildly years!
For active sports, for pleasing rest,
This is the time to be possest;
The best is but in season best.

The 'pointed hour of promis'd bliss,
    The pleasing whisper in the dark,
The half unwilling willing kiss,
    The laugh that guides thee to the mark,
When the kind Nymph wou'd coyness feign,
And hides but to be found again,
These, these are joyes the Gods for Youth ordain.

JOHN DRYDEN

An Ode
In imitation of Horace,
Ode IX. Lib. I.

Vides ut alta, etc.

Bless me, 'tis cold! how chill the Air!
    How naked does the World appear!
But see (big with the Off-spring of the North)
    The teeming Clouds bring forth.
  A Show'r of soft and fleecy Rain,
  Falls, to new-cloath the Earth again.
  Behold the Mountain-Tops, around,
  As if with Fur of Ermins crown'd:
    And lo! how by degrees
The universal Mantle hides the Trees,
    In hoary Flakes, which downward fly,
As if it were the *Autumn* of the Sky;
    Whose Fall of Leaf would theirs supply:

Trembling, the Groves sustain the Weight and bow
    Like aged Limbs, which feebly go
Beneath a venerable Head of Snow.

Diffusive Cold does the whole Earth invade,
Like a Disease, through all its Veins 'tis spread,
And each late living Stream, is num'd and dead.
Let's melt the frozen Hours, make warm the Air;
Let cheerful Fires *Sol*'s feeble Beams repair;
    Fill the large Bowl with sparkling Wine;
    Let's drink, till our own Faces shine,
      Till we like Suns appear,
    To light and warm the Hemisphere.
Wine can dispence to all both Light and Heat,
    They are with Wine incorporate:
That pow'rful Juice, with which no Cold dares mix,
Which still is fluid, and no Frost can fix:
    Let that but in abundance flow,
And let it storm and thunder, hail and snow,
    'Tis Heav'ns Concern; and let it be
    The Care of Heaven still for me:
These Winds, which rend the Oaks and plough the Seas;
    Great *Jove* can, if he please,
With one commanding Nod appease.

    Seek not to know to Morrow's Doom;
    That is not ours, which is to come.
    The present Moment's all our Store:
      The next, should Heav'n allow,
      Then this will be no more:
So all our Life is but one instant *Now*.
      Look on each Day you've past
    To be a mighty Treasure won:
    And lay each Moment out in haste;
      We're sure to live too fast,
      And cannot live too soon.
    Youth does a thousand Pleasures bring,
    Which from decrepid Age will fly;

The Flow'rs that flourish in the Spring,
In *Winter*'s cold Embraces dye.

Now Love, that everlasting Boy, invites
To revel while you may, in soft Delights:
Now the kind Nymph yields all her Charms,
Nor yields in vain to youthful Arms.
Slowly she promises at Night to meet,
But eagerly prevents the Hour with swifter Feet.
To gloomy Groves and obscure Shades she flies,
There vails the bright Confession of her Eyes.
Unwillingly she stays,
Would more unwillingly depart,
And in soft Sighs conveys
The Whispers of her Heart.
Still she invites and still denies,
And vows she'll leave you if y'are rude;
Then from her Ravisher she flies,
But flies to be pursu'd:
If from his Sight she does herself convey,
With a feign'd Laugh she will herself betray,
And cunningly instruct him in the way.

WILLIAM CONGREVE

To a Perjur'd Mistress;
the 8th. Ode of Horace,
lib. II. Imitated.

Falsest of fair ones, swear again,
And add to thy Trandscending store,
Of prosperous Perjuries Ten Thousand more.
Dull Truth becomes thee not, it looks too plain:
Did Heaven those mortal sins resent,
But with some Venial Punishment;
Were the least blemish on thy face,

One Hair or Nail out of its place;
I should believe, but still you rise
More beautiful by Blasphemies;
By Disobedience made divine,
The more you swear, the more you shine;
As if the Gods had nought to do,
But to be wrong'd, and thankful too.
  Then swear, and shine again,
Let each false Oath augment thy Lovers' Train,
  And make this Wonder plain,
That Mankind never has more Piety
Than when they least believe their Deity.

SIR FRANCIS FANE

The Eighth Ode of the Second Book of Horace

Did any Punishment attend
  Thy former Perjuries,
I should believe a second time,
  Thy charming Flatteries:
Did but one Wrinkle mark this Face,
Or hadst thou lost one single Grace.

No sooner hast thou, with false Vows,
  Provok'd the Powers above;
But thou art fairer than before,
  And we are more in love.
Thus Heaven and Earth seem to declare,
They pardon Falshood in the Fair.

Sure 'tis no Crime vainly to swear,
  By every Power on high,
And call our bury'd Mother's Ghost
  A Witness to the Lye:
Heaven at such Perjury connives,
And *Venus* with a Smile forgives.

The Nymphs and cruel *Cupid* too,
  Sharp'ning his pointed Dart
On an old Hone, besmear'd with Blood,
  Forbear thy perjur'd Heart.
Fresh Youth grows up, to wear thy Chains,
And the old Slave no Freedom gains.

Thee, Mothers for their eldest Sons,
  Thee, wretched Misers fear,
Lest thy prevailing Beauty should
  Seduce the hopeful Heir:
New-marry'd Virgins fear thy Charms
Should keep their Bridegroom from their Arms.

SIR CHARLES SEDLEY

From Horace *Ode* 29 *Book* 3

Happy the Man, and happy he alone,
  He, who can call to day his own:
  He, who secure within, can say
Tomorrow do thy worst, for I have liv'd today.
  Be fair, or foul, or rain, or shine,
The joys I have possest, in spight of fate are mine.
  Not Heav'n it self upon the past has pow'r;
But what has been, has been, and I have had my
    hour.

    Fortune, that with malicious joy,
      Does Man her slave oppress,
    Proud of her Office to destroy,
      Is seldome pleas'd to bless.
    Still various and unconstant still;
But with an inclination to be ill;
    Promotes, degrades, delights in strife,
    And makes a Lottery of life.
    I can enjoy her while she's kind;

But when she dances in the wind,
And shakes her wings, and will not stay,
I puff the Prostitute away:
The little or the much she gave, is quietly resign'd:
Content with poverty, my Soul, I arm;
And Vertue, tho' in rags, will keep me warm.

What is 't to me,
Who never sail in her unfaithful Sea,
If Storms arise, and Clouds grow black;
If the Mast split and threaten wreck,
Then let the greedy Merchant fear
For his ill gotten gain;
And pray to Gods that will not hear,
While the debating winds and billows bear
His Wealth into the Main.
For me secure from Fortune's blows,
(Secure of what I cannot lose)
In my small Pinnace I can sail,
Contemning all the blustring roar;
And running with a merry gale,
With friendly Stars my safety seek
Within some little winding Creek;
And see the storm ashore.

JOHN DRYDEN

Part of an Ode of Horace Paraphras'd by the Duke of Buckingham, 1680

Fortune made up of Toyes and Impudence
That common Jade that has not common sence
But fond of business insolently dares
Pretend to Rule and spoiles the World's affaires,
She fluttering up and downe her favours throws ⎫
On the next Trull not minding what she does ⎬
Nor why, nor whom she helps or Injures knowes. ⎭

First she speakes faire then like a fury raves
And seldome truly loves but fools or knaves;
Let her Love whom she please, I scorn to wooe her:
Whilst she stayes with me I'le be Civil to her;
But if she offers once to move her wings
I'le fling her back all her Vain gugaw things
And armd with Virtue will more glorious stand
Than if the Bitch stil bowd att my Comand.
I'le Marrye Honesty tho ne're so poore
Rather than follow such a blind dull Whore.

GEORGE VILLIERS, 2ND DUKE OF BUCKINGHAM

From *The Sixth Book of the* Aeneis
The Golden Bough

An ancient Wood, fit for the Work design'd,
(The shady Covert of the Salvage Kind)
The *Trojans* found: The sounding Ax is ply'd:
Firs, Pines, and Pitch-Trees, and the tow'ring Pride
Of Forest Ashes, feel the fatal Stroke:
And piercing Wedges cleave the stubborn Oak.
Huge Trunks of Trees, fell'd from the steepy Crown
Of the bare Mountains, rowl with Ruin down.
Arm'd like the rest the *Trojan* Prince appears:
And, by his pious Labour, urges theirs.
Thus while he wrought, revolving in his Mind,
The ways to compass what his Wish design'd,
He cast his Eyes upon the gloomy Grove;
And then with Vows implor'd the Queen of Love.
O may thy Pow'r, propitious still to me,
Conduct my steps to find the fatal Tree,
In this deep Forest; since the Sibyl's Breath
Foretold, alas! too true, *Misenus'** Death.

*The trumpeter of Aeneas, drowned by a sea-god for his impious boasting.

Scarce had he said, when full before his sight ⎫
Two Doves, descending from their Airy Flight, ⎬
Secure upon the grassy Plain alight. ⎭
He knew his Mother's Birds: And thus he pray'd:
Be you my Guides, with your auspicious Aid:
And lead my Footsteps, till the Branch be found,
Whose glitt'ring Shadow guilds the sacred Ground:
And thou, great Parent! With Coelestial Care,
In this Distress, be present to my Pray'r.
Thus having said, he stop'd: With watchful sight,
Observing still the motions of their Flight,
What course they took, what happy Signs they shew. ⎫
They fed, and flutt'ring by degrees, withdrew ⎬
Still farther from the Place; but still in view. ⎭
Hopping, and flying, thus they led him on
To the slow Lake; whose baleful Stench to shun,
They wing'd their Flight aloft; then, stooping low,
Perch'd on the double Tree, that bears the golden Bough.
Thro' the green Leafs the glitt'ring Shadows glow;
As on the sacred Oak, the wintry Misleto:
Where the proud Mother views her precious Brood;
And happier Branches, which she never sow'd.
Such was the glitt'ring; such the ruddy Rind,
And dancing Leaves, that wanton'd in the Wind.
He seiz'd the shining Bough with griping hold;
And rent away, with ease, the ling'ring Gold.

The Destiny of Rome

Let others better mold the running Mass ⎫
Of Mettals, and inform the breathing Brass; ⎬
And soften into Flesh a Marble Face: ⎭
Plead better at the Bar; describe the Skies,
And when the Stars descend, and when they rise.
But, *Rome*, 'tis thine alone, with awful sway, ⎫
To rule Mankind; and make the World obey; ⎬
Disposing Peace, and War, thy own Majestick Way. ⎭

To tame the Proud, the fetter'd Slave to free;
These are Imperial Arts, and worthy thee.

JOHN DRYDEN

Ovid, *Amores*, I. viii.
To Corinna's *Chamber-maid*

Dear skilfull *Betty*, who dost far excell
My Lady's other Maids in dressing well:
Dear *Betty*, fit to be preferr'd above
To *Juno*'s Chamber, or the Queen of Love;
Gentile, well bred, not rustically coy,
Not easie to deny desired Joy,
Through whose soft Eyes still secret wishes shine,
Fit for thy Mistress' Use, but more for mine;
Who, *Betty*, did the fatal Secret see,
Who told *Corinna*, you were kind to me?
Yet when she chid me for my kind Embrace,
Did any guilty Blush spread o'er my Face?
Did I betray thee, Maid, or could she spy
The least Confession in my conscious Eye?
Not that I think it a disgrace to prove
Stoln sweets, or make a Chamber-maid my Love.
Achilles wanton'd in *Briseis*'* Armes;
Atrides bow'd to fair *Cassandra*'s Charms.
Sure I am less than these, then what can bring
Disgrace to me, that so became a King?
But when she lookt on you, poor harmless Maid
You blusht, and all the kind Intrigue betray'd:
Yet still I vow'd, I made a stout defence,
I swore, and lookt as bold as Innocence:
Damme, I gad, all that, and let me dye; ⎫
Kind *Venus*, do not hear my perjury, ⎬
Kind *Venus*, stop thy Ears when Lovers lye. ⎭

*The concubine of Achilles, and the principal object of his dispute
with Agamemnon, who himself later received Cassandra as part of
the spoils of Troy.

Now, *Betty*, how will you my Oaths requite?)
Come prethee lets compound for more delight, }
Faith I am easie, and but ask a Night.)
What! Start at the proposal? how! deny?
Pretend fond Fears of a Discovery?
Refuse lest some sad Chance the thing betray?
Is this your kind, your damn'd Obliging way?
Well, deny on, I'll lye, I'll swear no more,
Corinna now shall know thou art a Whore;
I'll tell, since you my fair Address forbid,
How often, when, and where, and what we did.

THOMAS CREECH

Ovid, *Amores*, II. xix.

If for thy self thou wilt not watch thy Whore,
Watch her for me that I may love her more;
What comes with ease we nauseously receive,
Who but a Sot wou'd scorn to love with leave?
With hopes and fears my Flames are blown up higher,
Make me despair, and then I can desire.
Give me a Jilt to tease my Jealous mind,
Deceits are Vertues in the Female kind.
Corinna my Fantastick humour knew,
Play'd trick for trick, and kept her self still new:
She, that next night I might the sharper come,
Fell out with me, and sent me fasting home;
Or some pretence to lye alone wou'd take,
When e'er she pleas'd her head and teeth wou'd ake:
Till having won me to the highest strain,
She took occasion to be sweet again.
With what a Gust, ye Gods, we then imbrac'd!
How every kiss was dearer than the last!

Thou whom I now adore be edify'd,
Take care that I may often be deny'd.
Forget the promis'd hour, or feign some fright,

209

Make me lye rough on Bulks each other Night.
These are the Arts that best secure thy reign,
And this the Food that must my Fires maintain.
Gross easie Love does like gross diet, pall,
In squeasie Stomachs Honey turns to Gall.
Had *Danae* not been kept in brazen Tow'rs,
Jove had not thought her worth his Golden Show'rs.
When *Juno* to a Cow turn'd *Io*'s Shape,
The Watchman helpt her to a second Leap.
Let him who loves an easie Whetstone* Whore,
Pluck leaves from Trees, and drink the Common Shore.
The Jilting Harlot strikes the surest blow,
A truth which I by sad Experience know.
The kind poor constant Creature we despise,
Man but pursues the Quarry while it flies.

But thou dull Husband of a Wife too fair,
Stand on thy Guard, and watch the pretious Ware;
If creaking Doors, or barking Dogs thou hear,
Or Windows scratcht, suspect a Rival there;
An Orange-wench wou'd tempt thy Wife abroad,
Kick her, for she's a Letter-bearing Bawd:
In short be Jealous as the Devil in Hell;
And set my Wit on work to cheat thee well.
The sneaking City Cuckold is my Foe,
I scorn to strike, but when he Wards the blow.
Look to thy hits, and leave off thy Conniving,
I'll be no Drudge to any Wittall living;
I have been patient and forborn thee long,
In hope thou wou'dst not pocket up thy wrong:
If no Affront can rouse thee, understand
I'll take no more Indulgence at thy hand.
What, ne'er to be forbid thy House and Wife!
Damn him who loves to lead so dull a life.
Now I can neither sigh, nor whine, nor pray,
All those occasions thou hast ta'ne away.

*Whetstone Park, a lane in Holborn, was a well known gathering-place of prostitutes.

Why art thou so incorrigibly Civil?
Doe somewhat I may wish thee at the Devil.
For shame be no Accomplice in my Treason,
A Pimping Husband is too much in reason.

Once more wear horns before I quite forsake her,
In hopes whereof I rest thy Cuckold-maker.

JOHN DRYDEN

The Vices of Women
from *The Sixth Satyr* of Juvenal

You ask from whence proceed these monstrous Crimes;
Once Poor, and therefore Chast in former times,
Our Matrons were: No Luxury found room
In low-rooft Houses, and bare Walls of Lome;
Their Hands with Labour hard'ned while 'twas Light,
And Frugal sleep supply'd the quiet Night.
While pincht with want, their Hunger held 'em straight,
When *Hannibal* was Hov'ring at the Gate:
But wanton now, and lolling at our Ease,
We suffer all th'invet'rate ills of Peace;
And wastful Riot, whose Destructive Charms
Revenge the vanquish'd World, of our Victorious Arms.
No Crime, no Lustful Postures are unknown;
Since Poverty, our Guardian-God, is gone:
Pride, Laziness, and all Luxurious Arts,
Pour like a Deluge in, from Foreign Parts:
Since Gold Obscene, and Silver found the way,
Strange Fashions with strange Bullion to convey,
And our plain simple Manners to betray.
What care our Drunken Dames to whom they spread?
Wine, no distinction makes of Tail or Head.
Who lewdly Dancing at a Midnight-Ball,
For hot Eringoes, and Fat Oysters call:

Full Brimmers to their Fuddled Noses thrust;
Brimmers the last Provocatives of Lust:
When Vapours to their swimming Brains advance,
And double Tapers on the Tables Dance.

Now think what Bawdy Dialogues they have,
What *Tullia* talks to her confiding Slave;
At Modesty's old Statue: when by Night,
They make a stand, and from their Litters light;
The Good Man early to the Levee goes,
And treads the Nasty Paddle of his Spouse.

The Secrets of the Goddess nam'd the Good,*
Are even by Boys and Barbers understood:
Where the Rank Matrons, Dancing to the Pipe,
Gig with their Bums, and are for Action ripe;
With Musick rais'd, they spread abroad their Hair;
And toss their Heads like an enamour'd Mare:
Laufella lays her Garland by, and proves
The mimick Leachery of Manly Loves.
Rank'd with the Lady, the cheap Sinner lies;
For here not Blood, but Virtue gives the prize.
Nothing is feign'd, in this Venereal Strife;
'Tis downright Lust, and Acted to the Life.
So full, so fierce, so vigorous, and so strong;
That, looking on, wou'd make old *Nestor* Young.
Impatient of delay, a general sound,
An universal Groan of Lust goes round;
For then, and only then, the Sex sincere is found.
Now is the time of Action; now begin,
They cry, and let the lusty Lovers in.
The Whoresons are asleep; Then bring the Slaves
And Watermen, a Race of strong-back'd Knaves.

JOHN DRYDEN

*The rites of the *Bona Dea* were celebrated every December, usually in the house of a consul. Only women were supposed to be present.

Portraits and Histories

Resolution in four Sonnets,
of a Poetical Question put to me by a Friend,
concerning four Rural Sisters.*

I

Alice is tall and upright as a Pine,
White as blaunch'd Almonds, or the falling Snow,
Sweet as are Damask Roses when they blow,
And doubtless fruitful as the swelling Vine.

Ripe to be cut, and ready to be press'd,
Her full cheek'd beauties very well appear,
And a year's fruit she loses e'ery year,
Wanting a man t'improve her to the best.

Full fain she would be husbanded, and yet,
Alass! she cannot a fit Lab'rer get
To cultivate her to her own content:

Fain would she be (God wot) about her task,
And yet (forsooth) she is too proud to ask,
And (which is worse) too modest to consent.

II

Marg'ret of humbler stature by the head
Is (as it oft falls out with yellow hair)
Than her fair Sister, yet so much more fair,
As her pure white is better mixt with red.

*The substance of the question is left to the imagination of the reader.

This, hotter than the other ten to one,
Longs to be put unto her Mother's trade,
And loud proclaims she lives too long a Maid,
Wishing for one t'untie her Virgin Zone.

She finds Virginity a kind of ware,
That's very very troublesome to bear,
And being gone, she thinks will ne'er be mist:

And yet withall, the Girl has so much grace,
To call for help I know she wants the face,
Though ask'd, I know not how she would resist.

III

Mary is black, and taller than the last,
Yet equal in perfection and desire,
To the one's melting snow, and t'other's fire,
As with whose black their fairness is defac'd.

She pants as much for love as th'other two,
But she so vertuous is, or else so wise,
That she will win or will not love a prize,
And but upon good terms will never doe:

Therefore who her will conquer ought to be
At least as full of love and wit as she,
Or he shall n'eer gain favour at her hands:

Nay, though he have a pretty store of brains,
Shall only have his labour for his pains,
Unless he offer more than she demands.

IV

Martha is not so tall, nor yet so fair
As any of the other lovely three,
Her chiefest Grace is poor simplicity,
Yet were the rest away, she were a Star.

She's fair enough, only she wants the art
To set her Beauties off as they can doe,
And that's the cause she ne'er heard any woo,
Nor ever yet made conquest of a heart:

And yet her bloud's as boiling as the best,
Which, pretty soul, does so disturb her rest,
And makes her languish so, she's fit to die.

Poor thing, I doubt she still must lie alone,
For being like to be attack'd by none,
Sh'as no more wit to ask than to deny.

CHARLES COTTON

The Enemies of David*
from *Absalom and Achitophel* (1681)

Of these the false *Achitophel*† was first:
A Name to all succeeding Ages Curst.
For close Designs, and crooked Counsels fit;
Sagacious, Bold, and Turbulent of wit:
Restless, unfixt in Principles and Place;
In Power unpleas'd, impatient of Disgrace.
A fiery Soul, which working out its way,⎫
Fretted the Pigmy Body to decay: ⎬
And o'r inform'd the Tenement of Clay.⎭
A daring Pilot in extremity;
Pleas'd with the Danger, when the Waves went high
He sought the Storms; but for a Calm unfit,
Would Steer too nigh the Sands, to boast his Wit.
Great Wits are sure to Madness near ally'd;
And thin Partitions do their Bounds divide:
Else, why should he, with Wealth and Honour Blest,

*Charles II.
†Anthony Ashley Cooper, first Earl of Shaftesbury.

Refuse his Age the needful hours of Rest?
Punish a Body which he could not please;
Bankrupt of Life, yet Prodigal of Ease?
And all to leave, what with his Toyl he won,
To that unfeather'd, two Leg'd thing, a Son:
Got, while his Soul did hudled Notions try;
And born a shapeless Lump, like Anarchy.
In Friendship False, Implacable in Hate:
Resolv'd to Ruine or to Rule the State.
To Compass this the Triple Bond* he broke;
The Pillars of the publick Safety shook:
And fitted *Israel* for a Foreign Yoke.
Then, seized with Fear, yet still affecting Fame,
Usurp'd a Patriott's All-attoning Name.
So easie still it proves in Factious Times,
With publick Zeal to cancel private Crimes:
How safe is Treason, and how sacred ill,
Where none can sin against the People's Will:
Where Crouds can wink; and no offence be known,
Since in another's guilt they find their own.
Yet, Fame deserv'd, no Enemy can grudge;
The States-man we abhor, but praise the Judge.
In *Israel*'s Courts ne'r sat an *Abbethdin*
With more discerning Eyes, or Hands more clean:
Unbrib'd, unsought, the Wretched to redress;
Swift of Dispatch, and easie of Access.
Oh, had he been content to serve the Crown,
With vertues only proper to the Gown;
Or, had the rankness of the Soyl been freed
From Cockle, that opprest the Noble seed:
David, for him his tunefull Harp had strung,
And Heaven had wanted one Immortal song.
But wilde Ambition loves to slide, not stand;
And Fortune's Ice prefers to Vertue's Land:
Achitophel, grown weary to possess
A lawfull Fame, and lazy Happiness;

---

*The alliance of 1668 with Holland and Sweden. Shaftesbury was
one of the most determined advocates of the Third Dutch War (1672–4).

Disdain'd the Golden fruit to gather free,
And lent the Croud his Arm to shake the Tree.

Some of their Chiefs were Princes of the Land:
In the first Rank of these did *Zimri** stand:
A man so various, that he seem'd to be
Not one, but all Mankind's Epitome.
Stiff in Opinions, always in the wrong;
Was every thing by starts, and nothing long:
But, in the course of one revolving Moon,
Was Chymist, Fidler, States-Man, and Buffoon:
Then all for Women, Painting, Rhiming, Drinking;
Besides ten thousand freaks that dy'd in thinking.
Blest Madman, who coud every hour employ,
With something New to wish, or to enjoy!
Rayling and praising were his usual Theams;
And both (to shew his Judgment) in Extreams:
So over Violent, or over Civil,
That every man, with him, was God or Devil.
In squandring Wealth was his peculiar Art:
Nothing went unrewarded, but Desert.
Begger'd by Fools, whom still he found too late:
He had his Jest, and they had his Estate.
He laught himself from Court, then sought Releif
By forming Parties, but coud ne're be Chief:
For, spight of him, the weight of Business fell
on *Absalom* and wise *Achitophel*:
Thus, wicked but in will, of means bereft,
He left not Faction, but of that was left.

Shimei,† whose Youth did early Promise bring
Of Zeal to God, and Hatred to his King;
Did wisely from Expensive Sins refrain,
And never broke the Sabbath, but for Gain:
Nor ever was he known an Oath to vent,
Or Curse unless against the Government.

*George Villiers, second Duke of Buckingham. See biographical note.
†Slingsby Bethell, the Whig Sheriff.

Thus, heaping Wealth, by the most ready way
Among the Jews, which was to Cheat and Pray;
The City, to reward his pious Hate
Against his Master, chose him Magistrate:
His Hand a Vare of Justice did uphold;
His Neck was loaded with a Chain of Gold.
During his Office, Treason was no Crime.
The Sons of *Belial* had a glorious Time:
For *Shimei*, though not prodigal of pelf,
Yet lov'd his wicked Neighbour as himself:
When two or three were gather'd to declaim ⎫
Against the Monarch of *Jerusalem*, ⎬
Shimei was always in the midst of them. ⎭
And, if they Curst the King when he was by,
Woud rather Curse, than break good Company.
If any durst his Factious Friends accuse,
He pact a Jury of dissenting Jews:
Whose fellow-feeling, in the godly Cause,
Would free the suffring Saint from Human Laws.
For Laws are only made to Punish those,
Who serve the King, and to protect his Foes.
If any leisure time he had from Power,
(Because 'tis Sin to misimploy an hour)
His business was, by Writing, to Persuade,
That Kings were Useless, and a Clog to Trade:
And, that his noble Stile he might refine,
No *Rechabite* more shund the fumes of Wine.
Chast were his Cellars, and his Shrieval Board
The Grossness of a City Feast abhor'd:
His Cooks, with long disuse, their Trade forgot;
Cool was his Kitchen, tho his Brains were hot.

To speak the rest, who better are forgot,
Would tyre a well breath'd Witness of the Plot:
Yet, *Corah*,* thou shalt from Oblivion pass;
Erect thy self thou Monumental Brass:

*Titus Oates.

High as the Serpent of thy mettall made,
While Nations stand secure beneath thy shade.
What tho his Birth were base, yet Comets rise
From Earthy Vapours ere they shine in Skies.
Prodigious Actions may as well be done
By Weaver's issue, as by Prince's Son.
This Arch-Attestor for the Publick Good
By that one Deed Enobles all his Bloud.
Who ever ask'd the Witnesses' high race,
Whose Oath with Martyrdom did *Stephen* grace?
Ours was a *Levite*, and as times went then,
His Tribe were Godalmighty's Gentlemen.
Sunk were his Eyes, his Voyce was harsh and loud,
Sure signs he neither Cholerick was, nor Proud:
His long Chin prov'd his Wit; his Saintlike Grace
A Church Vermilion, and a *Moses*'s Face;
His Memory, miraculously great,
Could Plots, exceeding man's belief, repeat;
Which, therefore cannot be accounted Lies,
For human Wit could never such devise.
Some future Truths are mingled in his Book;
But, where the witness faild, the Prophet Spoke:
Some things like Visionary flights appear;
The Spirit caught him up, the Lord knows where:
And gave him his *Rabinical* degree
Unknown to Foreign University.*
His Judgment yet his Memory did excel;
Which peic'd his wondrous Evidence so well:
And suited to the temper of the times;
Then groaning under Jebusitick Crimes.
Let *Israel*'s foes suspect his heav'nly call,
And rashly judge his wit Apocryphal;
Our Laws for such affronts have forfeits made:
He takes his life, who takes away his trade.
Were I my self in witness *Corah*'s place,

*Oates claimed that while in Spain spying on the Jesuits he had been
awarded a Doctorate of Divinity by the University of Salamanca. This
was denied by the University.

The wretch who did me such a dire disgrace,
Should whet my memory, though once forgot,
To make him an Appendix of my Plot.

JOHN DRYDEN

From *The Second Part of Absalom and Achitophel* (1682)

Now stop your noses Readers, all and some,
For here's a tun of Midnight-work to come,
*Og** from a Treason Tavern rowling home.
Round as a Globe, and Liquor'd ev'ry chink,
Goodly and Great he Sayls behind his Link;
With all this Bulk there's nothing lost in *Og*
For ev'ry inch that is not Fool is Rogue:
A Monstrous mass of foul corrupted matter,
As all the Devils had spew'd to make the batter.
When wine has given him courage to Blaspheme,
He Curses God, but God before Curst him;
And if man cou'd have reason none has more,
That made his Paunch so rich and him so poor.
With wealth he was not trusted, for Heav'n knew
What 'twas of Old to pamper up a *Jew*;
To what wou'd he on Quail and Pheasant swell,
That ev'n on Tripe and Carrion cou'd rebell?
But though Heav'n made him poor (with rev'rence
    speaking)
He never was a Poet of God's making;
The Midwife laid her hand on his Thick Skull,
With this Prophetick blessing – *Be thou Dull*;
Drink, Swear and Roar, forbear no lewd delight
Fit for thy Bulk, doe any thing but write:
Thou art of lasting Make like thoughtless men,
A strong Nativity – but for the Pen;

*Shadwell.

Eat Opium, mingle Arsenick in thy Drink,
Still thou mayst live avoiding Pen and Ink.
I see, I see 'tis Counsell given in vain,
For Treason botcht in Rhime will be thy bane;
Rhime is the Rock on which thou art to wreck,
'Tis fatal to thy Fame and to thy Neck:
Why should thy Metre good King *David* blast?
A Psalm of his will Surely be thy last.*
Dar'st thou presume in verse to meet thy foes,
Thou whom the Penny Pamphlet foil'd in prose?
Doeg,† whom God for Mankind's mirth has made,
O'er-tops thy tallent in thy very Trade;
Doeg to thee, thy paintings are so Course,
A Poet is, though he's the Poet's Horse.
A Double Noose thou on thy Neck dost pull,
For Writing Treason, and for Writing dull;
To die for Faction is a Common evil,
But to be hang'd for Non-sense is the Devil:
Hadst thou the Glories of thy King exprest,
Thy praises had been Satyr at the best;
But thou in Clumsy verse, unlickt, unpointed,
Hast Shamefully defi'd the Lord's Anointed:
I will not rake the Dunghill of thy Crimes,
For who wou'd reade thy Life that reads thy rhimes?
But of King *David*'s Foes be this the Doom,
May all be like the Young-man *Absalom*;
And for my Foes may this their Blessing be,
To talk like *Doeg*, and to Write like Thee.

JOHN DRYDEN

*Metrical psalms were commonly sung at public executions while
the condemned was being escorted to the gallows.
†Elkanah Settle (1648–1724), an old theatrical rival of Dryden, and
Shadwell's associate as Whig propagandist.

*Pindarick**

Let Ancients boast no more
Their lewd Imperial Whore†
Whose everlasting Lust
Surviv'd her Body's latest thrust,
And when that Transitory dust
Had no more vigour left in Store
Was still as fresh and active as before.

Her glory must give place
To one of Modern *Brittish* race
Whose ev'ry dayly act exceeds
The other's most Transcendant deeds;
Shee has at length made good
That there is Human Flesh and Blood
Ev'n able to outdoe
All that their loosest Wishes prompt 'em to.

When shee has jaded quite
Her allmost boundless Appetite,
Cloy'd with the choicest Banquetts of delight,
She'l still drudge on in Tastless vice
As if shee sinn'd for Exercise
Disabling stoutest Stallions ev'ry hour,
And when they can perform no more
She'l rail at 'em and kick 'em out of door.

Monmouth and *Candish* droop
As first did *Henningham* and *Scroop*,
Nay Scabby *Ned* looks thinn and pale

*A mock-eulogy of Barbara Palmer, Duchess of Cleveland. The
poem is generally attributed to Rochester.
†Either Messalina, wife of the Emperor Claudius, or Lais, the
younger of two famous Greek courtesans of this name, who was
mistakenly regarded by some early sources as the concubine of
Alexander, by others as that of Pyrrhus. A temple of Aphrodite was
built in expiation of her death at the hands of the women of Thessaly.

And sturdy *Frank* himself begins to Fail.
    But Woe betide him if he does
    She'l sett her *Jocky* on his Toes
And he shall end the Quarell without Blows.

    Now tell me all ye Powers
Who e're could equall this lewd Dame of ours?
    Lais her self must yield
    And vanquish'd *Julia** quitt the Field,
    Nor can that Princess† one day fam'd
    As wonder of the Earth
    For *Minataurus*' gloryous Birth
With Admiration any more be nam'd.
These puny *Heroins* of History
Eclips'd by her shall all forgotten be
Whil'st her great Name confronts Eternity.

             B.M MS. Harl. 6913

A Panegyric
1681

Of a great Heroin I mean to tell,
And by what just degrees her Titles swell,
To Mrs. *Nelly* grown from Cinder *Nell*.
Much did she suffer first, on Bulk and Stage,
From the Black-guard, and Bullies of the Age:
Much more her growing Virtue did sustain,
While dear *Charles Hart* and *Buckhurst* sued in vain.‡

---

*The daughter of Augustus banished by him because of her immorality.
† Pasiphae.
‡ Charles Hart (d. 1683), one of the most celebrated of seventeenth-century actors, and Charles, Lord Buckhurst, later Earl of Dorset (see biographical note) were two of Nell's early lovers. She is said to have spoken of them as her Charles I and Charles II, the king being her Charles III.

In vain they su'd; curs'd be the envious Tongue
That her undoubted Chastity wou'd wrong!
For shou'd we Fame beleive, we then might say
That Thousands lay with her, as well as they.
But, Fame, thou ly'st; for her Prophetic mind
Foresaw her greatness, Fate had well design'd,
And her Ambition chose to be, before
A virtuous Countess, an Imperial Whore.
Ev'n in her native dirt, her Soul was high;
And did at Crowns, and Shining Monarchs fly:
Ev'n while she Cinders rak'd; her swelling brest
With thoughts of glorious Whoredom was possest.
Still did she dream (nor cou'd her birth withstand)
Of dandling Scepters in her dirty hand.
But first the Basket her fair Arm did sute,
Laden with Pippins and Hesperian fruit.
This first step rais'd, to th'wond'ring Pit she sold
The lovely fruit, smiling with Streaks of Gold.
Fate now for her did its whole force engage,
And from the Pit, she's mounted to the Stage.
There in full Lustre did her glories shine,
And, long eclips'd, spread forth their Light divine:
There *Hart*'s and *Rowley*'s Soul she did insnare,
And made a King the Rival to a Player.
The King o'rcomes; and to the Royal Bed
The Dunghill's Offspring is in Triumph led.
Nor let the envious her first rags object
To her that's now in taudry Gayness deck'd:
Her merit does from this much greater show,
Mounting so high that took her rise so low:
Less fam'd that *Nelly* was, whose Cuckold's rage
In ten years' Wars, did half the World ingage.*
She's now the Darling Strumpet of the Croud;
Forgets her State and talks to them aloud;
Lays by her Greatness and descends to prate
With those 'bove whom she's rais'd by wondrous fate:

*Helen of Troy.

226

True to the Protestant Interest and Cause,
True to th'Establish'd Government and Laws,
The choice delight of the whole Mobile,
Scarce *Monmouth*'s Self is more belov'd than She.
Was this the Cause that did their Quarrel move,
That both are Rivals in the People's Love?
No! 'twas her matchless Loyalty alone
That bid Prince *Perkin* pack up and be gone.
Ill bred thou art, says Prince. *Nell* does reply:
Was Mrs. *Barlow** better bred than I?
Thus sneak'd away the Nephew overcome,
By his Aunt in Law's Severer Wit struck dumb.
Her Virtue, Loyalty, Wit, and noble mind,
In the foregoing Dogrel you may find:
Now for her Piety, one touch; and then
To *Rymer** I'le resign my Muse and Pen.
'Twas this that rais'd her Charity so high
To visit those that did in durance lye:
From *Oxford* Prisons many did she free,⎫
There dy'd her Father and there gloried She,⎬
In giving others Life and Liberty.⎭
So pious a Remembrance still she bore,
Ev'n to the Fetters that her Father wore.
Nor was her Mother's Funeral less her Care;
No Cost, no Velvet did the Daughter spare.
Fine gilded Scutcheons did the Hearse inrich,
To celebrate this Martyr of the Ditch.
Burnt Brandy did in flaming Brimmers flow,
Drunk at her Funeral; while her well pleas'd Shade
Rejoic'd even in the Sober Feilds below,
At all the Drunkeness her Death had made.
Was ever Child with such a Mother blest?
Or ever Mother such a Child possest?
Nor must her Cousin be forgot, prefer'd
From many years' Command in the Black-guard

*Monmouth's mother.
†Thomas Rymer (1641–1713), poet and critic. His *A Short View of Tragedy* (1692) contains an attack on *Othello*.

To be an Ensign:
Whose Tatter'd Colours well do represent
His first Estate i'th Ragged Regiment.

Thus we in short have all the Virtues seen
Of the incomparable Madam *Guyn*:
Nor wonder others are not with her Shown;
She who no equal has must be alone.

B.M. MS. Harl. 7319

On the Dutchess of Portsmouth's* Picture

Had she but liv'd in *Cleopatra*'s Age,
When *Beauty* did the Earth's great Lords engage,
Brittain, not *Egypt*, had been Glorious made;
Augustus then, like *Julius*, had obey'd:
A Nobler Theam had been the Poet's boast,
That all the World for Love had well been lost.

Examen Poeticum

Upon Mr. Bennet, Procurer Extraordinary

Reader beneath this Marble Stone
Saint *Valentine*'s Adopted Son,
Bennet the Bawd now lies alone.

Here lies alone the Amorous Spark,
Who was us'd to lead them in the dark
Like Beasts by Pairs into the Ark.

If Men of Honour wou'd begin,
He'd ne'er stick out at any Sin,
For he was still for Sticking't in.

*Louise de Kerouaille, Duchess of Portsmouth, *maîtresse en titre* to
Charles II.

If Justice chiefest of the Bench
Had an occasion for a Wench,
His reverend Flames 'twas he cou'd quench.

And for his Son and Heir apparent,
He cou'd perform as good an errand
Without a Tipstaff or a Warrant.

Over the Clergy he'd such a lock,
That he could make a Spiritual Frock
Fly off at sight of Temporal Smock.

Like *Will'ith'wisp* still up and down
He led the Wives of *London* Town,
To lodge with Squires of high renown.

While they (poor Fools) being unaware,
Did find themselves in Mansion fair,
Near *Leic'ster Fields* or *James*'s *Square.*

Thus Worthy *Bennet* was imploy'd;
At last he held the Door so wide,
He caught a cold, so cough'd, and dy'd.

ALEXANDER RADCLIFFE

The Characters of the Wits
from *An Essay on Satyr*

And first behold the merriest Man alive*
Against his careless Genius vainly strive;
Quit his dear Ease some deep Design to lay,
Appoint the Hour, and then forget the Day.
Yet he will laugh, ev'n at his Friends, and be

*George Villiers, 2nd Duke of Buckingham.

Just as good Company as *Nokes*, or *Lee*;*
But when he would the Court, or Nation rule,
He turns himself the best to Ridicule.
When serious, few for great Affairs more fit;
But shew him Mirth, and bait that Mirth with Wit,
That Shadow of a Jest shall be enjoyed,
Tho' he left all Mankind to be destroyed . . .

Another sort of Wits shall now be shown,
Whose harmless Foibles hurt themselves alone;
Who think Excess of Luxury can please,
And Laziness call loving of their Ease;
Pleasure and Indolence their only aim;
Yet their whole Life's but intermitting Pain.
Such Head-Achs, Surfeits, Ails, their days divide,
They scarce perceive the little time beside.

Well-meaning Men, who make this gross Mistake,
And Pleasure lose, only for Pleasure's sake!
Each Pleasure hath its Price, and when we pay
Too much of Pain, we squander Life away.

Thus *Dorset*, purring like a thoughtful Cat,
Marry'd; but wiser *Puss* ne'er thinks on that.
Like *Pembroke*'s *Dog*, fierce at his fondest time,
At once he wooes, and worries her in Rhime;
To gain her Love, exposes all her Life,
A teeming Widow, but a barren Wife.
With tame submission to the will of Fate,
He lugg'd about the Matrimonial Weight;
Till Fortune, blindly kind as well as he,
Has ill restor'd him to his Liberty;
That is, to live in his old idle way
Smoking all Night, and dozing all the Day;
Dull as *Ned Howard*, whom his brisker Time†
Had fam'd for Nonsense in immortal Rhime.

---

* James Nokes and Anthony Leigh, comic actors.
† See *On Mr* Howard *upon his* British Princes ('Come on ye Critticks!
find one fault who dare . . .')

Mulgrave* had much ado to 'scape the Snare,
Tho' vers'd in all those Arts that cheat the Fair.
Beauty and Wit had seiz'd his Heart so fast,
That *Numps* himself seem'd in the Stocks at last.
Old injur'd Parents dry'd their weeping Eyes,
In hopes to see this Pirate made a Prize;
Th'impatient Town waited the wish'd for Change,
And Cuckolds sneer'd in hopes of sweet Revenge;
Till his Ambition set his Love aside,
And sav'd him, not by Prudence, but by Pride.
What tender Thoughts his harden'd Heart can move,
Who for a Shadow quits substantial Love?

And little *Sid*,† for Simile renown'd,
Pleasure has always sought, but seldom found:
Tho' Wine and Women are his only Care,
Of both he takes a lamentable Share.
The Flesh he lives on, is too rank and strong;
His Meat and Mistresses are kept too long.
But, sure, we all mistake the pious Man,
Who mortifies his Person all he can;
And what the World counts Lewdness, Vice, and Sin,
Are Penances of this odd Capuchin:
For never Hermit under grave pretence
Has liv'd more contrary to common Sense.
Expecting Supper is his chief Delight;
Like any Labourer, our little Knight
Toils all the Day, but to be drunk at Night;
When o'er his Cups this Night-Bird chirping sits,
Till he takes *Huett* and *Jack Howe*‡ for Wits.

Last enter *Rochester*, of sprightly Wit,
Yet not for Converse safe, or Business fit.

---

* John Sheffield, Earl of Mulgrave, later Duke of Buckinghamshire,
the author of the *Essay*. This passage was inserted, either by himself or
his adviser Dryden, in order to conceal his authorship.
 † Sir Charles Sedley.
 ‡ Sir George 'Beau' Hewitt, dandy and Whig, and John Grubham
Howe, a minor member of the Rochester circle celebrated in later life
for his extremism in the service of both political parties.

Mean in each Action; lewd in every Limb,
Manners themselves are mischievous in him.
A Gloss he gives to ev'ry foul Design,
And we must own his very Vices shine.
But of this odd Ill-nature to Mankind
Himself alone the ill effects will find:
So envious Hags in vain their Witchcraft try,
Yet for intended Mischief justly die.
For what a *Bessus** has he always liv'd,
And his own Kickings notably contriv'd?
For (there's the Folly that's still mix'd with Fear)
Cowards more Blows than any Heroes bear.
Of fighting Sparks Fame may her Pleasure say;
But 'tis a bolder thing to run away.
The World may well forgive him all his ill,
For ev'ry Fault does prove his Penance still.
Easily he falls into some dang'rous Noose,
And then as meanly labours to get loose:
A Life so infamous is better quitting,
Spent in base injuring, and low submitting.

JOHN SHEFFIELD,
DUKE OF BUCKINGHAMSHIRE,
with the assistance of John Dryden and Alexander Pope

My Lord All-Pride†

Bursting with Pride, the loath'd Impostume swells,
Prick him, he sheds his Venom strait and smells;
But 'tis so lewd a Scribler, that he writes,
With as much force to Nature, as he fights;
Hardned in shame, 'tis such a baffled Fop,
That ev'ry School-boy whips him like a Top:

---

*The cowardly soldier in Beaumont and Fletcher's *A King and No King*. Rochester had given signal proof of his courage during the Second Dutch War and the accusation made here may be quite unfair.
† John Sheffield, Duke of Buckinghamshire.

And with his Arme, and Head, his Brain's so weak,
That his starved fancy is compell'd to rake,
Among the Excrements of others' wit,
To make a stinking Meal of what they shit.
So Swine, for nasty Meat, to Dunghil run,
And toss their gruntling Snowts up when they've done:
Against his Stars, the Coxcomb ever strives,
And to be something they forbid, contrives.
With a Red Nose, Splay Foot, and Goggle Eye,
A Plough Man's looby Meene, Face all a wry,
With stinking Breath and ev'ry loathsome mark,
The *Punchianello*, sets up for a Spark.
With equal self conceit too, he bears Arms,
But with that vile successs his part performs,
That he Burlesques his Trade, and what is best
In others turns, like Harlequins, to jeast.

So have I seen at *Smithfield*'s wondrous Fair,
When all his Brother Monsters florish there,
A Lubbard *Elephant* divert the Town,
With making Legs, and shooting off a Gun.
Go where he will, he never finds a Friend,
Shame and derision all his steps attend;
Alike abroad, at home, 'ith' Camp, and Court,
This *Knight* o'th' *Burning Pestle* makes us sport.

JOHN WILMOT, EARL OF ROCHESTER

A Dialogue between Fleet Shepard *and* Will *the Coffee Man**

Shep.   Tell me, sage Will, Thou that the town around
        For Witt and Tea and Coffee art renown'd,
        Tell me, for as the common rumour goes

*Will's coffee house in Russell Street, Covent Garden, was the
meeting place of the wits. Dryden had a chair specially reserved for
him there.

Thy house is cramm'd eternally with Beaus,
How shall I that strange Animall define:
What are his marks, his virtue, or his sign?
Soe mayst Thou keep still in the Witts' good graces
And never lose a farthing more at races.
Soe Hee enquired, and thus sage Will reply'd:

Will. Hee that like Mumford* sings, like Sackvill writes,
Dresses like Russell, like Tredenham fights,
Like Harbert in a noe engagement swears,
Chatters like Durfey, squints like Welch at prayers,
Damns every thing besides his own dull jest,
That thing's a Beau.

Shep.   Why then The Beau's a Beast.

BM. MS. Add. 29497

On Rutt *the Judge*

Rutt, to the Suburb Beauties full well known,
Was from the bag scarce crept into a Gown,
When he, by telling of himself fine tales,
Was made a Judge, and sent away to *Wales*:
'Twas proper and most fit it should be so,
Whither should Goats but to the Mountains go?

CHARLES COTTON

To Scilla

Storm not, brave Friend, that thou hadst never yet
Mistress nor Wife that others did not swive,
But, like a Christian, pardon and forget,
For thy own Pox will thy Revenge contrive.

SIR CHARLES SEDLEY

*William Mountfort (1664(?)–92), comic actor. His singing is praised by his younger contemporary, Colley Cibber.

234

A Character of the Dutch
from A Description of Holland by Mr. Nevell*

Then first I observe from the French-Man *Des Cartes*,†
   Men in the beginning like Cabbages grew;
You may say this Quotation not worth a Fart is,
   Tho he knew it as well as my self to be true;
      But when all is done,
       'Tis as clear as the Sun,
That Dutch-Men had that beginning, or none;
For like Pumpkins, I tell you, they grew out of Bogs,
And learnt their first words from the croaking of Frogs.

Should no other Nation Plant Men in their Sisters,
   They wou'd not be reckon'd amongst Flesh and Blood,
Nor would have more Bones than our *Colchester* Oisters;
   For Dutch-Men at first were huge skins of Mud;
      At the top of which lay
      Some Froth of the Sea,
Which harden'd to Brains, as Curds come from Whey.
Which loosen'd at Bottom, away they did go,
Just such thinking Giants as Boys make of Snow.

You may wonder a little how I came to know it,
   But wonder's a sign of Ignorance still,
The Records of Nature, their Bodies, do shew it,
   As he that goes there may know if he will;
      And perhaps I might
      Prove *Hobbs* in the right,

*Presumably the Jacobite poet and playwright Henry Nevile Payne (1648?–1705?).

†This theory, deriving ultimately from Anaximander (early sixth century B.C.), is expounded by Lucretius in Book V, ll. 783–800 of *De rerum natura* and through him gained wide currency among seventeenth-century freethinkers. I have been unable to find any reference to it in Descartes.

That Mankind by Nature wou'd fall to't and Fight,
For these things no sooner each other did see,
But with Lobsters' Claws they began Snicker Snee.

That Love and good Nature some Strangers bring hither,
      With all their Arts they cou'd never inspire,
For Guelt* their sole God, they would hang their own
            Father,
      And Starving (if poor) would not make him a fire.
            The first word they spoke,
            (Or rather did Croke)
And their last too, was Guelt, which they throatled
            i'th'Throat;
All their Life-time a Bee's not more busie for Honey,
Than they are for raking, and scraping for Money.

Miscellany, Being a Collection of Poems (1685)

The Character of Sydrophel
from *Hudibras, the Second Part*

He had been long t'wards *Mathematicks,*
Opticks, Philosophy, and *Staticks,*
Magick, Horoscopie, Astrologie,
And was *old Dog* at *Physiologie*:
But, as a *Dog* that turns the spit,
Bestirs himself, and plys his feet,
To clime the *Wheel;* but all in vain,
His own weight brings him down again:
And still he's in the self same place,
Where at his setting out he was.
So in the *Circle* of the *Arts,*
Did he advance his nat'rall Parts;
Till falling back still, for retreat,
He fell to *Juggle, Cant,* and *Cheat*;

*Money.

236

For, as those *Fowls* that live in Water
Are never wet, he did but smatter;
What'ere he labour'd to appear,
His Understanding still was clear.
Yet none a deeper knowledg boasted,
Since old *Hodg Bacon*, and *Bob Grosted*.*
Th'*Intelligible world*† he knew,
And all men dream on't, to be true:
That in this *World*, there's not a *Wart*,
That has not there a Counterpart;
Nor can there on the *face* of Ground,
An Individuall *Beard* be found,
That has not, in that Forrain *Nation*,
A fellow of the self-same fashion;
So *cut*, so *colour'd*, and so *curl'd*,
As those are, in th'*Inferior World*.
H' had read *Dee*'s‡ Prefaces before
The *Dev'l*, and *Euclide* o're and o're,
And, all th'*Intregues*, 'twixt him and *Kelly*,
Lescus and th'*Emperor*, would tell yee;
But with the *Moon* was more familiar
Than e're was *Almanack-well-willer*;
Her Secrets understood so clear,
That some believ'd he had been there:
Knew when she was in fittest mood,
For cutting *Corns* or letting *blood*;
When for anoynting *Scabs* or *Itches*,
Or to the *Bum* applying *Leeches*;
When *Sows*, and *Bitches* may be spade,
And in what Sign best *Sider*'s made;

*Roger Bacon (1214–94) and Robert Grosseteste (d. 1253), philosophers famed for the breadth of their knowledge.

†O.E.D. quotes John Norris's definition: 'a world of a nature purely spiritual and intellectual, and such as is not sensible, but intelligible only.' *Essay towards the Theory of an Ideal and Intelligible World* (1701), I. i. 12.

‡John Dee (1527–1608), mathematician, alchemist and converser with spirits. Edward Kelley and Albert Laski were two of his associates.

Whether the *Wane* be, or *Increase*,
Best to sett *Garlick*, or sow *Pease*;
Who first found out the *Man 'ith' Moon*,
That to the *Ancients* was unknown;
How many *Dukes*, and *Earls*, and *Peers*,
Are in the *Planetary Spheres*,
Their *Aiery Empire* and Command,
Their sev'ral strengths by Sea and Land;
What factions th' have, and what they drive at
In publique Vogue, and what in private;
With what designs and Interests,
Each Party manages Contests.
He made an *Instrument* to know
If the *Moon* shine at full, or no,
That would as soon as e're she shon, streit
Whether 'twere Day or Night demonstrate;
Tell what her *D'ameter* t'an inch is,
And prove she is not made of *Green Cheese*.
It would demonstrate, that the *Man in
The Moon*'s a *Sea Mediterranean*,
And that it is no *Dog*, nor *Bitch*,
That stands behind him at his breech;
But a huge *Caspian Sea*, or *Lake*,
With *Arms* which men for *Legs* mistake.
How large a *Gulph* his *Tayl* composes,
And what a goodly *Bay* his *Nose* is;
How many *German* leagues by th'scale,
Cape-Snout's from *Promontory-Tayl*.
He made a *Planetary Gin*
Which *Rats* would run their own heads in,
And come of purpose to be taken,
Without th'expence of Cheese or Bacon;
With *Lute-strings* he would counterfeit
Maggots, that crawl on dish of meat,
Quote Moles and Spots, on any place
'O th' body, by the *Index-face*;
Detect lost *Maidenheads*, by sneezing,
Or breaking wind, of *Dames*, or pissing;

Cure *Warts* and *Corns*, with application
Of *Med'cines*, to th' *Imagination*;
Fright *Agues* into Dogs, and scare
With *Rimes*, the *Tooth-ach* and *Catarrh*;
Chase evil *spirits* away by dint
Of *Cickle*, *Horse-shoo*, *Hollow-flint*;
Spit fire out of a *Walnut-shell*,
Which made the *Roman* Slaves rebel,*
And fire a Mine in *China*, here
With Sympathetick *Gunpowder*.
He knew what'sever's to be known,
But much more than he knew, would own:
What *Med'cine* 'twas that *Paracelsus*†
Could make a man with, as he tells us;
What figur'd *Slats* are best to make,
On wat'ry surface, *Duck* or *Drake*;
What *Bowling-stones*, in running race
Upon a *Board*, have swiftest pace;
Whether a *Pulse* beat in the black
List, of a Dappled *Louse*'s back;
If *Systole* or *Diastole*‡ move
Quickest, when hee's in wrath, or love;
When two of them do run a race,
Whether they *gallop*, *trot*, or *pace*;
How many scores a *Flea* will jump,
Of his own length, from head to rump,
Which *Socrates*, and *Chaerephon*
In vain, assaid so long agon;§
Whether his *Snout* a perfect *Nose* is,
And not an Elephant's *Proboscis*;
How many different *Specieses*

*One of the conjuring tricks used by Eunus, a Syrian, to incite the slaves of Sicily to rebellion against their Roman masters in 135 B.C.

†Philippus Aureolus Theophrastus Bombastus ab Hohenheim (1493–1541), occult philosopher and pioneer of modern chemistry.

‡The rhythmical contraction and expansion of the organs of the body, especially the heart.

§A subject of debate at Socrates' 'think-shop' as represented by Aristophanes in *The Clouds*.

Of Maggots breed in Rotten Cheese,*
And which are next of kin to those,
Engendred in a *Chaundler*'s nose,
Of those not seen, but understood,
That live in *Vineger* and *Wood*.

SAMUEL BUTLER

Portrait of a Physician†
from *The Dispensary*

Long has he been of that amphibious Fry,
Bold to prescribe, and busie to apply.
His Shop the gazing Vulgar's Eyes employs
With forreign Trinkets, and domestick Toys.
Here, *Mummies* lay most reverendly stale,
And there, the *Tortois* hung her Coat o'Mail;
Not far from some huge *Shark*'s devouring Head,
The flying Fish their finny Pinions spread.
Aloft in rows large Poppy Heads were strung,
And near, a scaly Alligator hung.
In this place, Drugs in Musty heaps decay'd,
In that, dry'd Bladders, and drawn Teeth were laid.
An inner Room receives the numerous Shoals
Of such as pay to be reputed Fools.
Globes stand by Globes, Volumns on Volumns lie,
And Planitary Schemes amuse the Eye.

The Sage, in Velvet Chair, here lolls at ease,
To promise future Health for present Fees.
Then, as from *Tripod*, solemn shams reveals,
And what the Stars know nothing of, foretels.

*The invention of the microscope had given Restoration scientists
an interest in the smaller forms of life which their contemporaries
could not help but find ridiculous. Cf. Shadwell's *The Virtuoso*,
IV. iii. 192–228.

†Francis Bernard (1627–98) of St Bartholomew's Hospital, a sup-
porter of the apothecaries in their opposition to a proposal to set up a
free dispensary for the poor.

One asks how soon *Panthea* may be won,
And longs to feel the Marriage Fetters on.
Others, convinc'd by Melancholy proof,
Wou'd know how soon kind Fates will strike 'em off.
Some, by what means they may redress the wrong,
When Fathers the Possession keep too long.
And some wou'd know the issue of their Cause,
And whether Gold can sodder up its flaws.
Poor pregnant *Laijs* his advice wou'd have,
To lose by Art what fruitful Nature gave:
And *Portia* old in expectation grown,
Laments her barren Curse, and begs a Son.
Whilst *Iris*, his cosmetick Wash must try,
To make her Bloom revive, and Lovers dye.
Some ask for Charms, and others Philters choose
To gain *Corinna*, and their Quartans* loose.
Young *Hylas,* botch'd with Stains too foul to Name,
In Cradle† here, renews his Youthful Frame:
Cloy'd with Desire, and surfeited with Charms,
A Hot-house he prefers to *Julia*'s arms.
And old *Lucullus* wou'd th' *Arcanum* prove,
Of kindling in cold Veins the sparks of Love.

SIR SAMUEL GARTH

On an Indian *Tomineios, the Leaſt of* Birds

I'me made in sport by *Nature*, when
   Shee's tir'd with the stupendious weight
Of forming *Elephants* and Beasts of State;
Rhinocerots, that love the Fen;
   The *Elkes*, that scale the hills of Snow,
And *Lions* couching in their awfull Den:
   These do work Nature hard, and then
   Her wearied Hand in Me doth show,
What she can for her own Diversion doe.

---

*Fevers which recurred every four days.
†A sweating tub, used in the treatment of venereal disease.

Man is a little World ('tis said)
   And I in *Miniature* am drawn,
A Perfect Creature, but in Short-hand shown.
   The *Ruck*, in *Madagascar* bred,
   (If new Discoveries Truth do speak)
Whom greatest Beasts and armed Horsemen dread,
   Both Him and Me one Artist made:
   Nature in this Delight doth take,
That can so Great and Little Monsters make.

   The *Indians* me a *Sunbeam* name,
   And I may be the Child of one:
So small I am, my Kind is hardly known.
   To some a sportive *Bird* I seem,
   And some believe me but a *Fly*;
Tho me a Feather'd *Fowl* the Best esteem:
   What er'e I am, I'me Nature's Gemm;
   And, like a *Sunbeam* from the Sky,
I can't be follow'd by the quickest Eye.

   I'me the true *Bird of Paradise*,
   And heavenly Dew's my only Meat:
My Mouth so small, 'twill nothing else admit.
   No Scales know how my weight to poise,
   So Light, I seem condensed Air;
And did at th'End of the *Creation* rise,
   When Nature wanted more Supplies,
   When she could little Matter spare,
But in Return did make the work more *Rare*.

THOMAS HEYRICK

Town and Country

The Morning Quatrains

The Cock has crow'd an hour ago,
'Tis time we now dull sleep forgo;
Tir'd Nature is by sleep redress'd,
And Labour's overcome by Rest.

We have out-done the work of Night,
'Tis time we rise t'attend the Light,
And e'er he shall his Beams display,
To plot new bus'ness for the day.

None but the slothfull, or unsound,
Are by the Sun in Feathers found,
Nor, without rising with the Sun,
Can the World's bus'ness e'er be done.

Hark! Hark! the watchfull Chanticler,
Tells us the day's bright Harbinger
Peeps o'er the Eastern Hills, to awe
And warn night's sov'reign to withdraw.

The Morning Curtains now are drawn,
And now appears the blushing dawn;
Aurora has her Roses shed,
To strew the way *Sol*'s steeds must tread.

Xanthus and *Æthon* harness'd are,
To roll away the burning Carr,
And, snorting flame, impatient bear
The dressing of the Chariotier.

The sable Cheeks of sullen Night
Are streak'd with Rosie streams of light,
Whilst she retires away in fear,
To shade the other Hemisphere.

The merry Lark now takes her wings,
And long'd-for day's loud wellcome sings,
Mounting her body out of sight,
As if she meant to meet the light.

Now doors and windows are unbar'd,
Each-where are chearfull voices heard,
And round about Good-morrows fly
As if Day taught Humanity.

The Chimnies now to smoke begin,
And the old Wife sits down to spin,
Whilst *Kate*, taking her Pail, does trip
Mull's swoln and stradl'ing Paps to strip.

Vulcan now makes his Anvil ring,
Dick whistles loud, and *Maud* doth sing,
And *Silvio* with his Bugle Horn
Winds an Imprime unto the Morn.

Now through the morning doors behold
Phœbus array'd in burning Gold,
Lashing his fiery Steeds, displays
His warm and all enlight'ning Rays.

Now each one to his work prepares,
All that have hands are Labourers,
And Manufactures of each trade
By op'ning Shops are open laid.

Hob yokes his Oxen to the Team,
The Angler goes unto the stream,
The Wood-man to the Purlews highs,
And lab'ring Bees to load their thighs.

Fair *Amarillis* drives her Flocks,
All night safe folded from the Fox,
To flow'ry Downs, where *Collin* stays,
To court her with his Roundelays.

The Traveller now leaves his Inn
A new day's Journey to begin,
As he would post it with the day,
And early rising makes good way.

The slick-fac'd School-boy Sachel takes,
And with slow pace small riddance makes;
For why, the haste we make, you know,
To Knowledge and to Vertue's slow.

The Fore-horse gingles on the Road,
The Waggoner lugs on his Load,
The Field with busie People snies,*
And City rings with various cries.

The World is now a busie swarm,
All doing good, or doing harm;
But let's take heed our Acts be true,
For Heaven's eye sees all we doe.

None can that piercing sight evade,
It penetrates the darkest shade,
And sin, though it could scape the eye,
Would be discover'd by the Cry.

CHARLES COTTON

The Streets of London
from *A Satyr in Imitation of the Third of Juvenal*

If you walk out in Bus'ness ne'er so great,
Ten thousand stops you must expect to meet:
Thick Crowds in every Place you must charge thro,
And storm your Passage, wheresoe're you go:
While Tides of Followers behind you throng,
And, pressing on your heels, shove you along:

*Abounds.

247

One with a Board or Rafter hits your Head,
Another with his Elbow bores your side;
Some tread upon your Corns, perhaps in sport,
Mean while your Legs are cas'd all o're with Dirt.
Here you the March of a slow Funeral wait,
Advancing to the Church with solemn State:
There a Sedan, and Lacquies stop your way,
That bears some Punk of Honor to the Play:
Now you some mighty piece of Timber meet,
Which tott'ring threatens ruin to the Street:
Next a huge *Portland* Stone, for building *Pauls*,
It self almost a Rock, on Carriage rowls:
Which, if it fall, would cause a Massacre,
And serve at once to murder, and interr.

If what I've said can't from the Town affright,
Consider other dangers of the Night:
When Brickbats are from upper Stories thrown,
And emptied Chamber-pots come pouring down
From Garret Windows: you have cause to bless
The gentle Stars, if you come off with Piss:
So many Fates attend, a man had need,
Ne'er walk without a Surgeon by his side:
And he can hardly now discreet be thought,
That does not make his Will, e're he go out.

If this you scape, twenty to one, you meet
Some of the drunken Scowrers of the Street,
Flush'd with success of warlike Deeds perform'd,
Of Constables subdu'd, and Brothels storm'd:
These, if a Quarrel, or a Fray be mist,
Are ill at ease a nights, and want their Rest.
For mischief is a Lechery to some,
And serves to make them sleep like *Laudanum*.
Yet heated, as they are, with Youth, and Wine,
If they discern a train of Flamboes shine,
If a Great Man with his gilt Coach appear,
And a strong Guard of Foot-boys in the rere,)
The Rascals sneak, and shrink their Heads for fear.)
Poor me, who use no Light to walk about,

Save what the Parish, or the Skies hang out,
They value not: 'tis worth your while to hear
The scuffle, if that be a scuffle, where
Another gives the Blows, I only bear:
He bids me stand: of force I must give way,
For 'twere a senseless thing to disobey,
And struggle here, where I'd as good oppose
My self to *Pembroke** and his Mastiffs loose.
Who's there? he cries, and takes you by the Throat,
Dog! are you dumb? Speak quickly, else my Foot
Shall march about your Buttocks: whence d'ye come,
From what Bulk-ridden Strumpet reeking home?
Saving your reverend Pimpship, where d'ye ply?
How may one have a Job of Lechery?
If you say any thing, or hold your peace,
And silently go off; 'tis all a case:
Still he lays on: nay well, if you scape so:
Perhaps he'l clap an Action on you too
Of Battery: nor need he fear to meet
A Jury to his turn, shall do him right,
And bring him in large Damage for a Shooe
Worn out, besides the pains, in kicking you.
A Poor Man must expect nought of redress,
But Patience: his best in such a case
Is to be thankful for the Drubs, and beg
That they would mercifully spare one leg,
Or Arm unbroke, and let him go away
With Teeth enough to eat his Meat next day.

JOHN OLDHAM

*Philip Herbert, seventh Earl of Pembroke (1653–83), a homicidal
brawler. 'This present Earl of Pembroke (1680) has at Wilton, 52
Mastives and 30 Grey-hounds, some Beares, and a Lyon, and a matter
of 60 fellowes more bestiall than they.' (Aubrey)

Wrote in the Banquetting-House in Grayes-Inn-Walks

Here Damsel sits disconsolate,
Cursing the Rigor of her Fate,
Till Squire Insipid having spy'd her,
Takes Heart of Grace, and squats beside her.
    He thus accosts, – Madam, By Gad
You are at once both fair and sad.
She innocently does submit
To all the Tyrants of his Wit.
The Bargain's made, she first is led
To the three Tuns, and so to Bed.

But yonder comes a graver Fop,
With heavy Shoe, and Boot-hose-top;
To him repairs a virtuous Sir,
Whose Question is, What News does stir?
With Face askrew, he then declares
The probability of Wars:
And gives an ample satisfaction
Of *English*, *French*, and *Dutch* Transaction.
Thus chattering out three houres Tale,
They tread to th' Mag-pye, to drink Ale.

ALEXANDER RADCLIFFE

Satyr

A. What *Timon* does old Age begin t'approach
That thus thou droop'st under a Night's debauch?
Hast thou lost deep to needy Rogues on Tick
Who ne're cou'd pay, and must be paid next Week?
    Tim. Neither alas, but a dull dining Sot,
Seiz'd me i'th' *Mall*, who just my name had got;
He runs upon me, cries dear Rogue I'm thine,

With me some Wits of thy acquaintance dine.
I tell him I'm engag'd, but as a Whore,
With modesty enslaves her Spark the more,
The longer I deny'd, the more he prest,
At last I e'ne consent to be his Guest.
He takes me in his Coach, and as we go,
Pulls out a Libel, of a Sheet or two;
Insipid as *The praise of pious Queens*,
Or *Shadwell*'s unassisted former Scenes;*
Which he admir'd, and prais'd at e'vry Line,
At last it was so sharp, it must be mine.
I vow'd I was no more a Wit than he,
Unpractic'd and unblest in Poetry:
A Song to *Phillis*, I perhaps might make,
But never Rhym'd, but for my Pintle's sake:
I envy'd no Man's fortune, nor his fame,
Nor ever thought of a revenge so tame.
He knew my Stile, he swore, and 'twas in vain,
Thus to deny the Issue of my Brain.
Choak'd with his flattr'y, I no answer make,
But silent leave him to his dear mistake.
Of a well meaning *Fool*, I'm most afraid,
Who sillily repeats what was well said.
But this was not the worst, when he came home,
He askt are *Sidley*, *Buckhurst*, *Savill* come?
No, but there were above *Halfwit* and *Huffe*,
Kickum, and *Dingboy*. Oh 'tis well enough.
They're all brave Fellows cryes mine Host, let's Dine,
I long to have my Belly full of Wine:
They'll write, and fight I dare assure you,
They're Men, *Tam Marte quam Mercurio*.†
I saw my error, but 'twas now too late,
No means, nor hopes, appear of a retreat.

*Cf. *Mac Flecknoe*, ll. 163–4: 'But let no alien *Sedley* interpose / To lard with wit thy hungry *Epsom* prose.' This was a stock accusation of anti-Shadwell satire and had some slight justification.

†Devotees of both Mars the god of war and Mercury the god of eloquence.

Well we salute, and each Man takes his Seat.
Boy (says my Sot) is my Wife ready yet!
A Wife good Gods! A Fop and Bullys too!
For one poor Meale, what must I undergo?
In comes my Lady strait, she had been Fair,
Fit to give love, and to prevent despair.
But Age, Beauty's incureable Disease,
Had left her more desire than pow'r to please.
As Cocks will strike, although their Spurrs be gone,
She with her old bleer Eyes to smite begun:
Though nothing else, she (in despight of time)
Preserv'd the affectation of her prime;
How ever you begun, she brought in love,
And hardly from that Subject wou'd remove.
We chanc'd to speak of the *French King*'s success;
My Lady wonder'd much how *Heav'n* cou'd bless,
A Man, that lov'd Two Women at one time;
But more how he to them excus'd his Crime.
She askt *Huffe*, if *Love*'s flame he never felt?
He answer'd bluntly – do you think I'm gelt?
She at his plainness smil'd, then turn'd to me,
Love in young Minds, preceeds ev'n Poetry.
You to that passion can no Stranger be,
But Wits, are giv'n to inconstancy.
She had run on I think till now, but Meat
Came up, and suddenly she took her seat.
I thought the Dinner wou'd make some amends,
When my good Host cryes out – y'are all my Friends,
Our own plain Fare, *and the best* Terse* *the* Bull
Affords, I'll give you and your Bellies *full*:
As for French Kickshaws, Cellery, *and* Champoon,
Ragous *and* Fricasses, *introth we've none.*
Here's a good Dinner towards thought I, when strait
Up comes a piece of Beef, full Horsman's weight;
Hard as the Arse of Mosely,† under which

---

*Claret, from the size of barrel (a third of a pipe) in which it was customarily sold.

†Mother Mosely, a procuress.

The Coachman sweats, as ridden by a Witch.
A Dish of Carrets, each of 'em as long,
As Tool, that to fair *Countess* did belong;
Which her small Pillow cou'd not so well hide,
But Visiters his flaming Head espy'd.
Pig, Goose, and Capon, follow'd in the Rear,
With all that Country Bumpkins call good Cheer:
Serv'd up with Sauces all of Eighty-Eight,
When our tough *Youth* wrestled and threw the Weight.
And now the Bottle briskly flies about,
Instead of Ice, wrapt in a wet Clowt.
A Brimmer follows the third bit we eat,
Small Beer becomes our drink, and Wine our Meat.
The Table was so large, that in less space,
A Man might safe six old *Italians* place:
Each Man had as much room as *Porter Blunt*,
Or *Harris* had in *Cullen*'s Bushel Cunt.
And now the Wine began to work, mine Host
Had been a *Collonel* we must hear him boast
Not of Towns won, but an Estate he lost
For the *King*'s Service, which indeed he spent
Whoring and Drinking, but with good intent.
He talkt much of a Plot, and Money lent
In *Cromwell*'s time. My Lady she
Complain'd our love was course, our Poetry
Unfit for modest Eares, small Whores and Play'rs
Were of our Hair-brain'd Youth, the only cares;
Who were too wild for any virtuous League,
Too rotten to consummate the Intrigue.
Falkland, she prais'd, and *Suckling*'s* easie Pen,
And seem'd to taste their former parts again.
Mine Host drinks to the best in Christendome,
And decently my Lady quits the Room.
Left to our selves, of several things we prate,
Some regulate the *Stage*, and some the *State*.

*Lucius Cary, second Viscount Falkland (1610(?)–43) and Sir
John Suckling (1609–42), cavalier lyrists.

Halfwit cries up my Lord of *Orrerey*,*
Ah how well *Mustapha*, and *Zanger* dye!
His sense so little forc'd, that by one Line,
You may the other easily divine.
　'*And which is worse, if any worse can be,*
　'*He never said one word of it to me.*
There's fine Poetry! you'd swear 'twere Prose,
So little on the Sense, the Rhymes impose.
Damn me (says *Dingboy*) in my mind Gods-zounds
Etheridge writes Airy Songs, and soft Lampoons,
The best of any Man; as for your Nowns,
Grammar, and Rules of Art, he knows 'em not,
Yet writ two taking Plays without one Plot.
　Huffe was for Settle,† and *Morocco* prais'd,
Said rumbling words, like Drums, his courage rais'd.
　'*Whose broad-built-bulks, the boyst'rous Billows bear,*
　'*Zaphee and Sally, Mugadore, Oran,*
　'*The fam'd Arzile, Alcazer, Tituan.*
Was ever braver Language writ by Man?
　Kickum for *Crown*‡ declar'd, said in Romance,
He had out done the very Wits of *France*.
Witness *Pandion*, and his *Charles the Eight*;
Where a young Monarch, careless of his Fate,
Though Forreign Troops, and Rebels, shock his State,
Complains another sight afflicts him more.
(*Viz.*) '*The* Queen's Galleys *rowing from the* Shore,
　'*Fitting their Oars and Tackling to be gon*
　'*Whilst sporting Waves smil'd on the rising Sun.*
Waves smiling on the Sun! I am sure that's new,
And 'twas well thought on, give the Devil his due.
　Mine Host, who had said nothing in an hour,
Rose up, and prais'd the *Indian Emperor*.§
　'*As if our Old* World, *modestly withdrew,*

---

*Roger Boyle, first Earl of Orrery (1621–79), author of nine tedious
tragedies in rhymed couplets and two comedies.
　†Elkanah Settle (1648–1724). His *Empress of Morocco* appeared in
1673.　　‡John Crowne (1640–1712). See biographical note.
　§ A tragedy by Dryden (1665).

'*And here in private had brought forth a New.*
There are two Lines! who but he durst presume
To make the old World, a new withdrawing Room,
Where of another World she's brought to Bed!
What a brave Midwife is a *Laureat*'s head!

But pox of all these Scriblers, what do'e think.
Will *Zouches** this year any *Champoone* drink?
Will *Turene* fight him? without doubt says *Huffe*,
When they two meet, their meeting will be rough.
Damn me (says *Dingboy*) the *French*, Cowards are,
They pay, but the *English*, *Scots*, and *Swiss* make War.
In gawdy Troops, at a review they shine,
But dare not with the *Germans* Battel joyn;
What now appears like courage, is not so,
'Tis a short pride, which from success does grow;
On their first blow, they'll shrink into those fears,
They shew'd at *Cressy*, *Agincourt*, *Poytiers*;
Their loss was infamous, Honor so stain'd,
Is by a Nation not to be regain'd.
What they were then I know not, now th'are brave,
He that denies it lyes and is a Slave
(Says *Huffe* and frown'd) says *Dingboy*, that do I,
And at that word, at t'others Head let fly
A greasie *Plate*, when suddenly they all,
Together by the Eares in Parties fall.
Halfwit, with *Dingboy* joynes, *Kickum* with *Huffe*,
Their Swords were safe, and so we let 'em cuff
Till they, mine Host, and I, had all enough.
Their rage once over, they begin to treat,
And Six fresh Bottles must the peace compleat.
I ran down Stairs, with a Vow never more
To drink Beer Glass, and hear the *Hectors* roar.

JOHN WILMOT, EARL OF ROCHESTER†

*Commander of the Imperial army during part of 1674. Turenne
was the commander of the opposing French army.

† The attribution is not entirely certain. Two normally reliable
contemporary sources give the poem to Sedley. See D. M. Vieth,
Attribution in Restoration Poetry (New Haven, 1963), pp. 281–92.

On the London Fire's Monument

Here stand I,
I know not why:
And if I fall,
Have at you all.

GEORGE VILLIERS,
SECOND DUKE OF BUCKINGHAM

A Call to the Guard by a Drum

Rat too, rat too, tat too, rat tat too, rat tat too,
With your Noses all scabb'd and your Eyes black and
    blew,
All ye hungry poor Sinners that Foot Souldiers are,
Though with very small Coyn, yet with very much Care,
From your Quarters in Garrets make haste to repair,
       To the Guard, to the Guard.

From your sorry Straw Beds and your bonny white Fleas,
From your Dreams of Small Drink and your very small
    ease,
From your plenty of stink, and no plenty of room,
From your Walls daub'd with Phlegm sticking on 'em like
    Gum,
And Ceilings hung with Cobwebs to stanch a cut Thumb,
       To the Guard, &c.

From your crack'd Earthen Pispots where no Piss can
    stay,
From Roofs bewrit with Snuffs in Letters the wrong way;
From one old broken Stool with one unbroken Leg,
One Box with ne'er a Lid to keep ne'er a Rag,
And Windows that of Storms more than your selves can
    brag,
       To the Guard, &c.

With trusty Pike and Gun, and the other rusty Tool;
With Heads extremely hot, and with Hearts wondrous
    cool;
With Stomachs meaning none (but Cooks and Sutlers)
    hurt;
With two old tatter'd Shooes that disgrace the Town
    Dirt;
With forty shreds of Breeches, and not one shred of Shirt,
        To the Guard, &c.

See they come, see they come, see they come, see they
    come,
With Allarms in their Pates to the call of a Drum;
Some lodging with Bawds (whom the modest call Bitches)
With their Bones dry'd to Kexes, and Legs shrunk to
    Switches;
With the Plague in the Purse, and the Pox in the Breeches,
        To the Guard, &c.

Some from snoring and farting, and spewing on Benches,
Some from damn'd fulsom Ale, and more damn'd fulsom
    Wenches;
Some from Put, and Size Ace, and Old Sim, this way
    stalk;
Each man's Reeling's his gate, and his Hickup his talk,
With two new Cheeks of Red from ten old Rows of
    Chalk,
        To the Guard, &c.

Here come others from scuffling, and damning mine Host,
With their Tongues at last tam'd, but with Faces that
    boast
Of some Scars by the Jordan, or Warlike Quart Pot,
For their building of Sconces and Volleys of Shot,
Which they charg'd to the mouth, but discharg'd ne'er a
    Groat,
        To the Guard, &c.

Hey for Valour in black too, the Chaplain does come!
From his preaching o'er Pots now to pray o'er a Drum.
All ye whoring and swearing old Red Coats draw near,
Like to Saints in Red Letters listen and give ear,
And be godly awhile ho, and then as you were,
     To the Guard, &c.

After some canting terms, To your Arms, and the like,
Such as Poysing your Musquet, or Porting your Pike;
To the right, To the left, or else Face about;
After ratling your Sticks, and your shaking a Clout,
Hast your Infantry Troops that mount the Guard on foot,
     To the Guard, &c.

Captain *Hector* first marches, but not he of *Troy*,
But a Trifle made up of a Man and a Boy;
See the Man scant of Arms in a Scarf does abound,
Which presages some swaggering, but no bloud nor
     wound;
Like a Rainbow that shews the World shan't be drown'd;
     To the Guard, &c.

As the Tinker wears Rags whilst the Dog bears the
     Budget,
So the Man stalks with Staff whilst the Footboy does
     trudge it
With the Tool he should work with (that's Half Pike
     you'll say);
But what Captain's so strong his own Arms to convey,
When he marches o'er loaden with ten other men's Pay?
     To the Guard, &c.

In his March (if you mark) he's attended at least
With Stinks sixteen deep, and about five abreast,
Made of Ale and Mundungus, Snuff, Rags, and brown
     Crust Sir,

While he wants twenty Taylors to make up the cluster,
Which declares that his Journey's not now to the
   Muster,*
               But To the Guard, &c.

Some with Musquet and Belly uncharg'd march away,
With Pipes black as their Mouths are, and short as their
   Pay;
Whilst their Coats made of holes shew like Bone-lace
   about 'em,
And their Bandeliers hang like to Bobbins without 'em,
And whilst Horesmen do cloath 'em, these Footscrubs do
   clout 'em,
               For the Guard, &c.

Some with Hat ty'd on one side, and Wig ty'd on neither;
Wear gray Coats and gray Cattle, see their Wenches run
   hither,
For to peep through Red Lattice and dark Cellar doors,
To behold 'em wear Pikes rusty just like their Whores,
As slender as their Meals and as long as their Scores,
               To the Guard, &c.

Some with Tweedle, wheedle, wheede; whilst we beat
   Dub a Dub;
Keep the base *Scotish* noise, and as base *Scotish* scrub:†
Then with Body contracted, a Rag open spread,
Comes a thing with red Colours, and Nose full as red;
Like an Ensign to the King, and to the King's Head,
               Towards the Guard, &c.

Two Commanders come last, the Lieutenant perhaps,
Full of Low Country Stories and Low Country Claps.
To be next him the other takes care not to fail,

---

   *The captain is keeping the unit ten men under strength so as to
have their pay for himself.

   †The Coldstream Guards, Monck's regiment, had been formed in
1650 for service in Scotland.

Powder Monkey by name, that vents stink by whole sale,
For where should the Fart be but just with the Tail
     Of the Guard? &c.

And now hey for the King Boys, and hey for the Court,
Which is guarded by these as the Tower is by Dirt;
These *Whitehall* must admit and such other unhouse ye,
Each day lets in the drunk, whilst it lets out the drowsie,
And no place in the world shifts so oft to be lowsie.
     Thank the Guard, &c.

Some to *Scotland-Yard* sneak, and the Sutler's wife kisses;
But despairing of Drink till some Countryman pisses,
And pays too (for no place in the Court must be given)
To the Can-office then, all a *Foot-Soldier's* Heav'n,
Where he finds a foul *Fox*, soon, and curses Sir Stephen.*
     On the Guard, &c.

Some at Shite-house publick (where a Rag always goes)
At once empty their Guts and diminish their Clothes.
Though their Mouths are poor Pimps (Whore and Bacon
    being all
Their chief Food) yet their Bums we true Courtiers may
    call,
For what they eat in the Suburbs, they shite at *Whitehall*,
     For the Guard, &c.

Such a like Pack of Cards to the *Park* making entry,
Here and there deal an Ace, which the *Jews* call a Centry,
Which in bad Houses of Boards stand to tell what a clock
    'tis,
Where they keep up tame Redcoats as men keep up tame
    Foxes,
Or Apothecaries lay up their Dogs' Turds in Boxes.
     Oh the Guard, &c.

---

*The guardsman finds that his beer has 'the fox' (i.e. is spoiled) and
curses Sir Stephen Fox, Charles II's Paymaster General, for buying it.

Some of these are planted (though it has been their lucks
Oft to steal Country Geese) now to watch the King's
  Ducks;
While some others are set in the side that has Wood in,
To stand Pimps to black Masques that are oft thither
  footing,
Just as Huswives set Cuckolds to tend their Black
  Pudding.
    Oh the Guard, &c.

Whilst another true *Trojan* to some passage runs,
As to keep in the Debtors, so to keep out the Duns;
Or a Prentice, or his Mistress, with Oaths to confound,
Till he hyes him from the Park as from forbidden ground,
Cause his Credit is whole, and his Wench may be sound,
    And quits the Guard, &c.

Now it's night, and the Patrole in Alehouse drown'd,
For nought else but the Pot and their Brains walk the
  round;
Whilst like Hell the Commander's Guard-chamber does
  shew,
There's such damning themselves and all else of the
  Crew,
For though these cheat the Men, they give the Devil his
  due,
    On the Guard, &c.

Whilst a Main after Main at old Hazard they throw,
And their Quarrels grow high as their Money grows
  low;
Strait they threaten hard (using bad Faces for Frowns)
To revenge on the Flesh, the default of the Bones,
But the Blood's in their Hose, and in Oaths all their
  Wounds.
    Like the Guard, &c.

In the Morning they fight, just as much as they pray;
For some one to the King does the Tidings convey
For preventing of *Murder*; Oh 'tis a wise way!
Though not one of 'em knows (as a thousand dare say)
What belongs to a dead man, unless in his pay
                    For the Guard, &c.

With their Skins they march home no more hurt than
    their Drums,
But for scratching of Faces, or biting of Thumbs;
And now hey for fat *Alewives*, and *Tradesmen* grown lean;
For the Captain grown *Bankrupt*, recruits him again,
With sending out Tickets, and turning out Men
                    From the Guard, &c.

Strait the poor Rogue's cashier'd with a Cane, and a
    Curse,
Fall from wounding no Men, now to cut ev'ry Purse:
And what then? Man's a *Worm*; those we Glow-worms
    may name:
For as they'r dark of Body, have Tails all of flame.*
So tho' those liv'd in Oaths, yet they die with a *Psalm*.†
                    Farewell Guard, &c.

                              ALEXANDER RADCLIFFE

New Prison‡

You *Squires* o'th'shade, that love to tread
In gloomy Night, when *Day*'s in bed;
That court the *Moon*, supposing she
Likes such a watchful Industry:

*The Guards' red coats.
†i.e. are hanged.
‡This could either be the New Prison of the Gatehouse, adjoining
New Palace Yard, Westminster, or the New Prison at Clerkenwell
subsequently visited by Humphrey Clinker.

Read here a Story; it will make
Your Eye-lids droop, when she's awake.
'Tis not the horrid noise of Wars,
Consequent Chances, Wounds and Scars,
The dangers of the foaming Deep,
Nor all the *Bug-bear Fates*, that keep
Fond Men in awe, *Hobgoblins*, *Sprites*,
Dire Dreams in dark and tedious Nights,
A troubled Conscience, nor the sence
Of man's despairing Diffidence,
That can present so sad a face
Of black Affliction, as this place.

The sneaking *Rascals*, lowsie *Whores*,
The creaking of the dismal Doors,
That stink of stinks that fumes within,
(Symptoms of *Beasts* that dwell therein)
So rot the Air, *Cameleons** cou'd
Not live unpoyson'd with such Food.
There's reason for't, no Mortal can
Step from the Excrement of Man;
And that which should howe're be sweet,
Is like the rest; I mean, their meat.
The Locusts of the wilderness
Are Sweet-meats to their Nasty Mess.
  I could say more; the Place provokes me,
  But that the vile *Tobacco* choaks me.

CHARLES COTTON

*The chameleon was popularly supposed to live on air.

Second *DIALOGUE between* Crab *and* Gillian

from *The Bath, or the Western Lass*

Crab.	Where Oxen do low,
	And Apples do grow,
	Where Corn is sown,
	And Grass is Mown,
	Where Pidgeons do fly,
	And Rooks nestle high,
	Fate give me for Life a Place;
Gill.	Where Hay is well Cockt,
	And Udders are stroakt;
	Where Duck and Drake,
	Cry quack, quack, quack;
	Where Turkeys lay Eggs,
	And Sows suckle Pigs,
	Oh, there I would pass my days.
Crab.	On nought we will feed,
Gill.	But what we do breed;
Crab.	And wear on our backs,
Gill.	The Wool of our Flocks.
Crab.	And though Linen feel
Gill.	Rough spun from the Wheel,
	'Tis cleanly, though coarse it comes.
Crab.	Town Follys and Cullies,
	And *Mollys*, and *Dollys*,
	For ever adieu, and for ever;
Gill.	And Beaus, that in Boxes,
	Lie nuzzling the Doxies,
	In Wigs that hang down to their Bums.
Crab.	Adieu the *Pall-Mall*,
	The Park and Canal;
	St. *James*'s-*Square*,
	And Flaunters there.

> The Gaming-house too,
> Where high Dice and low*
> Are manag'd by all degrees.

Gill.   Godb'w'e to the Knight,
       Was bubl'd last Night;
       That keeps a Blowze,
       And beats his Spouse,
       And now in great haste,
       To pay what he lost,
> Sends home to cut down the Trees.

Crab.   And hey for the Lad,
Gill.   Improves e'ery Clod:
Crab.   That ne'er set his Hand
Gill.   To bill or to Bond,
Crab.   Nor barters his Flocks,
Gill.   For wine or the Pox,
> To chouse him of half his Days;

Crab.   But Fishing and Fowling,
       Hunting and Bowling,
       His Pastimes are ever and ever;

Gill.   Whose Lips when ye buss 'em,
       Smell like the Bean Blossom;
> Ah, he 'tis, shall have my Praise.

Crab.   To Taverns where grow,
       Sowr Apple and Sloe,
       A long adieu,
       And farewel too
       The House of the Great,
       Whose Cook has no Meat
> And Butler can't quench my Thirst;

Gill.   Godb'w'e to the *Change,*
       Where Rantipols range,
       Farewel cold Tea,
       And Ratafie,†

---

*Dice weighted to favour high or low numbers.
†Peach or apricot brandy.

> *Hide-Park* too, where Pride
> In Coaches will Ride,
> Although they be choak'd with Dust.

Crab. Farewel the Law-Gown,
Gill. The Plague of the Town,
Crab. And Friends of the Crown,
Gill. Cry'd up or run down,
Crab. And City Jack Daws,
Gill. That fain would make Laws
> To measure by Yards and Ells;
Crab. Stock-jobbers and Swobbers,
> And Toasters and Roasters;
> For ever adieu, and for ever.
Gill. We find what you're doing,
> And home we're a going,
> And so you may ring the Bells.

THOMAS DURFEY

From *Epistle to* John Bradshaw Esq.

Know then with Horses twain, one sound, one lame,
On *Sunday*'s Eve I to St. *Alban*'s came,
Where, finding by my Body's lusty state
I could not hold out home at that slow rate,
I found a Coach-man, who, my case bemoaning,
With three stout Geldings, and one able Stoning,
For eight good Pounds did bravely undertake,
Or for my own, or for my Money's sake,
Through thick and thin, fall out what could befall,
To bring me safe and sound to *Basford-hall.*
Which having drank upon, he bid good-night,
And (Heaven forgive us) with the Morning's light,
Not fearing God, nor his Vice-gerent Constable,*
We roundly rowling were the Road to *Dunstable,*

*The parish constable or beadle was empowered to apprehend
travellers during the hours of divine service.

Which, as they chim'd to Prayers, we trotted through,
And 'fore elev'n ten minutes came unto
The Town that *Brickhill* height, where we did rest,
And din'd indifferent well both man and beast.
'Twixt two and four to *Stratford*, 'twas well driven,
And came to *Tocester* to lodge at Even.
Next day we din'd at *Dunchurch*, and did lie
That night four miles on our side *Coventry*.
Tuesday at Noon at *Lichfeild* Town we baited,
But there some Friends, who long that hour had waited,
So long detain'd me, that my Chariotier
Could drive that night but to *Uttoxiter*.
And there the *Wedn'sday*, being Market-day,
I was constrain'd with some kind Lads to stay
Tippling till afternoon, which made it night
When from my *Hero*'s Tow'r* I saw the light
Of her Flambeaux, and fanci'd as we drave
Each rising Hillock was a swelling wave,
And that I swimming was in *Neptune*'s spight
To my long long'd-for Harbour of delight.

   And now I'm here set down again in peace,
After my troubles, business, Voyages,
The same dull Northern clod I was before,
Gravely enquiring how Ewes are a Score,
How the Hay-Harvest, and the Corn was got,
And if or no there's like to be a Rot;
Just the same Sot I was ere I remov'd,
Nor by my travel, nor the Court improv'd;
The same old fashion'd Squire, no whit refin'd,
And shall be wiser when the Devil's blind:
But find all here too in the self-same state,
And now begin to live at the old rate,
To bub old Ale, which nonsense does create,
Write leud Epistles, and sometimes translate
Old Tales of Tubs, of *Guyenne* and *Provence*,

*The beacon tower Cotton had built at Beresford-Hall to guide him home after dark, here compared to the torch used by Hero to guide Leander across the Hellespont.

And keep a clutter with th'old Blades of *France*,
As *D'Avenant* did with those of *Lombardy*,*⎫
Which any will receive, but none will buy, ⎬
And that has set *H.B.*† and me awry.   ⎭
My River still through the same Chanel glides,
Clear from the Tumult, Salt, and dirt of Tides,
And my poor Fishing-house, my Seat's best grace,
Stands firm and faithfull in the self-same place
I left it four months since, and ten to one
I go a Fishing ere two days are gone:
So that (my Friend) I nothing want but thee
    To make me happy as I'd wish to be;
And sure a day will come I shall be bless'd
In his enjoyment whom my heart loves best;
Which when it comes will raise me above men
Greater than crowned Monarchs are, and then
I'll not exchange my Cottage for *White-hall*,
Windsor, the *Lauvre*, or th'*Escurial*.

CHARLES COTTON

A Ballad of Andrew *and* Maudlin

Andrew and *Maudlin*, *Rebecca* and *Will*
    Margaret and *Thomas*, and *Jocky* and *Mary*,
Kate o'th' Kitchin, and *Kit* of the Mill,
    Dick the Plow-man, and *Joan* of the Dairy,
To solace their Lives, and to sweeten their Labour,
All met on a time with a Pipe and a Tabor.

Andrew was Cloathed in Shepherd's Gray,
    And *Will* had put on his Holy-day Jacket,
Beck had a Coat of *Popin-jay*,
    And *Madge* had a Ribbond hung down to her Placket;

---

*A reference to the setting of Davenant's romantic epic *Gondibert* (1650).

†Identified by John Buxton as Cotton's publisher Henry Brome.

Megg and *Moll* in Frize, *John* and *Jocky* in Leather,
And so they began all to Foot it together.

Their Heads, and their Arms about them they flung,
   With all the might and force they had;
Their Legs went like Flayls, and as loosely hung,
   They Cudgel'd their Arses as if they were Mad:
Their Faces did shine, and there Fires did kindle,
While the Maids they did trip and turn like a Spindle.

Andrew Chuck'd *Maudlin* under the Chin,
   Simper she did like a Furmity Kettle;
The twang of whose blobber-lips made such a din,
   As if her Chaps had been made of Bell-mettle.
Kate laughed heartily at this same smack,
And loud she did answer it with a Bum-crack.

At no *Whitsun-Ale* there e'er yet had been
   Such Fraysters and Friskers as these Lads and Lasses;
From their Faces the Sweat ran down to be seen,
   But sure I am, much more from their Arses.
For had you but seen't, you then would have sworn,
You never beheld the like since you were born.

Here they did Fling, and there they did Hoist;
   Here a hot Breath, and there went a Savor;
Here they did glance, and there they did gloist;
   Here they did Simper, and there they did Slaver.
Here was a Hand, and there was a Placket,
Whilst, hey! their Sleeves went Flicket-a-flacket.

The Dance being ended, they sweat and they stunk.
   The Maidens did smirk it, the Youngsters did Kiss 'em;
Cakes and Ale flew about, they clapp'd hands and drunk,
   They laugh'd and they gigl'd until they Be-pist 'em.
They laid the Girls down, and gave each a green Mantle,
While their Breasts and their Bellies went a-Pintle
   a-Pantle.

THOMAS DURFEY

To my Friend Mr. John Anderson
From the Countrey

You that the *City* Life embrace,
  And in those Tumults run your race,
Under th'aspect of the Celestial face
                    Of your bright *Lady*:
You, that to *Masks*, and *Plays* resort,
  As if you would rebuild the *Court*,
We here can match you with our *Countrey*-sport,
                    As neer as may be.

For, though 'tis good to be so nigh
  Rich wine, and excellent Company:
Yet, *John*, those Pleasures you full dear do buy
                    Some times, and seasons.
For you but *Tributaries* are,
  Aw'd by the furious men of War:
We *Countrey-Bumkins* then are happier far
                    For many reasons.

First, we have here no bawling *Duns*,
  Nor those fierce things ycleped *Bums*,
No *Cuckold-Constable*, or *Watch* here comes
                    To apprehend us.
And then we've no unwholsome *Dames*
  To broil us in their bawdy flames,
Nor need enquire after *Physicians* names,
                    That may befriend us.

And next, we have excelling *Ale*,
  Most high and mighty, strong and stale:
And, when we go, we need no other *Bail*
                    Than our own word, *Sir*,
When you all Day are fain to sit,
  Send Paper-pellets of small wit,
Your Tickets; and, when none of them will hit,
                    Pawn Cloak or Sword, *Sir*.

Then we out-do your *Beauties*, that
You Entertain with Cost and Chat,
That make you spend your precious *Time* and *Fat*,
         And yet are stedfast:
  We here have homely willing *Winn*,
  With bucksome *Bess*, and granting *Jinn*,
All full and plump without, and warm within,
         That crackt the Bed fast.

And then, for Mirth, we have much more
  Than you, for all your various store,
For we prefer *Bag-pipes*, so loud, before
         Lute, or *Cremona*.*
  We caper with *Tom Thump*, i'th'*Hall*,
  Measures beyond *Corant*, or *Brawl*;
And when we want a match, for *Ciceley* call,
         A roba bona.

We have too errant *Knights* so stout,
  As honest *Hobinol* and *Clout*,
With many an other stiff and sturdy Lout,
         That play at wasters,
  Shooe the wild Mare, and lick the board,
  That for stiff Tuck, or cutting Sword,
For Man, or Woman, care not of a *Turd*,
         But their own *Masters.*

Thus every of our petty toys
  Outvies your greatest dear-bought joys:
Then to thy freedom from the *City*-noise,
         I'll drink a *Beer-jack*:
  And now the *Spring* comes on apace,
  Sweet flowers crown the *Earth*'s green face,
Nor can I doubt, but thou wilt have the grace
         To wish thee here, *Jack.*

CHARLES COTTON

*Cremona was the home of the Stradivari and other famous violin makers.

The Battle between a Cock *and a* Capon
Lamport 1682

Let other Poets treat of lofty Things,
The rise of States and fall of Captive Kings:
A lower subject doth my Muse invite,
An humbler Theme, but of no less Delight.
   A bloody Battle late was fought between
Two Combatants of different hopes and Meine.
One, the proud Captain of the brooding Race,
That doth the Yard o'th' carefull *Houswife* grace:
With tender Chuck calls the admiring Rout,
And proudly leads th'obsequious *Hens* about:
The drowsie Peasant's Clock, whose wakefull throat
Doth Midnight's shades and Day's approach denote:
Calls up from his coarse Bed the snoring Hind, ⎞
Whom Sleep's strong fetters do securely bind, ⎟
While guilty Greatness can no Quiet find: ⎠
The Creature, whom enjoyment can't appease, ⎞
But Raves in lust, and Rivals all his Race; ⎟
Not a *Seraglio* his Desires can please. ⎠
Impatient Lust doth in his Visage lie,
And deadly Rage dwells in his bloody Eye.
   The *Other* of the Combatants was one
Of meaner hopes and expectation:
Not much unlike in shape, but much in Meine,
Not Male, nor Female, but a sort between.
Monster! not made by Nature, but by Art;
Whose sex the carefull *Housewife* did impart:
Who conscious, *Lust* did fret the Nerves away,
And on Life's Balsame did too freely prey,
With bloody Knife did rob him of the prize,
Where *Love* is plac'd, and some say, *Courage* lies.
Angry with all the World for th'Inju'ry done, ⎞
A melancholly sullen Creature grown, ⎟
He Consort shuns, and loves to be alone. ⎠
Ghastly and pale he look'd, whether for fear,

Or rage at the Misfortunes, he did bear,
Or want of generous spirits and active fires,
Which daring uncontrouled Love inspires:
Each part unseemly look'd, but most of all
The bending Feathers of his useless *Tail*.
    The Combat nois'd, to the unusual Sport
A gallant Train of Noble Youth resort.
All do the *Castrate*'s sneaking looks deride,
And give their suffrage o'th'proud Champion's side.
Till from the rest *One** born of noble Race,
Whom *Honour, Beauty, Wit,* and *Worth* did grace;
Whether it was his perspicacious Eye   ⎫
Did growing sparks of hidden Valour spy;   ⎬
(And who of Valour greater Judge than *He*?)⎭
Or that he scorn'd to walk i'th' beaten road,
The common Path, that all the Vulgar trod;
Or that, as generous Spirits do, He chose ⎫
To lend his help unto the weaker cause,   ⎬
As *Cato* did thô Gods did him oppose: ⎭
Castrate's Defence he took, and thus he spoke.
'*Narses*† did once an Empire's fate revoke:
'Renown with Kingdoms he did bravely win,
'And Victory sat on his beardless Chin.
'*Europe* and *Asia* still deplore the fate,
'That *Sinan Bassa*'s Valour did create!
'Both fill'd with Fame and Honourable scars;
'Unfit for *Venus*', fit for *Mars*'s Wars.
O're *Castrate*'s Soul the pleasing Accents spread,
And lifted up his long-dejected Head.
Great thoughts in his depressed Mind did grow,
And glowing Heat thrô every Limb did flow,
From valiant Race he sprung (if Fame says true),
And his Descent from bloody Warriours drew:
Till Numerous Injuries and long Disgrace   ⎫
(Scorn'd and contemn'd by all the female Race)⎬
His high-born generous Spirit did debase.   ⎭

*Sʳ
Justinian
Isham.

*Narses (472–568) was the Armenian eunuch who conquered Italy
for Justinian. Synan Pasha was a sixteenth-century Turkish general.

But now swell'd up by Praise to bloody Fight,
Praise, that the Coward doth to Fame excite,
With deep Revenge his Soul doth inward bleed,
And Jealousie doth on his Liver feed,
A Jealousie from Impotence that's bred.
Rage, Madness, and Revenge his soul possess,
And his torn Heart to mighty Acts address.

Fierce *Chanticleer* with haughty scornfull Pride
And mix'd Disdain over the Pit did stride,
And did th'Unworthy Combatant deride:
But, see'ing at last he did to fight prepare,
He gives the signal to th'unlucky Warr,
With that shrill Note, that ope's the *Morning*'s Eye,
That dreadfull Note, that makes even *Lions* fly:
And with Revenge, which his proud Soul did swell,
He like a Tempest on his Enemy fell.
Both met, both other's heightned Courage try'd,
And in deep Gore their shining Weapons died.

The Cautious *Castrate* let his eager Foe
In haughty Vaunts and scorn his strength bestow:
Disgrace and long-felt Shame had made him wise,
Taught him grave Arts and usefull Policies:
How to beguile a fierce and eager Foe,
How to ward off, and how return a Blow;
With circling winding Course his Foe deceive,
And deadly and unlook'd-for wounds to give.
To make his Enemie's fierceness useless still,
To fly and wound, and *Parthian-like* to kill.
With various fortune the event they try,
One doth on Force, th'other on Fraud rely,
And *Victory* with equal wings doth fly.
Besmeard with gore, with blood and fury red,
Blood they drink down, and showers of blood they shed.

With loss of blood at length the *Cock* grows faint,
And doth, too late, those fiery spirits want,
Which he so prodigally spent to please
The Lust of all his Speckled Mistresses:
Finds, what his glory was, his shame doth grow,

And *Lust*, that heightens, doth enervate too.
Yet scorning longer a base Foe to'engage,
He summons the remains of force and rage:
One blow he with united Forces made,
And *Castrate* senseless on the Pavement laid.
   Netled with the Disgrace, brave *Castrate* rose:
Disgrace, that sparks of hidden Valour blows,
Ferments within, and wakes the sleeping seeds,
That many years lay dead, to gallant deeds.
All, that from Rage or wrankled Malice flow,
All, that Revenge or Jealousie can show,
All, that past Scorn, Disgrace, or biting Slight;
All in one fatal bloody Blow unite;
Which strow'd the *Cock* supinely on the ground,
While Blood and Life flow'd from the gaping wound.
Castrate on his fall'n Foe with pride did tread,
And lifting up his late-dejected Head,
He would have *Crow'd*, to show the Victory;
But barr'd by former wrongs that faculty,
He *Cackled* something out, which those, that know
The Tongue, he spoke in, do interpret so.
'Here the Insulting Conquerour doth lie,
'Mighty in *Venus*' School, that could supply
'The Love of twenty *Hens*, and every Morn
'With fiery Lust his blushing Cheeks adorn.
'*Venus* and *Mars* have different ways of fight;
'One doth in *Love*, th'other in *Rage* delight:
'*Courage* resides i'th' noble seat the *Heart*;
'But *Love*'s confin'd unto a *lower Part*.

THOMAS HEYRICK

Walking

To *walk* abroad is, not with Eys,
  But Thoughts, the Fields to see and prize;
    Els may the silent Feet,

Like Logs of Wood,
Mov up and down, and see no Good,
Nor Joy nor Glory meet.

Ev'n Carts and Wheels their place do change,
But cannot see; tho very strange
The Glory that is by:
Dead Puppets may
Mov in the bright and glorious Day,
Yet not behold the Sky.

And are not Men than they more blind,
Who having Eys yet never find
The Bliss in which they mov:
Like Statues dead
They up and down are carried,
Yet neither see nor lov.

To *walk* is by a Thought to go;
To mov in Spirit to and fro;
To mind the Good we see;
To taste the Sweet;
Observing all the things we meet
How choice and rich they be.

To note the Beauty of the Day,
And golden Fields of Corn survey;
Admire the pretty Flow'rs
With their sweet Smell;
To prais their Maker, and to tell
The Marks of His Great Pow'rs.

To fly abroad like activ Bees,
Among the Hedges and the Trees,
To cull the Dew that lies
On evry Blade,
From evry Blossom; till we lade
Our *Minds*, as they their *Thighs*.

Observ those rich and glorious things,
The Rivers, Meadows, Woods, and Springs,
  The fructifying Sun;
       To note from far
The Rising of each Twinkling Star
  For us his Race to run.

A little Child these well perceivs,
Who, tumbling among Grass and Leaves,
  May Rich as Kings be thought,
       But there's a Sight
Which perfect Manhood may delight,
  To which we shall be brought.

While in those pleasant Paths we talk
'Tis *that* tow'rds which at last we walk;
  But we may by degrees
       Wisely proceed
Pleasures of Lov and Prais to heed,
  From viewing Herbs and Trees.

THOMAS TRAHERNE

Elden-Hole

from The Wonders of the Peak

Hence two miles *East*, does a fourth *Wonder* lye,
Worthy the greatest curiosity,
Cal'd *Elden-Hole*; but such a dreadful place,
As will procure a tender *Muse* her grace,
In the description if she chance to fail,
When my hand trembles, and my cheeks turn pale.
Betwixt a verdant *Mountain*'s falling flanks,
And within bounds of easie swelling banks,
That hem the *Wonder* in on either side,
A formidable *Scissure* gapes so wide,
Steep, black, and full of horror, that who dare

Looks down into the *Chasme*, and keeps his hair
From lifting off his hat, either has none,
Or for more modish curls casheers his own.
It were injurious I must confess,
By mine to measure braver Courages:
But when I peep into't, I must declare,
My heart still beats, and eyes with horror stare;
And he, that standing on the brink of *Hell*,
Can carry it so unconcern'd, and well,
As to betray no fear, is, certainly,
A better *Christian*, or a worse, than I.

This yawning mouth is thirty paces long,
Scarce half so wide, within lin'd through with strong
Continuous Walls of solid perpend stone:
A Gulf wide, steep, black, and a dreadful one;
Which few, that come to see it, dare come near,
And the most daring still approach with fear.
Having with terror, here beheld a space
The gastly aspect of this dang'rous place,
Critical *Passengers* usually sound
How deep the threatning gulf goes under ground,
By tumbling down stones sought throughout the field,
As great as the officious *Boores* can wield,
Of which such *Millions* of *Tuns* are thrown,
That in a *Country*, almost all of stone,
About the place they something scarce are grown.
But being brought, down they'r condemn'd to go,
When *silence* being made, and ears laid low,
The first's turn'd off, which, as it parts the Air,
A kind of *sighing* makes as if it were
Capable of that useless passion, Fear.
Till the first hit strikes the astonisht ear,
Like *Thunder* under-ground; thence it invades,
With louder thunders, those *Tartarean* shades,
Which groan forth horror, at each ponderous stroke
Th'unnatural *issue* gives the *Parent* Rock;
Whilst, as it strikes, the sound by turns we note,

When nearer *flat*, *sharper* when more remote,
As the hard walls, on which it strikes, are found
Fit to reverberate the bellowing sound:
When, after falling long, it seems to hiss,
Like the old *Serpent* in the dark *Abyss*:
Till *Eccho*, tir'd with posting, does refuse
To carry to th'inquisitive *Perdu's*,*
That couchant lye above, the trembling news.
And there ends our Intelligence, how far
It travails further, no one can declare;
Though if it rested here the place might well
Sure be accepted for a *Miracle*.

Your *Guide* to all these Wonders, never fails
To entertain you with ridic'lous tales
Of this strange place – One of a *Goose* thrown in,
Which out of *Peaks-Arse* two miles off, was seen
Shell-naked sally, rifled of her plume;
By which a man may lawfully presume,
The owner was a woman grave, and wise,
Could know her *Goose* again in that disguise.

Another lying *Tale* the People tell,
And without smiling, of a pond'rous *Bell*
By a long Rope let down the *Pit* to sound.
When many hundred fadoms under-ground
It stopt; but though they made their sinews crack
All the men there could not once move it back;
Till, after some short space, the plundred line
With scores of curious knots made wond'rous fine,
Came up amain with easie motion:
But for the Jangling *Plummet*, that was gone.

But with these idle *Fables* feign'd of old,
Some modern truths, and sad ones too are told:
One of that mercenary *Fool* expos'd
His Life for gold, t'explore what lies enclos'd

*Sentinels; watchers.

279

In this obscure *Vacuity*, and tell
Of stranger sights than *Theseus* saw in *Hell*:
But the poor *Wretch* pay'd for his thirst of gain:
For being cran'd up with a distemper'd brain,
A fault'ring tongue, and a wild staring look,
(Whether by *damps* not known, or horror strook)
He raving languish'd a few days, and then
Di'd; peradventure to go down agen.
Now this man was confederate with *mischance*
'Gainst his own Life, his whole inheritance,
Which bates the pity human nature bears
To poor involuntary *Sufferers*:
But the sad tale of his severer fate
Whose story's next, compassion must create
In savages and in the silent deep,
Make the hard marble, that destroy'd him, weep.

A *Stranger*, to this day from whence not known,
Travelling this wild *Countrey* all alone,
And by the *Night* surpriz'd, by *Destiny*
(If such a thing, and so unkind there be)
Was guided to a *Village* near this place,
Where asking at a house how far it was
To such a *Town*, and being told so far;
Will, you my friend, t'oblige a Traveller,
Says the benighted *Stranger, be so kind*
As to conduct me thither; you will bind
My gratitude for ever, and in hand,
Shall presently receive what you'l demand.
The fellow hum'd, and haw'd, and scratch'd his pate,
And, to draw on good wages, said 'twas late,
And grew so dark, that though he knew the way,
He durst not be so confident, to say
He might not miss it in so dark a night:
But if his *Worship* would be pleas'd t'alight,
And let him call a Friend, he made no doubt,
But one of them would surely find it out.
The *Traveller* well pleased at any rate,

To have so expert *Guides*, dismounted straight,
Giving his horse up to the treach'rous slave,
Who having hous'd him, forthwith fell to heave
And poize the *Portmantu*, which finding fraight
At either end with lumps of tempting weight,
The *Devil* and *he* made but a short dispute
About the thing they soon did execute:
For calling th'other *Rogue*, who long had bin
His complice in preceding acts of sin,
He tells him of the prize, sets out the gain,
Shews how secure and easie to obtain;
Which prest so home, where was so little need,
The *stranger*'s ruine quickly was decreed.
Thus to the poor *proscrib*'d, the *Villains* go,
And with joynt confidence assure him so,
That with his hap to meet such friends content,
He put himself into their hands, and went.

The guilty *night*, as if she would express
Confederacy with such black purposes,
The sparkling *Hemisphear* had overspread
With darkest vapours from foul *Lerna*** bred;
The world was husht, all save a sighing wind,
That might have warn'd a more presaging mind,
When these two Sons of *Satan*, thus agreed,
With seeming wariness, and care proceed,
All the while mixing their amusing chat,
With frequent cautions of this step, and that;
Till having some six hundred paces gone,
Master here's but a scurvy grip, says one
Of the damn'd *Rogues* (and he said very right)
*Pray for more safety, Sir, be pleas'd t'alight,
And let him lead your Horse a little space,
Till you are past this one uneven place,
You'l need to light no more, Ile warrant you;*

*Marshes near Argos; the home of the Lernaean Hydra, a monster
killed by Hercules.

And still this *instrument of Hell* said true.
Forthwith alights the innocent *Trapan'd*,
One leads his Horse, the other takes his hand,
And, with a shew of care, conducts him thus
To these steep thresholds of black *Erebus*:
And there (O act of horror which out-vies
The direst of inhumane cruelties!)
Let me (my *Muse*) repeat it without sin,
The barb'rous *Villain* pusht him headlong in.
The frighted wretch, having no time to speak,
Forc'd his distended throat in such a skriek,
As, by the shrilness of the doleful cry,
Pierc'd through, and through th'immense *inanity*,
Enforming so the half-dead faller's Ear
What he must suffer, what he had to fear
When, at the very first befriending knock,
His trembling brains smear'd the *Tarpeian* Rock.*
The shatter'd carcass downward rattles fast,
Whilst thence dismist, the Soul with greater hast
From those infernal mansions does remove
And mounts to seek the happy seats above.
What bloody *Arab* of the fellest breed, ⎫
What but the yet more fell *Iudaen* seed, ⎬
Could once have meditated such a *Deed*? ⎭
But one of these *Heaven*'s vengeance did ere long
Call to account for this poor creature's wrong,
Who hang'd for other Crimes, amongst the rest
This horrid murther at his death confest:
Whilst th'other *Rogue*, to *Justice* foul disgrace,
Yet lives, 'tis said unquestion'd near the place.
How deep this *Gulph* does travel under ground,
Though there have been attempts, was never found:
But I my self, with half the *Peak* surrounded,
Eight hundred, fourscore, and four yards have sounded,
And, though of these fourscore return'd back wet,

* The rock at Rome from which criminals were thrown in ancient times.

The *Plummet* drew, and found no bottom yet:
Though when I went again another day,
To make a further, and a new essay,
I could not get the *lead* down half the way.

CHARLES COTTON

An Epistle from Mr Duke to Mr Otway
Cambridge

Dear *Tom*, how melancholly I am grown
Since thou hast left this learned dirty Town,
To thee by this dull Letter be it known.
Whilst all my Comfort under all this Care,
Are Duns and Punns, and Logick, and Small Beer.
Thou see'st I'm dull as *Shadwell*'s Men of Wit,
Or the Top Scene that *Settle* ever writ:
The sprightly Court that wander up and down,
From Gudgeons to a Race, from Town to Town,
All, all are fled; but them I well can spare,
For I'm so dull I have no Business there.
I have forgot whatever there I knew,
Why Men one Stocking tye, with Ribbon blue.*
Why others Medals wear, a fine gilt Thing,
That at their Breasts hang dangling by a String;
(Yet stay, I think that I to Mind recal,
For once a Squirt was rais'd by *Windsor* Wall.)†
I know no Officer of Court; nay more,
No Dog of Court, their Favourite before.
Shou'd *Veny* fawn, I shou'd not understand her;
Nor who committed Incest for *Legander*.‡

*The Garter.
† An apparatus built by Sir Samuel Morland to bring water from
Blackmore Park near Winkfield to the top of Windsor Castle.
‡ 'Veny' (= Venus?) and Legander would be two of the royal
spaniels.

Unpolish'd thus, and arrant Scholar grown, ⎫
What shou'd I do but sit and cooe alone, ⎬
And thee, my absent Mate, for ever moan. ⎭
Thus 'tis sometimes, and Sorrow plays its Part,
'Till other Thoughts of thee revive my Heart.
For whilst with Wit, with Women and with Wine,
Thy glad Heart beats, and noble Face does shine,
Thy Joys we at this Distance feel and know;
Thou kindly wishest it with us were so.
Then thee we name; this heard, cries *James*, for him,
Leap up thou sparkling Wine, and kiss the Brim.
Crosses attend the Man who dares to flinch;
Great as that Man deserves, who drinks not *Finch*.*
But these are empty Joys, without you two,
We drink your Names, alas! but where are you?
My Dear, whom I more cherish in my Breast,
Than by thy own soft Muse can be exprest,
True to thy Word, afford one Visit more,
Else I shall grow, from him thou lov'dst before,
A greasie Blockhead Fellow in a Gown,
(Such as is, Sir, a Cousin of your own);†
With my own Hair, a Band and ten long Nails,
And Wit that at a Quibble never fails.

RICHARD DUKE

On a Cock at Rochester

Thou cursed Cock, with thy perpetual Noise,
May'st thou be Capon made, and lose thy Voice,
Or on a Dunghil may'st thou spend thy Blood,
And Vermin prey upon thy craven Brood;
May Rivals tread thy Hens before thy Face,
Then with redoubled Courage give thee chase;

---

* Probably Duke's Cambridge contemporary, Edward Finch, son of
Heneage Finch, Earl of Nottingham.
† Otway's cousin Charles was a fellow of St John's.

May'st thou be punish'd for St. *Peter*'s Crime,
And on *Shrove-tuesday*, perish in thy Prime;
May thy bruis'd Carcass be some Beggar's Feast,
Thou first and worst Disturber of Man's Rest.

SIR CHARLES SEDLEY

Poet and Public

Advice to a Young Friend on the Choice of his Library

Thy Books shou'd, like thy Friends, not many be,
Yet such wherein Men may thy Judgment see.
In Numbers ev'n of Counsellors, the Wise
Maintain, that dangerous Distraction lies.
Then aim not at a Croud, but still confine
Thy Choice to such as do the Croud out-shine;
Such as thy vacant Hours may entertain,
And be thy Pastime, not thy Life constrain;
Not dark, mysterious, crabbed, or morose,
Useless and void, or stupidly Verbose,
Tho' witty, yet judicious and sincere,
And like true Friends, still faithful, tho' severe;
Books that may prove, in ev'ry Change of State,
Guides and Assistants to your shifting Fate:
That may to Virtue form your early Soul,
And the first Thought of unripe Guilt controul:
Friends, whose sage Wit, call'd up at each Extream,
May help you to converse on ev'ry Theme;
And when retir'd from Business, and alone,
Delight you with their Talk, and spare your own;
Make short the Season of the restless Night,
And force dull Hours to mend their ling'ring Flight;
Then, wheresoe'er your wand'ring Steps you guide,
May travel with you, and close up your Side:
Relieve you from the Pageantry of Courts,
Their gawdy Fopp'ries, and their irksom Sports:
Or, if some dire Necessity require,
With you to Dungeons for your Aid retire,
And still, like Friends, your Sadness to prevent
In Prison, Want, Distress, or Banishment.
     Like Friends, it matters not how great, but good;
Not how long known, but how well understood:
Imports not, though without they old appear,

If new and just the Thoughts within 'em are:
So that, like old Friends, still they ready be,
Open at Will, and of Instruction free;
Whose faithful Counsel soars above the Art
Of servil Flatt'ry, to seduce the Heart:
But its instructive, honest Dictates lends,
Void of Design, or mercenary Ends.
Unlike most other Friends, less tiresome too,
As with them still you more acquainted grow.

WILLIAM WYCHERLEY

To Nysus

How shall we please this Age? If in a Song
We put above six Lines, they count it long;
If we contract it to an Epigram,
As deep the dwarfish Poetry they damn;
If we write Plays, few see above an Act,
And those lewd Masks, or noisie Fops distract:
Let us write Satyr then, and at our ease
Vex th'ill-natur'd Fools we cannot please.

SIR CHARLES SEDLEY

A Dissuasive against Poetry
from A Satyr

But, grant thy Poetry should find success,
And (which is rare) the squeamish Criticks please;
Admit it read and prais'd and courted be
By this nice Age, and all Posterity;
If thou expectest ought but empty Fame;
Condemn thy Hopes, and Labors to the Flame:

The rich have now learn'd only to admire,⎫
He, who to greater Favours does aspire,⎬
Is mercenary thought, and writes to hire:⎭
Would'st thou to raise thine, and thy Country's Fame,
Chuse some old *English* Hero for thy Theme,
Bold *Arthur*, or great *Edward*'s greater *Son*,
Or our fifth *Harry*, matchless in Renown,
Make *Agincourt* and *Cressy* Fields outvie
The fam'd *Lavinian* Shores and Walls of *Troy*;
What *Scipio*, what *Mæcenas* would'st thou find,
What *Sidney** now to thy great Project kind?
Bless me! how great his Genius! how each Line⎫
Is big with Sense! how glorious a Design⎬
Does thro the whole, and each Proportion shine!⎭
How lofty all his Thoughts, and how inspir'd!
Pity, such wond'rous Parts are not preferr'd:
Cries a gay wealthy Sot, who would not bail
For bare five Pounds the Author out of Jail,
Should he starve there, and rot; who if a Brief⎫
Came out the needy Poets to relieve,⎬
To the whole Tribe would scarce a Tester give.⎭
But fifty Guinnies for a Whore and Clap!
The Peer's well us'd, and comes off wond'rous cheap:
A Poet would be dear, and out o'th'way,
Should he expect above a Coach-man's pay:
For this will any dedicate, and lye,
And dawb the gaudy Ass with Flattery?
For this will any prostitute his Sense
To Coxcombs void of Bounty, as of Brains?
Yet such is the hard Fate of Writers now,
They're forc'd for Alms to each great Name to bow:
Fawn, like her Lap-dog, on her tawdry Grace,⎫
Commend her Beauty, and bely her Glass,⎬
By which she every morning primes her Face:⎭
Sneak to his Honor, call him Wity, Brave,
And Just, tho a known Coward, Fool, or Knave,
And praise his Lineage, and Nobility,

*Sir Philip Sidney.

Whose Arms at first came from the Company.
 'Tis so, 'twas ever so, since heretofore ⎫
The blind old *Bard*,* with Dog and Bell before, ⎬
Was fain to sing for Bread from door to door: ⎭
The needy Muses all turn'd Gipsies then,
And of the begging Trade e're since have been:
Should mighty *Sappho* in these days revive,
And hope upon her stock of Wit to live;
She must to *Creswel*'s† trudg to mend her Gains,
And let her Tail to hire, as well as Brains.
What Poet ever fin'd for Sheriff?‡ or who
By Wit and Sense did ever Lord Mayors grow?

*   *   *

Then be advis'd, the slighted Muse forsake,
And *Cook*, and *Dalton*§ for thy study take:
For Fees each Term sweat in the crowded Hall,
And there for Charters, and crack'd Titles bawl:
Where *Maynard*‖ thrives, and pockets more each year
Than forty Laureats of the Theater.
Or else to Orders and the Church betake
Thy self, and that thy future Refuge make:
There fawn on some proud Patron to engage
Th'Advowson of cast Punk, and Parsonage:**
Or sooth the Court, and preach up Kingly Right,
To gain a Prebend'ry and Mitre by't.
In fine, turn Pettifogger, Canonist,
Civilian, Pedant, Mountebank, or Priest,

---

*Homer.

† Mother Cresswell, a procuress patronized chiefly by the Whigs.

‡ Paid a forfeit in order to avoid having to serve for a year as Sheriff.

§ Sir Edward Coke (1552–1634), author of *The Institutes of the Laws of England*, and Michael Dalton (d. 1648?), author of *The Countrey Justice*.

‖ The King's Sergeant, Sir John Maynard, who appeared for the crown at most state trials.

** The accusation that landowners with livings in their gift would often use them to gain husbands for their servants and mistresses was a commonplace of anti-clerical satire in the seventeenth century.

Soldier, or Merchant, Fidler, Painter, Fencer,
Jack-pudding, Juggler, Player, or Rope-dancer:
Preach, Plead, Cure, Fight, Game, Pimp, Beg, Cheat, or
    Thieve;
Be all but Poet, and there's way to live.

JOHN OLDHAM

The Beggar *and* Poet

Happy the Man who free from Care and Strife,
With Dog and Bell gropes thro' the *Road* of Life!
Beggar *at large*, without or Fear, or Shame,
He'll all the World his *Benefactors* name.
He, like the famous ancient *Scythian* Race,
Shifts not *himself* as often as his *place*.
Tir'd with the *pillage* of *one* fruitful Plain,
He and his *Cattle* soon decamp again:*
He with a proud Repulse when warmly vext,
Throws you a hearty *Curse*, and tries the next.
No long *Harangues* to squeeze the stubborn *Pence*,⎞
No Oratorical Impertinence,   ⎬
Nor grateful *murd'ring* both of Truth and Sense.   ⎠
He'll in two Lines compendiously impart
The *System* of his truly *Liberal Art*;
𝔓𝔯𝔞𝔶 𝔖𝔦𝔯, 𝔱𝔥𝔢 𝔊𝔦𝔣𝔱: And when the Farthings stir,
𝔍 𝔥𝔬𝔭𝔢 𝔶𝔬𝔲'𝔩𝔩 𝔫𝔢𝔟𝔢𝔯 𝔩𝔦𝔟𝔢 𝔱𝔬 𝔴𝔞𝔫𝔱 𝔦𝔱 𝔖𝔦𝔯!
When *Beadle Death* does him at last attend,
Let him go where he will, in this he's sure to *mend*:
Death kindly *Land* and *House* provides him, more
Besides the *Cage*, than e're he had before.
    Thrice miserable they whom want and Fate
Eternal *Mumpers*† made at Learning's Gate:

---

*The beggar's cattle would be of the genus *pediculus*.

†Mumpers were beggars of a superior order who sometimes posed
as destitute gentlemen.

Their *Souls* indeed they *cram* with *notions high*,
But let poor *Colon* live by Sympathy:
To Honourable Beggars they give place,
Lean *younger Brothers* of the *lowsie* Race.

SAMUEL WESLEY

To
JULIAN
Secretary to the Muses,
A Consolatory Epistle
in his
CONFINEMENT*

Dear Friend, when those we love are in distress,
Kind Verse may *comfort*, though it can't *redress*:
Nor can I think such *Zeal* you'l discommend,
Since *Poesie* has been so much thy *Friend*:
On that thou'st liv'd and flourisht all thy Time,
Nay more, maintain'd a *Family* with *Rhime*:
And that's a mark which *Dryden* ne'r cou'd hit,
He lives upon his *Pension*, not his Wit.
Ev'n *gentle George*,† with flux in *Tongue* and *Purse*,
In shunning *one snare* run into a *worse*.
Want once may be reliev'd in a Man's Life,
But who can be reliev'd that has a Wife?
Otway can hardly *Guts* from *Jayl* preserve,
For though he's *very fat*, he's like to *starve*,
And Sing-song *Durfey*, plact beneath abuses,
Lives by his *Impudence*, not by the *Muses*.
Poor *Crown* too has his *third days* mixt with *Gall*;

---

*One of a number of satiric poems addressed to 'Colonel' Robert
Julian, a copyist and distributor of lampoons. In 1684 he was found
guilty of scandalous libel and sentenced to stand in the pillory.
   † Sir George Etherege.

He *lives so ill* he hardly *lives at all*.
Shadwell and *Settle*, who pretend to Reason,
Though paid so well for scribling *Dogrel Treason*,
Must now expect a very barren Season;
But chiefly he that made his *Recantation*;*
For *Villain* thrives best in his own *Vocation*.
Nat Lee in *Bedlam* now sees better days,
Than when applaus'd for writing *Bombast Plays*;
He knows no *care*, nor feels *sharp want* no more;
And that is what he ne'r cou'd say before.

Thus, while our *Bards* e'en *famish* by their *wit*,
Thou, who hast none at all, did'st *thrive* by *it*.

Wer't possible that *Wit* cou'd turn a penny,
Poets wou'd then grow rich as well as any:
For 'tis not *Wit* to have a *great Estate*,
(The blind Effects of Fortune and of Fate)
For oft we see a Coxcomb, dull and vain,
Brim full of *Cash* and *empty* in his *Brain*.
Nor is it *Wit* that makes the *Lawyer* prize
His *dagled Gown*, but *Knavery* in disguise,
To pluck down *honest men* that *he* may rise.
Nor is it *Wit* that makes the *Tradesman great*;
'Tis the compendious Art to ly and cheat.
The base-born Strumpet too may roar and rail,
But 'tis not *Wit* she lives by, 'tis her *Tail*.
Nor is it *Wit* that drills the Statesman on
To wast the sweets of Life, so quickly gone,
In toyling for Estates, then, like a Sot,
Dy, and leave *Fools* to spend what he has got.
Nor is it *Wit* for *Whigs* to scribble *Satyrs*,
No more than for their *Patriots* to be *Traytors*;
For *Wit* does never bring a Man to hanging:
That goes no further than a harmless banging.†
How justly then dost thou our Praise deserve,
That got thy Bread where all Men else wou'd starve?

*Settle abandoned the Whigs for the Tories in 1683, justifying his action in a much-ridiculed *Narrative*.

†Dryden's fate in the 'Rose-Alley' ambush of December, 1679.

And what's more strange, the Miracle was wrought
By him that han't the least pretence to *thought*;
And he that had no *meaning* to do wrong,
Can't suffer, sure, for his *No-meaning* long;
And that's the *Consolation* that I bring:
Thou art too dull to *think* a treach'rous thing,
And 'tis the *thoughtful Traytor* that offends his King.

ROBERT GOULD

An Allusion to Horace
The 10th *Satyr of the* 1st. *Book.*
Nempe incomposito Dixi pede &c.

Well Sir, 'tis granted, I said *Dryden*'s Rhimes,
Were stoln, unequal, nay dull many times:
What foolish Patron is there found of his,
So blindly partial, to deny me this?
But that his Plays, embroider'd up and down
With Wit and Learning, justly pleas'd the Town,
In the same Paper, I as freely own.
Yet having this allow'd, the heavy Mass
That Stuffs up his loose Volumns, must not pass:
For by that Rule, I might as wel admit
Crown's tedious Scenes for Poetry and Wit.
'Tis therefore not enough, when your false sense
Hits the false Judgment of an Audience
Of clapping Fools, assembling a vast Crowd,
Till the throng'd Play-house crack with the dull load;
Though ev'n that Talent merits in some sort,
That can divert the Rabble, and the Court:
Which blundring *Settle* never cou'd attain,
And puzling *Otway* labors at in vain.
But within due proportions circumscribe
What e're you write; that with a flowing Tide

The Style may rise, yet in its rise forbear
With useless words t'oppress the weary'd Ear.
Here be your Language lofty, there more light,
Your Rethorick with your Poetry unite:
For Elegance sake, sometimes allay the force
Of Epithets, 'twill soften the discourse;
A jeast in scorn points out and hits the thing
More home than the Morosest Satyr's sting.
Shake-spear and *Johnson* did herein excell,
And might in this be imitated well;
Whom refin'd *Etherege* coppy's not at all,
But is himself a sheer Original,
Nor that slow Drudge in swift Pindarick straines,⎫
Flatman, who *Cowley* imitates with pains,   ⎬
And rides a jaded Muse, whipt with loose Rains. ⎭
When *Lee* makes temp'rate *Scipio* fret and rave
And *Hannibal* a whining Amorous Slave,*
I laugh, and wish the hot-brain'd Fustian Fool,
In *Busby*'s hands, to be well lasht at School.†
Of all our Modern Wits none seems to me⎫
Once to have toucht upon true Comedy,   ⎬
But hasty *Shadwel*‡ and slow *Wicherley*.   ⎭
Shadwell's unfinish'd works do yet impart
Great proofs of force of Nature, none of Art:
With just bold strokes he dashes here and there,
Shewing great Mastery with little Care,
And scorns to varnish his good Touches o're,
To make the Fools, and Women, praise 'em more.
But *Wicherley* earnes hard what e're he gains,
He wants no judgment, nor he spares no pains;
He frequently excells, and at the least,
Makes fewer faults than any of the best.

---

*An allusion to Lee's *Sophonisba, or Hannibal's Overthrow* (1676).

†Richard Busby was master of Westminster School from 1639 until his death in 1695. Dryden and Locke were among his pupils but not Lee who was educated at Charterhouse.

‡Thomas Shadwell (1641(?)–92), the rival of Dryden, was the author of sixteen plays, some of them far from despicable.

Waller, by Nature for the Bays design'd,
With force and fire and fancy unconfin'd,
In Panegyricks does excell Mankind.
He best can turn, enforce, and soften things,
To praise great Conquerors, or to flatter Kings.*

For pointed Satyrs, I wou'd *Buckhurst*† choose,
The best good Man with the worst natur'd Muse;
For Songs and Verses mannerly obscene,
That can stir Nature up by spring unseen,
And without forcing blushes warm the Queen.

Sidley has that prevailing, gentle Art,
That can with a resistless Charm impart,
The loosest wishes to the chastest heart;
Raise such a conflict, kindle such a Fire,
Betwixt declining Virtue and Desire;
Till the poor vanquisht Maid dissolves away,
In Dreams all Night, in Sighs and Tears all day.

Dryden in vain try'd this nice way of wit,
For he to be a tearing Blade thought fit,
But when he wou'd be sharp, he still was blunt;
To frisk his frollique fancy, he'd cry Cunt;
Wou'd give the Ladies a dry Bawdy bob,
And thus he got the name of *Poet Squab*.
But to be just, 'twill to his praise be found,
His Excellencies more than faults abound;
Nor dare I from his sacred Temples tear
That Lawrel which he best deserves to wear.
But does not *Dryden* find ev'n *Johnson* dull?
Fletcher and *Beaumont* uncorrect, and full
Of lewd Lines, as he calls 'em? *Shake-spear*'s stile
Stiff and affected (to his own the while
Allowing all the justness that his Pride,
So Arrogantly had to these deny'd)?
And may not I have leave impartially,
To search and censure *Dryden*'s Works, and try
If those gross faults his choice Pen does commit,

---

*Waller had written in praise of both Cromwell and Charles II.
†The future Earl of Dorset (see biographical note).

Proceed from want of Judgment, or of Wit?
Or if his lumpish fancy does refuse,
Spirit and Grace to his loose slattern Muse?
Five Hundred Verses ev'ry Morning writ,
Proves you no more a Poet than a Wit:
Such scribling Authors have been seen before ⎫
Mustapha,* the *English Princess*,† forty more, ⎬
Were things perhaps compos'd in half an hour. ⎭
To write what may securely stand the Test
Or being well read over Thrice at least,
Compare each Phrase, examine ev'ry Line,
Weigh ev'ry Word, and ev'ry Thought refine;
Scorn all applause the vile Rout can bestow,
And be content to please those few who know.
Canst thou be such a vain mistaken Thing,
To wish thy Works might make a Play-house ring
With the unthinking Laughter and poor praise
Of Fops and Ladies, factious for thy Plays;
Then send a cunning Friend to learn thy doom,
From the shrewd Judges of the Drawing Room?
I've no Ambition on that idle score,
But say with Betty *Morris* heretofore,
When a Court Lady call'd her *Buckley*'s‡ Whore:
I please one Man of Wit, am proud on't too,
Let all the Coxcombs dance to Bed to you.
Shou'd I be troubled when the Pur-blind Knight,§ ⎫
Who squints more in his Judgment than his sight, ⎬
Picks silly faults, and censures what I write? ⎭
Or when the poor led Poets of the Town
For Scraps and Coach-room cry my Verses down?
I loath the Rabble, 'tis enough for me,

* A play by Roger Boyle, Earl of Orrerey, first performed in April 1665.

† A tragedy by John Caryl first performed in 1667. Rochester may actually have been thinking of Edward Howard's much-satirized historical poem *The British Princes* (1669).

‡ Henry Bulkeley, a minor wit and court official.

§ Rochester's poetical enemy, Sir Carr Scroop.

If *Sidley, Shadwell, Shepherd, Wicherley,*
Godolphin, Butler, Buckhurst, Buckingham,
And some few more, whom I omit to name,
Approve my sense, I count their censure Fame.

JOHN WILMOT, EARL OF ROCHESTER

First Prologue to *Secret Love,*
or the *Maiden Queen*

He who writ this, not without pains and thought
From *French* and *English* Theaters has brought
Th'exactest Rules by which a Play is wrought.

The Unities of Action, Place, and Time;
The Scenes unbroken; and a mingled chime
Of *Johnson*'s humour, with *Corneille*'s rhyme.

But while dead colours he with care did lay,
He fears his Wit, or Plot he did not weigh,
Which are the living Beauties of a Play.

Plays are like Towns, which howe're fortifi'd
By Engineers, have still some weaker side
By the o'reseen Defendant unespy'd.

And with that Art you make approaches now;
Such skilful fury in Assaults you show,
That every Poet without shame may bow.

Ours therefore humbly would attend your doom,
If Souldier-like, he may have termes to come
With flying colours, and with beat of Drum.

JOHN DRYDEN

To
Sir George Etheridge,
On his shewing his Verses imperfect

Be wise, and ne'er to publick View produce
Thy undrest Mistress, or unfinisht Muse;
Since either, by that *Dishabilé*, seem
To hurt their Beauties in our good Esteem:
And easier far we kind Impressions make,
Than we can rooted Prejudices shake.
From Nature learn, which *Embrio*'s does conceal,
Thine, till they're perfect, never to reveal.

WILLIAM WYCHERLEY

From *A Letter from the Country to a Friend in Town, giving an Account of the Author's Inclinations to* Poetry

'Tis endless, Sir, to tell the many ways,
Wherein my poor deluded self I please:
How, when the Fancy lab'ring for a Birth,
With unfelt Throws brings its rude issue forth:
How after, when imperfect shapeless Thought
Is by the Judgment into Fashion wrought.
When at first search I traverse o're my mind,
Nought but a dark and empty Void I find:
Some little hints at length, like sparks, break thence,
And glimm'ring Thoughts just dawning into sence:
Confus'd a while the mixt Idea's lie,
With nought of mark to be discover'd by,
Like colours undistinguisht in the night,
Till the dusk images, mov'd to the light,

Teach the discerning Faculty to chuse,
Which it had best adopt, and which refuse.
Here rougher strokes, touch'd with a careless dash,
Resemble the first sitting of a face:
There finisht draughts in form more full appear,
And to their justness ask no further care.
Mean while with inward joy I proud am grown,
To see the work successfully go on:
And prize my self in a creating power,
That could make something, what was nought before.

JOHN OLDHAM

On Paradise Lost

When I beheld the Poet blind, yet bold,
In slender Book his vast Design unfold,
Messiash Crown'd, God's Reconcil'd Decree,
Rebelling Angels, the Forbidden Tree,
Heav'n, Hell, Earth, Chaos, All; the Argument
Held me a while misdoubting his Intent,
That he would ruine (for I saw him strong)
The sacred Truths to Fable and old Song
(So *Sampson* groap'd the Temples' Posts in spight
The World o'rewhelming to revenge his sight.)

    Yet as I read, soon growing less severe,
I lik'd his Project, the success did fear;
Through that wide Field how he his way should find
O're which lame Faith leads Understanding blind;
Lest he perplex'd the things he would explain,
And what was easie he should render vain.

    Or if a Work so infinite he spann'd,
Jealous I was that some less skilful hand
(Such as disquiet always what is well,
And by ill imitating would excell)
Might hence presume the whole Creation's day

To change in Scenes, and show it in a Play.*
   Pardon me, Mighty Poet, nor despise
My causeless, yet not impious, surmise.
But I am now convinc'd, and none will dare
Within thy Labours to pretend a share.
Thou hast not miss'd one thought that could be fit,
And all that was improper dost omit:
So that no room is here for Writers left,
But to detect their Ignorance or Theft.
   That Majesty which through thy Work doth Reign
Draws the Devout, deterring the Profane.
And things divine thou treatst of in such state
As them preserves, and thee, inviolate.
At once delight and horrour on us seise,
Thou singst with so much gravity and ease;
And above human flight dost soar aloft
With Plume so strong, so equal, and so soft.
The Bird nam'd from that Paradise you sing
So never flaggs, but always keeps on Wing.
   Where couldst thou words of such a compass find?
Whence furnish such a vast expence of mind?
Just Heav'n thee like *Tiresias*† to requite
Rewards with Prophesie thy loss of sight.
   Well mightst thou scorn thy Readers to allure
With tinkling Rhime, of thy own sense secure;
While the *Town-Bayes*‡ writes all the while and spells,
And like a Pack-horse tires without his Bells:
Their Fancies like our Bushy-points appear,
The Poets tag them, we for fashion wear.
I too transported by the Mode offend,
And while I meant to Praise thee must Commend.
Thy Verse created like thy Theme sublime,
In Number, Weight, and Measure, needs not Rhime.

ANDREW MARVELL

*A reference to Dryden's unacted *The State of Innocence* (1677).
Dryden visited Milton to request his permission for the enterprise.
†The comparison is made by Milton himself in Book 3, l. 36.
‡Dryden.

On
Dr. Woodford's *Paraphrase on the*
CANTICLES*

Well! since it must be so, so let it be,
For what do Resolutions signifie,
When we are urg'd to write by Destiny?

I had resolv'd, nay, and I almost swore,
My bedrid Muse should walk abroad no more:
Alas! 'tis more than time that I give o're.

In the Recesses of a private Breast,
I thought to entertain your charming Guest,
And never to have boasted of my Feast.

But see (my Friend) when through the world you go,
My Laquy-Verse must shadow-like pursue,
Thin and Obscure to make a Foyl for you.

'Tis true, you cannot need my feeble Praise,
A lasting Monument to your Name to raise,
Well-known in Heav'n by your Angeliqu' Layes.

There in indelible Characters they are writ,
Where no pretended Heights will easie sit,
But those of serious consecrated wit.

By immaterial defecated Love,
Your Soul its Heavenly Origin do's approve,
And in least dangerous Raptures soars above.

---

*Samuel Woodford (1636–1700) published paraphrases of the psalms in 1667 and the canticles in 1679. Flatman wrote commendatory verses for both.

How could I wish (dear Friend!) unsaid agen
(For once I rank'd my self with tuneful men)
Whatever dropt from my unhallowed Pen!

The triffling Rage of youthful heat, once past,
Who is not troubled for his wit misplac'd!
All pleasant Follies breed regret at last.

While Reverend *Don*'s, and noble *Herbert*'s Flame
A glorious immortality shall claim,
In the most durable Records of Fame,

Our modish Rhimes, like Culinary Fire,*
Unctuous and Earthy, shall in smoak expire;
In odorous Clouds your Incense shall aspire.

Let th'*Pagan*-world your pious verse defie,
Yet shall they envy when they come to dye,
Your wiser Projects on Eternity.

THOMAS FLATMAN

On *Mr* Edward Howard *upon his* British Princes†

Come on ye Critticks! find one fault who dare,
For read it backward, like a Witches' Pray'r,
'Twill do as well; throw not away your jeasts,
On solid Non-sense, that abides all Tests.
Wit, like Tierce Clarret, when't begins to pall,
Neglected lyes, and's of no use at all;
But in its full perfection of decay,
Turns Vinegar, and comes again in play.

*Culinary fire was that observed during the process of combustion. The purer elemental form was not directly evident to the senses.
†A heroic poem published in 1669. Howard (1624–1712) was Dryden's brother-in-law and the author of six undistinguished plays.

This Simile shall stand in thy defence,
'Gainst such dull Rogues, as now and then write sense.
He lyes dear *Ned*, who says thy Brain is barren,
Where deep conceits, like Vermin, breed in Carrin;
Thou hast a Brain, such as thou hast indeed,
On what else shou'd thy Worme of Fancy feed?
Yet in a Philbert, I have often known
Maggots survive, when all the Kernell's gone.
Thy Stile's the same, what ever be the Theame,
As some digestions turn all Meat to Phlegm.
Thy stumbling Founder'd Jade can Trot as high,
As any other Pegasus can fly.
As skillful Dyvers to the bottom fall
Sooner than those that cannot swim at all;
So in this way of writing without thinking
Thou hast a strange Alacrity in sinking.
Thou writ'st below even thy own nat'ral parts,
And with acquir'd dullness, and new Arts
Of study'd Non-sense, tak'st kind Readers' hearts.
So the dull Eele moves nimbler in the Mud,
Than all the swift finn'd Racers of the Flood.
Therefore dear *Ned*, at my advice forbear
Such loud complaints 'gainst Criticks to prefer,
Since thou art turn'd an Arrant Libeller:
Thou sett'st thy Name to what thy self dost write,
Did ever Libell yet so sharply bite?

CHARLES SACKVILLE, EARL OF DORSET

Upon the *Author* of a *Play call'd* Sodom*

Tell me, abandon'd *Miscreant*, prithee tell,
What damned Pow'r invok'd and sent from *Hell*
(If *Hell* were bad enough) did thee inspire,

---

* *Sodom, or the Quintessence of Debauchery*, the pornographic *hilaro-tragædia* which has been attributed to both Rochester and Christopher Fishbourne.

306

To write, what *Fiends* asham'd wou'd blushing hear?
Hast thou of late embrac'd some *Succubus*?
And us'd the lewd *Familiar* for a *Muse*?
Or didst thy Soul, by Inch o'th' *Candle* sell,
To gain the glorious Name of *Pimp* to *Hell*?
If so; go, and its vow'd *Allegiance* swear,
Without Press-Money, be its *Voluntiere*:
May he who envies thee deserve thy fate,
Deserve both *Heav'n*'s and *Mankind*'s scorn and hate.
Disgrace to *Libels*! Foyle to very shame,
Whom 'tis a scandal to vouchsafe to damn!
What foul discriptions foul enough for thee,
Sunk quite below the reach of infamy?
Thou covet'st to be lewd, but want'st the might,
And art all over *Devil*, but in Wit.
Weak feeble *Strainer* at meer ribaldry,   )
Whose *Muse* is impotent to that degree,   }
'T had need like Age, be whipt to *Lechery*.)
Vile *Sot*! who clapt with *Poetry* art sick,
And void'st Corruption, like a *Shanker'd Prick*.
Like *Ulcers*, thy impostum'd Addle Brains,
Drop out in *Matter*, which thy Paper stains:
Whence nauseous *Rhymes*, by filthy *Births* proceed,
As *Maggots*, in some *Turd*, ingendring breed.
Thy *Muse* has got the *Flow'rs*, and they ascend,
As in some *Green-sick Girl*, at upper end.
Sure *Nature* made, or meant at least t'have don't,
Thy Tongue a *Clytoris*, thy Mouth a *Cunt*:
How well a *Dildoe* wou'd that place become,
To gag it up, and make't for ever dumb!
At least it shou'd be syring'd
Or wear some stinking *Merkin*,* for a Beard,
That all from its base converse might be scar'd:
As they a *Door* shut up, and mark'd beware,
That tells infection and the *Plague* is there.
Thou *Moorfields Author*, fit for *Bawds* to quote

---

*'Counterfeit hair for the private parts of a woman' (Grose).

(If *Bawds* themselves, with Honor safe may do't)
When *Suburb Prentice* comes to hire delight,
And wants incentives to dull Appetite;
There *Punk*, perhaps, may thy brave works rehearse,
Frigging the senseless thing, with Hand and Verse;
Which after shall (preferr'd to *Dressing Box*)
Hold *Turpentine*, and *Medicines* for the *Pox*.
Or (if I may ordain a *Fate* more fit)
For such foul, nasty, *Excrements* of *Wit*,
May they condemn'd to th'publick *Jakes* be lent,⎫
(For me I'd fear the *Piles* in vengeance sent ⎬
Shou'd I with them prophane my *Fundament*) ⎭
There bugger wiping *Porters*, when they shite,
And so thy *Book* it self turn *Sodomite*.

                                        JOHN OLDHAM

Song *A-la-Mode*

O're the Desert, cross the Meadows,
    Hunters blew the merry Horn;
Phoebus chas'd the flying Shadows:
    Eccho, she reply'd, in scorn;
        Still adoring,
        And deploring:
Why must *Thirsis* lose his Life?

Rivers murmur'd from their Fountains,
    Acorns dropping from the Oaks,
Fawns came tripping o're the Mountains,
    Fishes bit the naked Hook;
        Still admiring,
        And desiring:
When shall *Phillis* be a Wife.

                                SIR CHARLES SEDLEY

Mac Flecknoe

All human things are subject to decay,
And, when Fate summons, Monarchs must obey:
This *Fleckno** found, who, like *Augustus*, young
Was call'd to Empire, and had govern'd long:
In Prose and Verse, was own'd, without dispute
Through all the Realms of *Non-sense*, absolute.
This aged Prince now flourishing in Peace,
And blest with issue of a large increase,
Worn out with business, did at length debate
To settle the succession of the State:
And pond'ring which of all his Sons was fit
To Reign, and wage immortal War with Wit;
Cry'd, 'tis resolv'd; for Nature pleads that He
Should onely rule, who most resembles me:
Shadwell† alone my perfect image bears,
Mature in dullness from his tender years.
Shadwell alone, of all my Sons, is he
Who stands confirm'd in full stupidity.
The rest to some faint meaning make pretence,
But *Shadwell* never deviates into sense.
Some Beams of Wit on other souls may fall,
Strike through and make a lucid intervall;
But *Shadwell*'s genuine night admits no ray,
His rising Fogs prevail upon the Day:
Besides his goodly Fabrick fills the eye,
And seems design'd for thoughtless Majesty:
Thoughtless as Monarch Oakes, that shade the plain,
And, spread in solemn state, supinely reign.
Heywood and *Shirley*‡ were but Types of thee,
Thou last great *Prophet* of Tautology:
Even I, a dunce of more renown than they,

*Richard Flecknoe (d. 1678?), playwright and poetaster.
†Thomas Shadwell (1640–92), comic dramatist.
‡Thomas Heywood (c. 1574–1641) and James Shirley (1596–1666), dramatists.

Was sent before but to prepare thy way;
And coursly clad in *Norwich* Drugget came
To teach the Nations in thy greater name.
My warbling Lute, the Lute I whilom strung
When to King *John* of *Portugal* I sung,
Was but the prelude to that glorious day,*
When thou on silver *Thames* did'st cut thy way,
With well tim'd Oars before the Royal Barge,
Swell'd with the Pride of thy Celestial charge;
And big with Hymn, Commander of an Host,
The like was ne'er in *Epsom* Blankets† tost.
Methinks I see the new *Arion* Sail,
The Lute still trembling underneath thy nail.
At thy well sharpned thumb from Shore to Shore
The Treble squeaks for fear, the Bases roar:
Echoes from *Pissing-Ally*, *Shadwell* call,
And *Shadwell* they resound from *Aston Hall*.
About thy boat the little Fishes throng,
As at the Morning Toast, that Floats along.
Sometimes as Prince of thy Harmonious band
Thou weild'st thy Papers in thy threshing hand;
St. *Andre*'s feet ne'er kept more equal time,
Not ev'n the feet of thy own *Psyche*'s‡ rhime:
Though they in number as in sense excell;
So just, so like tautology they fell,
That, pale with envy, *Singleton* forswore
The Lute and Sword which he in Triumph bore,
And vow'd he ne'er would act *Villerius* more.
Here stopt the good old *Syre*; and wept for joy

---

*This and the following twenty-two lines appear to refer to an occasion, not otherwise recorded, on which Shadwell, a skilled amateur lutenist, had attached himself to the orchestra during a royal progress on the Thames.

†Tossing itinerant fiddlers in a blanket was a popular late-evening exercise among aristocratic topers. Rochester had been involved in a fatal brawl at Epsom on one such occasion. There are also allusions to the title of Shadwell's comedy, *Epsom Wells* (1673), and the fate of a counterfeit fiddler in *The Virtuoso* (1676).

‡A musical play of 1675 adapted from Molière.

In silent raptures of the hopefull boy.
All arguments, but most his Plays, perswade,
That for anointed dullness he was made.

    Close to the Walls which fair *Augusta** bind,
(The fair *Augusta* much to fears inclin'd)
An ancient fabrick, rais'd t'inform the sight,
There stood of yore, and *Barbican* it hight:
A watch Tower once; but now, so Fate ordains,
Of all the Pile an empty name remains.
From its old Ruins Brothel-houses rise,
Scenes of lewd loves, and of polluted joys.
Where their vast Courts the Mother-Strumpets keep,
And, undisturb'd by Watch, in silence sleep.
Near these a Nursery† erects its head,
Where Queens are form'd, and future Heroes bred;
Where unfledg'd Actors learn to laugh and cry,⎫
Where infant Punks their tender Voices try, ⎬
And little *Maximins*‡ the Gods defy. ⎭
Great *Fletcher* never treads in Buskins here,
Nor greater *Johnson*§ dares in Socks appear.
But gentle *Simkin* just reception finds
Amidst this Monument of vanisht minds:
Pure Clinches,‖ the suburbian Muse affords;
And *Panton* waging harmless War with words.
Here *Fleckno*, as a place to Fame well known,
Ambitiously design'd his *Shadwell*'s Throne.
For ancient *Decker* prophesi'd long since, ⎫
That in this Pile should Reign a mighty Prince, ⎬
Born for a scourge of Wit, and flayle of Sense: ⎭
To whom true dulness should some *Psyches* owe,
But Worlds of *Misers* from his pen should flow;
Humorists and Hypocrites it should produce,
Whole *Raymond* families, and Tribes of *Bruce*.**

*London. †The theatre at which young actors were trained.
  ‡The villain of Dryden's *Tyrranic Love* (1670).
  §Ben Jonson ‖Puns.
  **A character in Shadwell's comedy *The Virtuoso* (1676), as are
'Longvil' and 'Sir Formal' mentioned subsequently.

Now Empress *Fame* had publisht the renown,
Of *Shadwell*'s Coronation through the Town.
Rows'd by report of Fame, the Nations meet,
From near *Bun-Hill*, and distant *Watling-street*.
No *Persian* Carpets spread th'Imperial way,
But scatter'd Limbs of mangled Poets lay:
From dusty shops neglected Authors come,
Martyrs of Pies, and Reliques of the Bum.
Much *Heywood*, *Shirly*, *Ogleby** there lay,
But loads of *Shadwell* almost choakt the way.
Bilkt *Stationers* for Yeomen stood prepar'd,
And *Herringman*† was Captain of the Guard.
The hoary Prince in Majesty appear'd,
High on a Throne of his own Labours rear'd.
At his right hand our young *Ascanius*‡ sat
Rome's other hope, and pillar of the State.
His Brows thick fogs, instead of glories, grace,
And lambent dullness plaid arround his face.
As *Hannibal* did to the Altars come,
Sworn by his *Syre* a mortal Foe to *Rome*;
So *Shadwell* swore, nor should his Vow bee vain,
That he till Death true dullness would maintain;
And in his father's Right, and Realm's defence,
Ne'er to have peace with Wit, nor truce with Sense.
The King himself the sacred Unction made,
As King by Office, and as Priest by Trade:
In his sinister hand, instead of Ball,
He plac'd a mighty Mug of potent Ale;
Love's Kingdom§ to his right he did convey,
At once his Sceptre and his rule of Sway;
Whose righteous Lore the Prince had practis'd young,
And from whose Loyns recorded *Psyche* sprung.
His Temples last with Poppies were o'erspread,

---

*John Ogilby (1600–76), cartographer, theatrical entrepreneur and translator.

†A bookseller who published many of Dryden's writings.

‡The son of Aeneas. Cf. *Aeneid*, ii, 682–4.

§A play by Flecknoe (1664)

That nodding seem'd to consecrate his head:
Just at that point of time, if Fame not lye,
On his left hand twelve reverend *Owls* did fly.
So *Romulus*, 'tis sung, by *Tyber's Brook*,
Presage of Sway from twice six Vultures took.
Th'admiring throng loud acclamations make,
And Omens of his future Empire take.
The *Syre* then shook the honours of his head,
And from his brows damps of oblivion shed
Full on the filial dullness: long he stood, ⎫
Repelling from his Breast the raging God; ⎬
At length burst out in this prophetick mood: ⎭

    Heavens bless my Son, from *Ireland* let him reign
To farr *Barbadoes* on the Western main;
Of his Dominion may no end be known,
And greater than his Father's be his Throne.
Beyond Love's Kingdom let him stretch his Pen;
He paus'd, and all the people cry'd *Amen*.
Then thus, continu'd he, my Son advance
Still in new Impudence, new Ignorance.
Success let others teach, learn thou from me
Pangs without birth, and fruitless Industry.
Let *Virtuoso's* in five years be Writ;
Yet not one thought accuse thy toyl of wit.
Let gentle *George*** in triumph tread the Stage,
Make *Dorimant* betray, and *Loveit* rage;
Let *Cully, Cockwood, Fopling,* charm the Pit,
And in their folly shew the Writer's wit.
Yet still thy fools shall stand in thy defence,
And justifie their Author's want of sense.
Let 'em be all by thy own model made
Of dullness, and desire no foreign aid:
That they to future ages may be known,
Not Copies drawn, but Issue of thy own.
Nay let thy men of wit too be the same,
All full of thee, and differing but in name;
But let no alien *Sedley* interpose

            *Sir George Etherege.

To lard with wit thy hungry *Epsom* prose.
And when false flowers of *Rhetorick* thou would'st cull,
Trust Nature, do not labour to be dull;
But write thy best, and top; and in each line,
Sir *Formal*'s oratory will be thine.
Sir *Formal*,* though unsought, attends thy quill,
And does thy *Northern Dedications*† fill.
Nor let false friends seduce thy mind to fame,
By arrogating *Johnson*'s Hostile name.
Let Father *Fleckno* fire thy mind with praise,
And Uncle *Ogleby* thy envy raise.
Thou art my blood, where *Johnson* has no part;
What share have we in Nature or in Art?
Where did his wit on learning fix a brand,
And rail at Arts he did not understand?
Where made he love in Prince *Nicander*'s‡ vein,
Or swept the dust in *Psyche*'s humble strain?
Where sold he Bargains, Whip-stitch, kiss my Arse,§
Promis'd a Play and dwindled to a Farce?
When did his Muse from *Fletcher* scenes purloin,
As thou whole *Eth'ridg* dost transfuse to thine?
But so transfus'd as Oyls on Water flow,
His always floats above, thine sinks below.
This is thy Province, this thy wondrous way,
New Humours to invent for each new Play:
This is that boasted Byas of thy mind,
By which one way, to dullness, 'tis inclin'd.
Which makes thy writings lean on oneside still,
And in all changes that way bends thy will.
Nor let thy mountain belly make pretence
Of likeness; thine's a tympany of sense.
A Tun of Man in thy Large bulk is writ,
But sure thou'rt but a Kilderkin of wit.‖

*A prolix orator in *The Virtuoso*.
†An allusion to Shadwell's principal patrons, the Duke and Duchess of Newcastle.
‡One of the unsuccessful suitors in *Psyche*.
§Catch-phrases of Sir Samuel Hearty in *The Virtuoso*.
‖A tun was an exceptionally large barrel, a kilderkin a half-barrel.

Like mine thy gentle numbers feebly creep,
Thy Tragick Muse gives smiles, thy Comick sleep.
With whate'er gall thou sett'st thy self to write,
Thy inoffensive Satyrs never bite.
In thy fellonious heart, though Venom lies,
It does but touch thy *Irish* pen, and dyes.
Thy Genius calls thee not to purchase fame
In keen Iambicks, but mild Anagram:
Leave writing Plays, and chuse for thy command
Some peacefull Province in Acrostick Land.
There thou maist wings display and Altars raise,
And torture one poor word Ten thousand ways.
Or if thou would'st thy diff'rent talents suit,
Set thy own Songs, and sing them to thy lute.
He said, but his last words were scarcely heard,)
For *Bruce* and *Longvil* had a *Trap* prepar'd,   }
And down they sent the yet declaiming Bard.   )
Sinking he left his Drugget robe behind,
Born upwards by a subterranean wind.
The Mantle fell to the young Prophet's part,
With double portion of his Father's Art.*

JOHN DRYDEN

The Envious Critick

The Poor in Wit or Judgment, like all Poor,
Revile, for having least, those who have more:
So 'tis the Critick's Scarcity of Wit
Makes him traduce them who have most of it.
Since to their Pitch himself he cannot raise,
He them to his mean Level would debase.
Acting like Demons, that would All deprive
Of Heav'n, to which themselves can ne'er arrive.

WILLIAM WYCHERLEY

*In 2 Kings ii, 9–13, Elijah is carried off to heaven in a whirlwind, his mantle falling to his successor Elisha.

Mors Omnibus Communis*

*Motto written by Thomas Otway in the parish register at Woolbeding.

Song

Oh the sad Day,
When friends shall shake their heads and say
Of miserable me,
Hark how he groans, look how he pants for breath,
See how he struggles with the pangs of Death!
When they shall say of these poor eyes,
How Hollow, and how dim they be!
Mark how his breast does swell and rise,
Against his potent enemy!
When some old Friend shall step to my Bed-side,
Touch my chill face, and thence shall gently slide,
And when his next companions say,
How does he do? what hopes? shall turn away,
Answering only with a lift up hand,
Who can his fate withstand?
Then shall a gasp or two, do more
Than e're my Rhetorick could before,
Perswade the peevish World to trouble me no more!

THOMAS FLATMAN

The Meditation

It must be done (my Soul) but 'tis a strange,
A dismal and Mysterious Change,
When thou shalt leave this Tenement of Clay,
And to an unknown somewhere wing away;
When Time shall be Eternity, and thou
Shalt be thou know'st not what, and live thou
know'st not how.

Amazing State! no wonder that we dread
To think of Death, or view the Dead.
Thou'rt all wrapt up in Clouds, as if to thee

Our very Knowledge had Antipathy.
Death could not a more Sad Retinue find,
Sickness and Pain before, and Darkness all behind.

Some Courteous Ghost, tell this great Secrecy,
    What 'tis you are, and we must be.
You warn us of approaching Death, and why
May we not know from you what 'tis to Dye?
But you, having shot the Gulph, delight to see
Succeeding Souls plunge in with like uncertainty.

When Life's close Knot by Writ from Destiny,
    Disease shall cut, or Age unty;
When after some Delays, some dying Strife,
The Soul stands shivering on the Ridge of Life;
With what a dreadful Curiosity
Does she launch out into the Sea of vast Eternity.

So when the Spatious Globe was delug'd o're,
    And lower holds could save no more,
On th'utmost Bough th'astonish'd Sinners stood,
And view'd th'advances of th'encroaching Flood.
O're-topp'd at length by th'Element's encrease,
With horrour they resign'd to the untry'd Abyss.

                  JOHN NORRIS

Superstition

      I care not tho it be
By the preciser sort thought Popery;
   We Poets can a Licence shew
     For every thing we do,
Hear then my little Saint, I'll pray to thee.

If now thy happy mind
Amidst its various joys can leasure find
　　T'attend to any thing so low
　　As what I say or do,
Regard, and be what thou wast ever, kind.

　　Let not the Blest above
Engross thee quite, but sometimes hither rove;
　　Fain would I thy sweet image see
　　And sit, and talk with thee,
Nor is it Curiosity but Love.

　　Ah what delight 'twou'd be
Would'st thou sometimes by stealth converse with me!
　　How should I thy sweet commerce prize
　　And other joys despise!
Come then, I ne'r was yet denyed by thee.

　　I would not long detain
Thy Soul from Bliss, nor keep thee here in pain.
　　Nor should thy fellow-Saints ere know
　　Of thy escape below,
Before thou'rt miss'd, thou should'st return again.

　　Sure heaven must needs thy love
As well as other qualitys improve.
　　Come then and recreate my sight
　　With rays of thy pure light,
'Twill chear my eyes more than the lamps above.

　　But if Fate's so severe
As to confine thee to thy blissful Sphere,
　　(And by thy absence I shall know
　　Whether thy state be so)
Live happy, but be mindful of me there.

JOHN NORRIS

Seneca's Troas, *Act* 2.
Chorus.

After Death, nothing is, and Nothing, Death,
  The utmost Limit of a Gasp of Breath:
  Let the ambitious Zealot lay aside,
His hopes of Heav'n (whose Faith is but his Pride)
  Let Slavish Souls lay by their Fear,
  Nor be concern'd, which way, or where
  After this life they shall be hurl'd;
Dead, we become the Lumber of the World;
And to that Mass of Matter shall be swept,
Where things Destroy'd, with things Unborn are kept.
  Devouring time swallows us whole,
Impartial Death confounds Body and Soul.
  For Hell, and the foul Fiend that rules
  God's everlasting fiery Goales,
  Devis'd by Rogues, dreaded by Fools;
(With his grim griezly Dog, that keeps the Door)
  Are sensless Stories, idle Tales,
  Dreams, Whimseys, and no more.

JOHN WILMOT, EARL OF ROCHESTER

The Death of Dives
from *Madness*

How sad doth *Dives* look? how deep he groans?
His Mammon god now will not hear his cries;
Mony and Friends now answer not his moans,
For all his wealth, he trembles, faints and dies.

The greatest Lord and Prince must now submit,
Crowns, Titles, Mony will not ease his pain;
Forced repentance seems to have some wit,
Preachers may speak now without proud disdain.

He calls for Mercy, he forgiveth all,
Instead of Fire and Sword, he speaks for Peace,
His wit revives as Flesh and Strength do fall,
Not from a Holy change, but for his ease.

Now he talks how he'd live; when life's near gone,
He seemeth wise, and promiseth to mend;
He thinks what Time is for, when time is done,
Begins to think of living at his end.

Might he be sav'd now for a frightned wish,
When guilt and terror cause his heart to faint;
When worldly pleasures all forsake his flesh,
He'd have the end and portion of a Saint.

Now take an Inventory of his Wealth,
This Corps was once the Body of a Man:
It liv'd in Pleasure, Honour, Ease and Health,
Goes Naked hence, as Naked Life began.

That frightful Earthly Face was wont to smile,
And with proud Scorn on hated Persons frown,
It Comely seem'd, which now is Black and Vile,
That it's the same, can hardly now be known.

Those closed Eyes, the Casements were of Lust,
There enter'd Worldly Vanity and Sin,
That Mouth, those Lips that now must Rot to Dust,
Have taken many a pleasant Morsel in.

That Throat, his Fellow-Creatures did Devour,
Made Sumptuous Feasts his Body to maintain,
With pleasant Liquors, many a merry Hour,
He did exhilerate both Heart and Brain.

Those Ears have heard, Jests, Plays and Melody,
Men's flattering Praise, and many a merry Song,
The welcom news of their Calamity,
Whom Wrath and Malice did delight to Wrong.

That Mouth hath utter'd many a merry Jest,
Vain Worldly talk, Strife, News and feigned Story,
Oaths, Lies and wanton Speeches, were its Feast,
Threats, and proud Boasts, and Scorning were its Glory.

That Nose delighted was with pleasant smell.
That Black and Sallow Skin was smooth and white;
On Eyes and Countenance did Grandure dwell,
The Just did flie; the Poor crowch'd at his sight.

Those Limbs could move; those hands had nimble Joints,
The Corps which now lies Dead, did Ride and Run,
All did perform what Lust and Pride appoints,
Many successful Actions he hath done.

Many deep Plodding Thoughts that Brain hath hatch'd,
How to grow Rich, and Great, and have his Will,
For Means and Seasons, he hath wisely watch'd,
All his Desires and Pleasure to fulfil.

And now what's left? To keep him from Men's sight,
A Shrowd and Coffin's all that he must have,
And these unknown, afford him no delight,
But serve their turn, who bring him to a Grave.

RICHARD BAXTER

A Wish

Whatever Blessing you my Life deny,
Grant me kind Heaven this one thing when I dye.
    I charge thee guardian Spirit hear,
And as thou lov'st me, further this my Prayer.

When I'm to leave this grosser Sphere, and try
Death, that amazing Curiosity,
    When just about to breathe my last,
Then when no Mortal joy can strike my tast,

Let me soft melting strains of Music hear
Whose Dying sounds may speak Death to my ear,
    Gently the Bands of Life unty,
Till in sweet raptures I dissolve and dye.

How soft and easy my new Birth will be
Help'd on by Music's gentle Midwifery!
    And I who 'midst these charms expire
Shall bring a Soul well tuned to Heaven's Quire.

JOHN NORRIS

From The Innocent Usurper

Sweet Harmony of Life, just Musick flows
From Souls, and strings, by stops that interpose;
Always intranc'd is never to be blest,
Hunger delights, but Surfeits spoil the Taste.
Love were not Love, nor wou'd yon Heav'n be dear,
If ever we enjoy'd such Raptures here.

JOHN BANKS

325

From *The Submarine Voyage*

There lies a Broken Anker, on whose Trust
The Lives of all the Nautick Crew were Weigh'd;
That scarcely bore the first impetuous Gust,
But them to Rocks and Gaping Sands betray'd,
    Or to the dreaded Strand:
There Heaps of Bodies under Hills of Sand,
    (The *Mummies* of the Sea)
    That at the *Resurrection*-Day
Need take no Pains to make their Members hit,
    Their Scatter'd Parts again to Knit;
But once inform'd with Heat and Active Fire,
    Their Bodies will be found Entire,
And in one Moment be for *Rising* fit.
Here *Guns* and *Swords* and Instruments of War,
That Death do give *near hand*, or from *afar*,
    With those they slew, One Fortune ran:
Peaceably now they ly and *would* do so,
    They of themselves no Mischief do,
Nor *would*, without the Cruel Hand of Man.

    There Two, that strugling Sank into the Deep,
With Deadly Hate grasping Each Other fast,
    Ev'en Dead their Hostile Postures keep;
    The Enmity yet seems to last:
    The senseless Bones Each Other hold,
Not Death th'unkind Embraces could unfold:
    But when the Raging Tempests blow,
    And Tydes move all the Deep below;
    The Clashing Bones yet seem to Jar,
    And keep up a Perpetual War.
    Another lies hard by,
That o'rboard fell with a far-stretch'd-out Blow,
    Aim'd at his Eager Foe,
And i'th' same Posture fell, i'th' same doth ly.

His Threatning Arm his Deadly Sword doth wield,
  Menacing Death i'th' watry Field;
And to Express His Ranker'd Hate within,
  Dead He retains a Ghastly Grin.

THOMAS HEYRICK

Description of a Sea-battle
from The Unhappy Favourite

   When the first Broad sids were giv'n,
A tall brave Ship, the tallest of the Rest,
That seem'd the Pride of all their big Half-moon,
Whether by Chance, or by a luckey Shot
From us, I know not, but she was Blown up,
Bursting like Thunder, and almost as high,
And then did Shiver in a Thousand Pieces,
Whilst from her Belly Crouds of Living Creatures
Broak like untimely Births, and fill'd the Skye:
Then might be seen a *Spanyard* catch his Fellow,
And Wrestling in the Air fall down together;
A Priest for safety Riding on a Cross,
Another that had none, crossing himself;
Fryers with long big sleeves like Magpyes' Wings
That bore them up, came gently Sailing down:
One with a Don that held him by the Arms,
And Cry'd, Confess me straight; but as he just
Had spoke the Words, they Tumbled down together.

JOHN BANKS

From *The Ambitious Statesman*

> Whilst th'iron Hand
> Of Death broke this fair Diamond in pieces,
> What Sparks flew round, each Richer than a World?

JOHN CROWNE

From *To the Society of the Beaux-Esprits*

Unhappy, foolish, wilful Man,
Preposterous! from thy self thy Woes began:
Of all created things none are so curst as *Thee*,
So curst by their Simplicity:
The Feather'd and four-footed kind,
Without those helps we boast to find,
Endure Heav'n's wrath, excessive heat and cold,
Yet grow, according to their *Natures*, old;
Nor are among themselves at strife,
How to abridge the little span of Life,
Which of it self, alas! is quickly gone,
And flies too fast to be pusht faster on:
But *Man*, vain *Man* has found a *thousand Keys*
To open that *one Lock* that ends his Days;
Or if *Sword*, *Fire*, the *Plague* and *Tempest* fail,
They're not *Physician-proof*, he'll certainly prevail.

ROBERT GOULD

To the Pious Memory
Of the Accomplisht Young LADY
MRS ANNE KILLIGREW*
Excellent in the two Sister-Arts of Poesie,
and Painting
An ODE

Thou Youngest Virgin-Daughter of the Skies,
  Made in the last Promotion of the Blest;
Whose Palmes, new pluckt from Paradise,
In spreading Branches more sublimely rise,
Rich with Immortal Green above the rest:
Whether, adopted to some Neighbouring Star,
Thou rol'st above us, in thy wand'ring Race,
  Or, in Procession fixt and regular,
  Mov'd with the Heavens' Majestick Pace;
  Or, call'd to more Superiour Bliss,
Thou tread'st, with Seraphims, the vast Abyss:
What ever happy Region be thy place,
Cease thy Celestial Song a little space;
(Thou wilt have Time enough for Hymns Divine,
  Since Heav'ns Eternal Year is thine.)
Hear then a Mortal Muse thy Praise rehearse,
  In no ignoble Verse;
But such as thy own voice did practise here,
When thy first Fruits of Poesie were giv'n;
To make thy self a welcome Inmate there:
  While yet a young Probationer,
    And Candidate of Heav'n.

*Daughter of Dr Henry Killigrew, Almoner to the Duke of York
and Master of the Savoy. She died of smallpox in 1685 aged twenty-
five.

If by Traduction* came thy Mind,
  Our Wonder is the less to find
A Soul so charming from a Stock so good;
Thy Father was transfus'd into thy Blood:
So wert thou born into the tuneful strain,
(An early, rich, and inexhausted Vain.)
    But if thy Præexisting Soul
      Was form'd, at first, with Myriads more,
It did through all the Mighty Poets roul,
  Who *Greek* or *Latine* Laurels wore,
And was that *Sappho* last, which once it was before.
  If so, then cease thy flight, *O Heav'n-born Mind!*
Thou hast no Dross to purge from thy Rich Ore:
Nor can thy Soul a fairer Mansion find,
Than was the Beauteous Frame she left behind:
Return, to fill or mend the Quire, of thy Celestial kind.

  May we presume to say, that at thy Birth,
New joy was sprung in Heav'n, as well as here on Earth.
  For sure the Milder Planets did combine
  On thy Auspicious Horoscope to shine,
  And ev'n the most Malicious were in Trine.†
    Thy Brother-Angels at thy Birth
    Strung each his Lyre, and tun'd it high,
    That all the People of the Skie
  Might know a Poetess was born on Earth.
    And then if ever, Mortal Ears
    Had heard the Musick of the Spheres!
    And if no clust'ring Swarm of Bees
On thy sweet Mouth distill'd their golden Dew,
    'Twas that, such vulgar Miracles,
    Heav'n had not Leasure to renew:
  For all the Blest Fraternity of Love
Solemniz'd there thy Birth, and kept thy Holyday above.

---

*Believers in 'traduction' held that both soul and body were propagated by the parents.

†i.e. 120° apart, the position in which their rays were least harmful.

O Gracious God! How far have we
Prophan'd thy Heav'nly Gift of Poesy?
Made prostitute and profligate the Muse,
Debas'd to each obscene and impious use,
Whose Harmony was first ordain'd Above
For Tongues of Angels, and for Hymns of Love?
O wretched We! why were we hurry'd down
 This lubrique and adult'rate age,
 (Nay added fat Pollutions of our own)
 T'increase the steaming Ordures of the Stage?
What can we say t'excuse our *Second Fall*?
Let this thy *Vestal*, Heav'n, attone for all!
Her *Arethusian* Stream* remains unsoil'd,
Unmixt with Forreign Filth, and undefil'd,
Her Wit was more than Man, her Innocence a Child!

 Art she had none, yet wanted none;
 For Nature did that Want supply,
 So rich in Treasures of her Own,
 She might our boasted Stores defy:
Such Noble Vigour did her Verse adorn,
That it seem'd borrow'd, where 'twas only born.
Her Morals too were in her Bosome bred
 By great Examples daily fed,
What in the best of Books, her Father's Life, she read.
 And to be read her self she need not fear,
 Each Test, and ev'ry Light, her Muse will bear,
 Though *Epictetus*† with his Lamp were there.
 Ev'n Love (for Love sometimes her Muse exprest)
Was but a *Lambent-flame* which play'd about her Brest:
 Light as the Vapours of a Morning Dream,
 So cold herself, whilst she such Warmth exprest,
 'Twas *Cupid* bathing in *Diana*'s Stream.

*The water nymph Arethusa passed through the sea unpolluted in her attempt to escape the pursuit of Alpheus.

†Dryden means Diogenes who went out with a lamp in broad daylight to look for an honest man.

Born to the Spacious Empire of the *Nine*,
One would have thought, she should have been content
To manage well that Mighty Government:
But what can young ambitious Souls confine?
   To the next Realm she stretcht her Sway,⎫
   For *Painture* neer adjoyning lay,   ⎬
A plenteous Province, and alluring Prey. ⎭
*A Chamber of Dependences** was fram'd,
  (As Conquerors will never want Pretence,
   When arm'd, to justifie the Offence)
And the whole Fief, in right of Poetry she claim'd.
The Country open lay without Defence:
For Poets frequent In-rodes there had made,
   And perfectly could represent
The Shape, the Face, with ev'ry Lineament;
And all the large Demains which the *Dumb-sister* sway'd,
   All bow'd beneath her Government,
   Receiv'd in Triumph wheresoe're she went.
Her Pencil drew, what e're her Soul design'd,
And oft the happy Draught surpass'd the Image in her
      Mind.

The *Sylvan* Scenes of Herds and Flocks,
And fruitful Plains and barren Rocks,
Of shallow Brooks that flow'd so clear,
The Bottom did the Top appear;
Of deeper too and ampler Flouds,
Which as in Mirrors, shew'd the Woods;
Of lofty Trees with Sacred Shades,
And Perspectives of pleasant Glades,
Where Nymphs of brightest Form appear,⎫
And shaggy Satyrs standing neer,   ⎬
Which them at once admire and fear; ⎭
The Ruines too of some Majestick Piece,
Boasting the Pow'r of ancient *Rome* or *Greece*,
Whose Statues, Freezes, Columns broken lie,

* (1) Subject territories or provinces (2) *hung* pictures (Lat. *dependere*).

And though defact, the Wonder of the Eie,
What Nature, Art, bold Fiction e're durst frame,
Her forming Hand gave Shape unto the Name.
So strange a Concourse ne're was seen before,
But when the people'd Ark the whole Creation bore.

The Scene then chang'd, with bold Erected Look
Our Martial King* the Eye with Reverence strook:
For not content t'express his Outward Part,
Her hand call'd out the Image of his Heart,
His Warlike Mind, his Soul devoid of Fear,
His High-designing Thoughts, were figur'd there,
As when, by Magick, Ghosts are made appear.
    Our Phenix Queen was portrai'd too so bright,
Beauty alone could Beauty take so right:
Her Dress, her Shape, her matchless Grace,
Were all oberv'd, as well as heav'nly Face.
With such a Peerless Majesty she stands,
As in that Day she took the Crown from Sacred hands;
Before a Train of Heroins was seen
In *Beauty* foremost, as in Rank, the Queen!
    Thus nothing to her *Genius* was deny'd,
But like a Ball of Fire the further thrown,
    Still with a greater Blaze she shone,
And her bright Soul broke out on ev'ry side.
What next she had design'd, Heaven only knows,
To such Immod'rate Growth her Conquest rose,
That Fate alone its Progress could oppose.

    Now all those Charmes, that blooming Grace,
The well-proportion'd Shape, and beauteous Face,
Shall never more be seen by Mortal Eyes;
In Earth the much lamented Virgin lies!
    Not Wit, nor Piety could Fate prevent;
    Nor was the cruel *Destiny* content
    To finish all the Murder at a Blow,
    To sweep at once her Life, and Beauty too;

* James II.

But, like a hardn'd Fellon, took a pride
   To work more Mischievously slow,
   And plunder'd first, and then destroy'd.
O double Sacriledge on things Divine,
To rob the Relique, and deface the Shrine!
   But thus *Orinda* dy'd:
Heav'n, by the same Disease, did both translate,
As equal were their Souls, so equal was their Fate.

Mean time her Warlike Brother on the Seas
   His waving Streamers to the Winds displays,
And vows for his Return, with vain Devotion, pays.
   Ah, Generous Youth, that Wish forbear,
   The Winds too soon will waft thee here!
   Slack all thy Sailes, and fear to come,
Alas, thou know'st not, Thou art wreck'd at home!
No more shalt thou behold thy Sister's Face,
Thou hast already had her last Embrace.
But look aloft, and if thou ken'st from far,
Among the *Pleiad's* a New-kindl'd Star,
If any sparkles, than the rest, more bright,
'Tis she that shines in that propitious Light.

When in mid-Aire, the Golden Trump shall sound,
   To raise the Nations under ground;
   When in the Valley of *Jehosaphat*,
The Judging God shall close the Book of Fate;
   And there the last Assizes keep,
   For those who Wake, and those who Sleep;
   When ratling Bones together fly,
From the four Corners of the Skie,
When Sinews o're the Skeletons are spread,
Those cloath'd with Flesh, and Life inspires the Dead;
The Sacred Poets first shall hear the Sound,
   And formost from the Tomb shall bound:
For they are cover'd with the lightest Ground!
And streight, with in-born Vigour, on the Wing,
Like mounting Larkes, to the New Morning sing.

There *Thou*, Sweet Saint, before the Quire shalt go,
As Harbinger of Heav'n, the Way to show,
The Way which thou so well hast learn'd below.

JOHN DRYDEN

An Epitaph on M.H.

In this cold *Monument* lies one,
That I know who has lain upon,
The happier *He*: her Sight would charm,
And Touch have kept *King David* warm.
Lovely, as is the dawning *East*,
Was this Marble's frozen *Guest*;
As soft, and Snowy, as that Down
Adorns the *Blow-balls* frizled Crown;
As straight and slender as the *Crest*,
Or *Antlet* of the one-beam'd Beast;
Pleasant as th'odorous *Month* of *May*:
As glorious, and as light as *Day*.

Whom I admir'd, as soon as knew,
And now her Memory pursue
With such a superstitious Lust,
That I could fumble with her Dust.

She all Perfections had, and more,
Tempting, as if design'd a *Whore*,
For so she was; and since there are
Such, I could wish them all as fair.

Pretty she was, and young, and wise,
And in her Calling so precise,
That Industry had made her prove
The sucking *School-Mistress* of *Love*:

And *Death*, ambitious to become
Her *Pupil*, left his Ghastly home,
And, seeing how we us'd her here,
The raw-bon'd *Rascal* ravisht her.

Who, pretty *Soul*, resign'd her Breath,
To seek new Letchery in Death.

CHARLES COTTON

To the Memory of Mr. Oldham

Farewel, too little and too lately known,
Whom I began to think and call my own;
For sure our Souls were near ally'd; and thine
Cast in the same Poetick mould with mine.
One common Note on either Lyre did strike,
And Knaves and Fools we both abhorr'd alike:
To the same Goal did both our Studies drive,
The last set out the soonest did arrive.
Thus *Nisus* fell upon the slippery place,
While his young Friend perform'd and won the Race.*
O early ripe! to thy abundant store
What could advancing Age have added more?
It might (what Nature never gives the young)
Have taught the numbers of thy native Tongue.
But Satyr needs not those, and Wit will shine
Through the harsh cadence of a rugged line.
A noble Error, and but seldom made,
When Poets are by too much force betray'd.
Thy generous fruits, though gather'd ere their prime
Still shew'd a quickness; and maturing time
But mellows what we write to the dull sweets of Rime.
Once more, hail and farewel; farewel thou young,

*In Book V of the *Aeneid*, Nisus, having fallen, trips another runner so that his friend Euryalus may win the prize.

336

But ah too short, *Marcellus** of our Tongue;
Thy Brows with Ivy, and with Laurels bound;
But Fate and gloomy Night encompass thee around.

JOHN DRYDEN

Epitaph on the Duke of Grafton†

                    Here
                    Lyes a Peer
                    Beneath this Place
                    Stil'd his Grace
                    The Duke of Grafton,
        A Blade as fine, as e're had Haft on.
        Markt with a Garter and a Star
        Forg'd out, and ground for War;
                    Of Mettle true
                    As ever drew,
                    Or made a Pass
                    At Lad or Lass.
        This Valiant Son of Mars
                    Ne're hung an Arse
                    With Sword or Tarse,
                    Nor turn'd his Tail,
                    Tho' Shots like Hail
                    Flew about his Ears
                    With Spikes and Spears
        So Thick, they'd hide the Sun.
                    He boldly forc'd his Way
                    Leading the Van
        More like the Devil than a Man:
        For why, he valu'd not a Fart a Gun.

*The adopted son of Augustus as seen by Aeneas in the underworld
(*Aeneid*, VI. 860–6).

†Henry Fitzroy, Duke of Grafton, natural son of Charles II and the
Duchess of Cleveland, was killed fighting for King William at the
siege of Cork in 1690.

He ne're wou'd Dread
Bullets of Lead,
Nor Cannon Ball
Nothing at all;
But a Bullet of Cork
Soon did his Work
Unhappy Pellet
With Greif I tell it
For with one Blow thou hast Undone
Great Cæsar's Son:
A Soldier foil'd
A Statesman Spoil'd.
God Rot him
That shot him
For a Son of a Whore,
Ile say no more,
But Here lyes Henry Duke of Grafton.

attrib. FLEETWOOD SHEPHERD

An Epitaph upon the Worthy and truly Vigilant, Sam. Micoe *Esq;*

Here Honest *Micoe* lies, who never knew
Whether the Parish Clock went false or true.
A true bred *English* Gentleman, for he
Never demanded yet *Quel heur est il?*
He valued not the Rise of Sun or Moon,
Nor e'er distinguish'd yet their Night from Noon.
Untill at last by chance he clos'd his Eyes,
And Death did catch him napping by surprize.
But first he thus spoke to the King of Fears,
Have I in Taverns spent my blooming years,
Outsate the Beadle nodding in his Chair,
Outwatch'd the Bulker and the Burglarer;
Outdrank all measure fill'd above the Seal,
When some weak Brethren to their Beds did reel;

338

And there when last night's Bottles were on board,
When Squires in Cloaks wrapt up in corners snoar'd;
I onely clad in my old Night Campain,
Call'd for more Wine and drank to 'em again?
Have I made Sir *John Robinson** to yield,
Sent haughty *Langston* staggering from the Field?
And unto meager Death now must I sink,
Death that eats all without a drop of Drink?
You steal my Life (grim Tyrant) 'cause you knew
Had I sate up I'd kill'd more men than you.
Quoth surly Death, *Statutum est, sic dico*;
Sat vigilasti – Bonos Nochios Micoe.

ALEXANDER RADCLIFFE

Epitaph on Mr *John Sprat, late Steward of* Grayes-Inn.†

Beneath this Stone, Reader, there lieth flat
Upon his Back the trusty *Steward Sprat*:
Disturb him not, for if he chance to stir,
He'll say, *When shall I wait upon you, Sir?*

ALEXANDER RADCLIFFE

*Sir John Robinson (1617–81), the royalist general, was like Radcliffe and, presumably, Micoe, a Gray's Inn man. Langston cannot be identified with certainty.

†Sprat became steward of Gray's Inn on 11 February 1667. His successor was appointed on 22 November 1676.

Envoi

The Leather Bottel

Now God alone that made all things,
Heaven and Earth, and all that's in,
The Ships that in the Seas do swim,
To keep out Foes from coming in,
Then every one does what he can,
All for the good, and use of man,
 And I wish in Heav'n his Soul may dwell,
 That first devis'd the Leather Bottel.

Now what d'ye say to Canns of Wood?
Faith they're naught, they cannot be good;
For when a man for Beer doth send,
To have them fill'd he doth intend,
The bearer stumbles by the way,
And on the ground the Beer doth lay;
Then doth the man begin to bann,
And swears 'twas long o'th woodden Cann,
But had it been in a Leather Bottel,
It had not been so, for all had been well,
And safe therein it would remain,
Until the man got up again,
 And I wish, &c.

What do you say to Glasses fine?
Faith they shall have no praise of mine,
For when a man's at Table set,
And by him sev'ral sorts of meat,
The one loves flesh, the other fish,
Then with your hand remove a Dish,
Touch but the Glass upon the brim,
The Glass is broke, and nought left in,
The Table-cloath though ne're so fine,
Is soil'd with Beer, or Ale, or Wine,
And doubtless for so small abuse,
A Servant may his Service loose,
 But I wish, &c.

What say you to the handled pot?
No praise of mine shall be its lot,
For when a man and wife's at strife,
As many have been in their life,
They lay their hands upon it both,
And break the same, although they're loath,
But woe to them shall bear the guilt,
Between them both the liquor's spilt,
For which they shall answer another day,
Casting so vainly their liquor away,
But if it had been Leather-bottel'd,
One might have tug'd, the other have held,
Both might have tug'd till their hearts should break,
No harm the Leather Bottel could take,
    Then I wish, &c.

What say you to Flagons of silver fine?
Why faith they shall have no praise of mine,
For when a Lord for Sack doth send,
To have them fild he doth intend,
The man with the Flagon runs away,
And never is seen after that day;
The Lord then begins to swear and ban,
For having lost both Flagon, and man,
But had it been either by Page or Groom,
With a Leather bottle it had come home,
    And I wish, &c.

And when this Bottel is grown old,
And that it will no longer hold,
Out o'th side you may cut a clout,
To mend your shooes when they're worn out,
Then hang the rest up on a pin,
'T will serve to put odd trifles in,
As Rings, and Awls, and Candles' ends,
For young beginners have such things,
      And I wish in Heaven his Soul may dwell,
      That first devis'd the Leather Bottel.

          The New Academy of Complements (1669)

To Amasia, *tickling a Gentleman*

Methinks, I see how the blest Swain was lay'd,
While round his sides your nimble Fingers play'd.
With pleasing softness did they swiftly rove,
Raising the Sweet, Delicious pangs of Love,
While, at each touch, they made his Heart strings move.
As round his Breast, his ravish'd Breast they crowd,
We hear their Musick, when he laughs aloud.
You ply him still, and as he melting lies,
Act your soft Triumphs, while your Captive dies.
Thus, he perceives, thou, Dearest, Charming Fair,
Without your Eyes, you can o'ercome him there.
Thus too he shews what's your unbounded skill,
You please, and charm us, tho' at once you kill.
Lodg'd in your Arms, he does in transport lie,
While thro' his Veins the fancy'd light'nings fly,
And, gush'd with vast delights, I see him hast to die.

JOHN HOPKINS

To the Laud and Praise *of a* Shock Bitch

Let lofty *Greek* and *Latin* go,
And *Priscian* crackt from *top to Toe*;
Since he at *School* full often so
        Misus'd us;

From *High and mighty Lines* I fall,
At powerful *Shock*'s imperious Call,
And now in downright *Doggrel* crawl
        My Muse does.

Tho' my *froze Hogs-Head* e'ne is burst,
I'le do what none before e're durst,
And on her Praises make the first
        Adventure;

345

O for some *Album-Græcum** now!
'Twould clear my musty *pipes* I trow;
Then would I yelp as loud as thou,
    Old Stentor!

Come hither *Shock*; I'll n'er complain,
Nor kick thee from my *Lap* again,
Tho' other Lips thy Mouth so dain-
    ty touches;

Give me one Buss, I'le prize thee more
Than *tinsil*'d Lord does *brazen* Whore;
Or then – or then – or then – or then
    No-body.†

Let *lowsie Poets* sit and chat
Of *Money*, and they know *not what*!
Of *Love*, and *Honour*, and all that
    So silly!

Let *Play-house-Hero*'s live or dy,
Or spew, or stink, or swear, or lye,
To court the *Glance* of one bright Eye
    From *Philly*!

Let the entranced *loving Ass*
A Picture wooe, and buss the Glass,
Covering his Mistress's surpas-
    sing Beauty!

Then steal from *Cowley*, or from *Don*,
(Since none will miss 'em when they're gon)
Two hundred thousand Stanza's on
    Her Shoo-ty!

*'The white and solid excrement of dogs, which subsist chiefly on bones, has been received as a remedy in the medical art, under the name of Album Graecum.' (W. Nicholson, *A Dictionary of Practical and Theoretical Chemistry*, 1808.) The principal reactive substance was calcium phosphate.

†Readers are invited to devise other ways of completing this stanza.

All other Fairs avaunt, avaunt,
For *Shock*'s sweet praise my *Muse* must *chaunt*,
And sweat, (ah, wou'd she wou'd!) in Rant
    Extatic.

'Tis *Shock* alone is my desire,
She does my addled pate inspire,
As much as any *Muse*, with Fire
    Poetic.

View every *Limb* in every part,
From *Head* to *Tail*, from *Rump* to *Heart*,
You'll find she not one *Pin* from Art
    Has gotten;

When Courtly *Dames* so gawdy, tho'
They dress their mouths in *pimlico*,
A *Dog won't touch 'em*, they are so
    Ripe-rotten.

Muse, what d'ye mean? what Flesh can stay,
And dive in *Helicon* to day,
Or swim in any Streams but *A-*
    qua-vitae?

Put up your Pipes, to dinner go,
Whilest I dismiss the *Guests* below:
You're welcome Gentlemen! and so,
    Good-buy-t'y'e!

                 SAMUEL WESLEY

Rochester to the Post Boy

Son of a whore, God dam you: Can you tell
A Peerless Peer the Readyest way to Hell?
Ive out swilld Baccus, sworn of my own make
Oaths wou'd fright furies and make Pluto quake;
Ive swived more whores more ways than Sodom's
    walls
Ere knew or the College of Rome's Cardinalls.
Witness Heroick scars, look here (ne're go)
Sear cloaths and ulcers from the top to toe:
Frighted at my own mischeifes I have fled
And bravely left my life's defender dead;*
Broke houses to break chastity and died
That floor with murder which my lust denyed.
Pox on it, why do I speak of these poor things?
I have blasphemed my God and libelld Kings.
The readyest way to Hell, come quick, ne're stirr!

Boy.   The readyest way my Lord's by *Rochester*.

Attrib. JOHN WILMOT, EARL OF ROCHESTER

On Fleet: Shepheard's takeing away a child's bread and butter

At that so pleasant Season of the Year,
When fields and meadowes fresh and gay appear,
The tender infant of some neighb'ring Swaine,
Eat bread and butter upon Brentford plaine,
Grac'd with glasse windowes in the Diamond cutt;
Such was his nice indulgence to his gutt:
Smileing hee sat, secure and unconcern'd,
When hungry Shepherd this poor child discern'd,

---

*A reference to a brawl at Epsom on 17 June 1676, in which one of Rochester's companions was killed by the watch.

Resolv'd to make him his lov'd morsell yeild,
Or swore hee'd kill him in the open field.
Thrice hee prepar'd for this unequall fight;
As oft the child secur'd himself by flight.
Hunger, and rage, at once his Soul inspire;
His lookes were fierce, and his red eyes struck fire.
So sparkled Turnus' eyes with furious rage,
When with Æneas hee did once engage;
So Ajax look'd, when hee with Hector strove,
And so look'd Capaneus defying Jove.
The child stood trembling, almost dead with fear,
Whilst he run at him with a full carreer,
Luxurious brat, hee cry'd, give me the bread,
Each hour you are by tender mother fed;
Here, free from hunger, and from harm secure,
You think not what wee travellers endure;
Then, like a Heroe, seiz'd upon the prize,
Whilst floods of teares ran from the infant's eyes,
And the plaine ecchoes with the mournfull cryes.

MATTHEW PRIOR

On Melting down the Plate: Or, the Piss-Pot's Farewel, 1697.

Maids need no more their Silver Piss-pots scoure,
They now must jog like Traytors to the Tower:
A quick dispatch! no sooner are they come,
But ev'ry Vessel there receives its Doom:
By Law condemn'd to take their fiery Tryal,
A sentence that admits of no denial.
Presumptuous Piss-Pot! how didst thou offend?
Compelling Females on the Hams to bend?
To Kings and Queens, we humbly bow the Knee;
But Queens themselves are forc'd to stoop to thee;
To thee they cringe, and with a straining Face,

They cure their Grief, by opening of their Case.
In times of need thy help they did implore,
And oft to ease their Ailments made thee roar.
Under their Bed thou still hadst been conceal'd,
And ne'er but on Necessity reveal'd;
When over charg'd, and in Extremity,
Their dearest Secrets they disclos'd to thee.
Long hast thou been a Prisoner close confin'd,
But Liberty is now for thee design'd,
Thou, whom so many Beauties have enjoy'd,
Now in another use shall be employ'd;
And with delight be handled ev'ry Day,
And oftener occupied a better way.
But crafty Workmen first must thee refine,
To purge thee from thy Soder and thy Brine.
When thou, transform'd into another shape,
Shalt make the World rejoyce at thy Escape;
And from the Mint in Triumph shall be sent,
New Coin'd, and Mill'd, to ev'ry Heart's content.
Welcome to all, then proud of thy new Vamp,
Bearing the Pasport of a royal Stamp;
And pass as currant, pleasant and as free,
As that which hath so often pass'd in thee.

State-Poems Continued (1703)

Biographical Notes*

JOHN BANKS (c. 1650–1706). Banks was a law student turned dramatist who is important historically as one of the popularizers of the pathetic 'she-tragedy'. His best known plays are *The Unhappy Favourite or the Earl of Essex* and *Vertue Betray'd or Anna Bullen* both published for the first time in 1682. Undiplomatic allusions to affairs of state led to three of his other plays being refused production.

RICHARD BAXTER (1615–91). The son of a 'mean freeholder' of Eaton-Constantine near Shrewsbury, Baxter was educated at the free school of Wroxeter. His early experiences of the negligence of the ministers of the Established Church inclined him to the Presbyterians though he accepted an Anglican ordination and was always a moderate in the dispute between the churches. His appointment in 1641 to the curacy of Kidderminster inaugurated an enormously influential career as a preacher and devotional writer. From 1643 to 1647 he served as a chaplain with the parliamentary army. As a strong advocate of the Restoration, Baxter was offered a bishopric by Charles II; however he refused to be reconciled to the Church of England and afterwards had to endure twenty-five years of official persecution. In 1685 he was sent to prison by Judge Jeffreys for an alleged libel on the church and remained there a year and a half before being released by James II as part of his plan to win the support of the non-conformists. Baxter was an extremely prolific writer – Wing's *Short-Title-Catalogue* identifies 279 editions of his various works published before 1700 – and he is still remembered today for *The Saints' Everlasting Rest* (1650) and his autobiography *Reliquiae Baxterianae* (1696). 'Madness' is one of the *Additions* to the second edition of his *Poetical Fragments* (1689).

APHRA BEHN (1640?–89). Aphra Behn was the daughter of an English official, possibly named Johnson, who is surmised to have died in 1653 while en route to take up an administrative

*All dates for plays given in these notes are those of publication, not performance.

post in Surinam. On her return to England she apparently married, her husband being variously identified as Joachim Beene of Hamburg, a member of the Bean family of Barham, and a city merchant of Dutch extraction. Our first definite information about her is contained in the records of a spying mission to the low countries she undertook on behalf of the English government in 1666 at the suggestion of the dramatist Thomas Killigrew. After the production of her first play, *The Forced Marriage or the Jealous Bridegroom* in 1670, she managed to establish herself as a professional writer and held her own in a highly competitive arena until her death. Her works comprise eighteen plays, a dozen short novels, some original poems, and a large number of prose and verse translations, principally from the French. There is an edition in six volumes by Montague Summers (1915).

SIR RICHARD BLACKMORE (1652–1729). Although a contemporary of Oldham at St Edmund Hall, Oxford, Blackmore waited till he was over forty and a prosperous physician to make his first appearance in print with his epic *Prince Arthur* (1695). His *Satire against Wit* (1700) earned him the enmity of the Tory satirists who continued for many years to extract matter for ridicule from his fondness for moralizing, his devotion to the principles of the Revolution, and the fecundity of his muse. *Prince Arthur*, the only one of nine lengthy works in verse still remembered, is the attempt of a vigorous but unmistakably minor talent on a genre and a subject to which Dryden had only dared aspire.

ALEXANDER BROME (1620–66). Brome, a lawyer by profession, was one of the second generation of the cavalier school who grew to poetic maturity during the interregnum, and never quite managed to digest the disappointments of the period immediately after the Restoration. He was a personal friend of Cotton and shares his conversational rhythms and fondness for Bacchanalian subjects. His *Songs and other Poems* was published in 1661 and reprinted in 1664 and 1668.

JOHN BUNYAN (1628–88). The son of a Bedford tinsmith, Bunyan fought in the civil wars and later, after a period of spiritual awakening lasting from his twenty-second to his twenty-fifth year, joined a Baptist congregation where he discovered his vocation as a preacher. From 1660 to 1672 he was imprisoned under the laws against non-conformity. *The Pilgrim's Progress* (1678 and 1684) remains the most widely read and deeply loved book of its age. Bunyan's other principal works are *Grace Abounding to the Chief of Sinners* (1666), *The Life and Death of Mr Badman* (1680), and the *Holy War* (1682).

SAMUEL BUTLER (1613–80). The earlier of the two homophonous satirists was born at Strensham near Worcester and educated at the King's School, Worcester. His friend Aubrey notes that 'When but a Boy he would make observations and reflections on every Thing one sayd or did, and censure it to be either well or ill'. Prevented by poverty from going on to the university, he became a justice's clerk and later a steward in two noble families. His fame is based chiefly on *Hudibras* (three parts, 1663, 1664 and 1678), a burlesque heroic poem in slangy tetrameters attacking the Puritans. Despite its popularity among Butler's contemporaries, it never brought him the preferments which he felt were his due and he died in poverty. The excerpts from *Hudibras* have been taken from Hugh Macdonald's copies of the earliest editions in the Sydney University Library. The standard edition is that of John Wilders (1967).

WILLIAM CONGREVE (1670–1729). Born at Bardsey in Yorkshire and educated at the free school at Kilkenny and Trinity College, Dublin, Congreve came to London to study law. In his early dealings with the theatre he was helped by Dryden and Southerne and his four comedies *The Old Bachelor* (1693), *The Double Dealer* (1694), *Love for Love* (1695) and *The Way of the World* (1700) are regarded along with Etherege's *The Man of Mode* and Wycherley's *The Country Wife* and *The Plain Dealer* as representing the supreme accomplishments of Restoration comedy. His tragedy *The Mourning Bride* (1697) was highly popular in its day. Congreve abandoned writing for the stage in disgust after the relative failure of *The Way of the World* and produced nothing else of any real significance. Congreve's poems have been edited by Montague Summers (1923) and Bonamy Dobrée (1929). The most recent edition of the plays is that of Herbert Davis (1966).

The text of the *Ode in imitation of Horace* is based on that in Gildon's *Miscellany Poems* (1692).

CHARLES COTTON (1630–87). Better known for his translation of Montaigne and his share in *The Compleat Angler* than for his poetry, Cotton nonetheless thoroughly deserved the admiration bestowed on his verse by Coleridge, Wordsworth and Lamb. Born at Beresford in Staffordshire, he was the son of a luminary of the court of Charles I from whom he inherited an unwavering devotion to the Stuart cause, the friendship of Izaak Walton and an estate which proved the least enduring of the three. He was married twice, in 1656 to his cousin Isabella who died in 1669, and in 1675 to Mary, dowager Countess of Ardglass. Cotton's later years were rendered difficult by money troubles, but nothing seems to have long interrupted his enjoyment of life, his fishing expeditions, or the steady stream of translations (principally from French) and miscellaneous prose with which he supplied the press. He preferred to withhold his poetry from the public, with the exception of *Scarronides* (1664), *Burlesque upon Burlesque* (1675) and *The Wonders of the Peak* (1681). An edition that he was said to have prepared shortly before his death never reached the printer. *The Poems on Several Occasions* of 1689, the last and not the least worthy monument of the cavalier school, is presumably derived from manuscripts circulating among his friends. A much earlier manuscript of this type in the Derby Public Library has been consulted along with the edition of 1689 in preparing texts for this edition. Selections of Cotton's verse have been published by John Beresford (1923) and John Buxton (1958).

ABRAHAM COWLEY (1618–67). Cowley blossomed early, so early that it is hard to believe that he was younger than Samuel Butler by six years. Born in London, the posthumous son of a wealthy stationer, he received his education at Westminster School and Trinity College, Cambridge. The publication of *The Mistress* (1647) established him in the popular consciousness as the foremost poet of his generation. Espousing the royal cause during the civil wars, he accompanied Queen Henrietta Maria into exile in 1646. Ten years later he returned to England, took an M.D. at Oxford, and published a collection of his poems, including the unfinished epic *Davideis*, before retiring once more to the continent. After the Restoration his sufferings were not rewarded as promptly as he expected, and it was only after several poetic complaints that he received a grant of Queen's land at Barn Elms. The principal achievement of his final years was his discovery of the Pindaric ode, which, despite the depths to which it descended in the hands of less talented imitators, proved an ideal vehicle for the mercurial cavalier. Texts of poems by Cowley are from Sprat's edition of 1668. The standard modern edition is that of A. R. Waller (1905–6).

THOMAS CREECH (1659–1700). The translator of Lucretius was born at Blandford in Dorset and educated at Sherbourne School and Wadham College, Oxford. His version of the *De rerum natura*, the great philosophical poem whose mechanistic doctrines and denial of immortality held a special fascination for the Restoration, was published anonymously in 1682 and reprinted in 1683 with commendatory verses by Evelyn, Otway, Aphra Behn, Richard Duke and Waller. It was also admired, and (some said) envied, by Dryden. Creech went on to publish a complete English version of Horace (1684) and to contribute to Dryden's *Miscellany Poems* (1684) and other collections. He died by his own hand. The text is that of the heavily revised second edition.

JOHN CROWNE (1640–1712). Born in Nova Scotia and an alumnus of Harvard, Crowne came to England shortly after the Restoration in an attempt to obtain compensation for a grant of land made to his father by Cromwell and later confiscated by the French. Unsuccessful in this, he became a professional dramatist. His tragedies, of which the most interesting are the grandiose two-part *The Destruction of Jerusalem* (1677) and the neo-Websterian *The Ambitious Statesman* (1679), contain lines and passages of remarkable power. His best comedy is *The City Politiques* (1683). *Sir Courtly Nice* (1685), written at the personal request of Charles II, was highly popular in its day. There is an edition in four volumes by J. Maidment and W. H. Logan (1873–7).

CHARLES DARBY (c.1635–1709). The author of *Bacchanalia, or a Description of a Drunken Club* (1680) was a fellow of Jesus College, Cambridge, and later rector of Kedington, Suffolk. He also published *The Psalms in English Metre* (1704). The text is from the edition of 1698.

SIR WILLIAM DAVENANT (1606–68). A native of Oxford, where his father kept an inn, Davenant had distinguished himself enough by 1638 as poet and dramatist to be awarded the laureateship on the death of Ben Jonson. He fought for the king in the civil war and accompanied the queen in the early years of her exile. In 1650 he was captured at sea by a parliamentary ship and having survived (possibly through the intervention of Milton) a proposal to have him executed, was permitted to live freely in England where he later persuaded the authorities to relax their ban on theatrical entertainment. His unfinished epic *Gondibert* appeared in 1651. In 1660, Davenant became proprietor of the Duke of York's servants, one of the two licensed dramatic companies, and was responsible for the introduction of women actors and elaborate scenic effects to the English stage. He made several adaptations of plays by Shakespeare, whom he remembered as a regular visitor to his father's inn on his journeys to and from Stratford and whom he was prone among friends to claim as his real father. A folio collected edition of his works was published in 1673. The most recent edition is that of Maidment and Logan (1872–4).

SIR JOHN DENHAM (1615–69). Denham, born at Dublin and educated at Trinity College, Oxford, and Lincoln's Inn, was the son of a royalist Judge and like Cowley and Waller was closely associated with the family of Charles I during the civil war and years of exile. *Coopers Hill* appeared in 1642. In 1652, having impoverished himself through gambling, he returned to England where he was tolerated by the government and enjoyed the patronage of the Earl of Pembroke. After the Restoration he obtained the valuable post of Surveyor-General of Works. In 1667 his second wife, who was the mistress of the Duke of York, died under suspicious circumstances and Denham, only recently recovered from a bout of insanity, was widely suspected of having poisoned her. As a poet, Denham is usually paired with Waller as one of the two popularizers of the heroic couplet. Texts are from *Poems and Translations with The Sophy* (1668). The standard modern edition is that of T. H. Banks (1928).

JOHN DENNIS (1657–1734). Dennis was the son of a London saddler and received his education at Harrow and Caius College and Trinity Hall, Cambridge (his transfer being the consequence of a duel). Although remembered today only as a critic, he was also active as a poet, dramatist, letter-writer and compiler of anthologies. *The Two Friends* is from his *Poems in Burlesque* published in 1692 with a dedication to Fleetwood Shepherd.

JOHN DRYDEN (1631–1700). The most eminent poet, critic and prose writer of his age and a dramatist of considerably greater distinction than is usually allowed him, Dryden was born at

Aldwinkle All Saints, Northamptonshire, and educated at Westminster School and Trinity College, Cambridge. In the late 1650s he appears to have held a minor post under Cromwell, whose death was the occasion of his first significant poem. After the Restoration, Dryden was able with the aid of some well-timed panegyrics to obtain the favour of the king whose cause he supported faithfully for the rest of his life and from whom he received the laureateship on the death of Davenant in 1668. His principal longer poems are *Annus Mirabilis* (1667), *Absalom and Achitophel* (1681), *The Medal* (1682), *Mac Flecknoe* (published 1682, written *c.* 1678), *Religio Laici* (1682), and *The Hind and the Panther* (1687); however, he also wrote a huge quantity of occasional verse – prologues and epilogues, songs, commendatory poems, elegies, etc. – most of it superbly tailored to its purpose and intended audience. After the Revolution, Dryden, who had been converted to Catholicism during the reign of James II, lost all his official posts, and the final decade of his life was devoted to his translations of the complete works of Juvenal and Persius (1693) and Virgil (1697) and the supervision of a series of *Miscellanies*, published by Jacob Tonson, containing original poems and further translations by himself and his protégés. His last major collection, *Fables Ancient and Modern* (1700), contained translations and adaptations from Boccaccio, Chaucer, Ovid, and Homer.

Always the professional, Dryden was forced to rely for income to a greater extent than he would have liked on the theatre. Between 1663 and 1693 he wrote twenty-four plays of which the best are *Secret Love or the Maiden Queen* (1668), *Tyrannick Love* (1670), the two parts of *The Conquest of Granada* (1672), *Marriage A-la-Mode* (1673), *All for Love* (1678), *Oedipus* (with Nathaniel Lee, 1679), and *Don Sebastian* (1690). His critical writing, with the exception of the essay *Of Dramatic Poesie* (1668), is principally contained in the often lengthy introductions to his plays and poems. He died in London on 1 May 1700, and is buried in Westminster Abbey.

The standard edition of Dryden's poems, that of James Kinsley (1958), is being progressively superseded by a complete edition of the works issued by the University of California Press.

RICHARD DUKE (1658–1711). Duke was a Londoner by birth and received his education at Westminster School and Trinity College, Cambridge. He was closely associated with the Tory wits during the closing years of the reign of Charles II. In 1685 he took orders and was appointed a prebendary of Gloucester and later rector of Blaby in Leicestershire. His death was seized upon by Swift as the occasion for an atrocious pun. Duke's *Poems on Several Occasions* were published in one volume with the poems of Roscommon in 1717. *A Panegyrick upon Oates* is taken from the broadside of 1679.

THOMAS DURFEY (1653–1723). Comic dramatist, buffoon, and balladmonger extraordinary, Durfey's principal claim to the gratitude of posterity is his association with the various volumes of the *Pills to Purge Melancholy* series, still the best source for the study (and performance) of Restoration popular music. He also wrote one tragedy, *The Siege of Memphis* (1676), and nearly thirty comedies, operas and burlesques.

SIR GEORGE ETHEREGE (1635?–91). 'Loose, wandering Etherege' was the eldest of six children of a small landowner at Maidenhead, Berkshire. Little is known of his life before 1664 when the success of his first play, *The Comical Revenge, or Love in a Tub*, brought him to the notice of the Buckingham circle. His second comedy, *She Wou'd if She Cou'd*, was produced in 1668. Later in the same year he travelled to Constantinople as secretary to the English ambassador, and would seem to have remained there until 1671 when he signalized his return to England by a duel with a fellow poet, Edmund Ashton. His one undeniably great comedy, *The Man of Mode*, was produced in 1676. The rest of Etherege's life is largely a tale of brawls and disasters, the most remarkable of the latter being his expedition to Ratisbon as James II's ambassador to the Imperial Diet in 1685, surely the most hilariously mismanaged diplomatic mission in English history. His own account of it is preserved in his *letterbooks* along with the disapproving remarks of his Puritan secretary. After the Revolution he fled to Paris. The circumstances of his death are not fully known.

SIR FRANCIS FANE (d. 1689). Fane was the eldest son of a younger son of the first Earl of Westmoreland, and was created a Knight of the Bath at the coronation of Charles II. He knew and admired Rochester, wrote a masque for his revision of Fletcher's *Valentinian*, and as early as 1675 was prepared to claim, apparently without irony, that he had been made a better Christian by his ill-reputed friend's conversation. Fane's *Love in the Dark, or the Man of Business* (1675) is one of the best of the second rank of Restoration comedies. He also wrote a tragedy *The Sacrifice* (1686). *To a Perjur'd Mistress* was published in Nahum Tate's *Poems by Several Hands* (1685).

THOMAS FLATMAN (1635–88). A lawyer by profession, a miniature painter of some distinction, and a fellow of the Royal Society, Flatman was descended from a Norfolk family and was educated at Winchester, New College, Oxford, and the Inner Temple. He married in 1672. He was a close friend of Cotton and of Shipman, whose verse he prepared for publication, and his style was formed in their school. All four editions of his *Poems and Songs* (1674, 1676, 1682 and 1686) have been consulted. Poems by Flatman are included in the third volume of Saintsbury's *The Caroline Poets* and in the life by F. A. Child (both 1921). I have omitted a stanza added to *The Retirement* in the edition of 1686.

SIR SAMUEL GARTH (1661–1719). The friend and advocate of the young Alexander Pope was a native of Bowland Forest in the West Riding of Yorkshire and was educated at Ingleton School, Peterhouse, Cambridge, and the University of Leyden in Holland, where he studied medicine. In 1693 he was elected a fellow of the College of Physicians. His satire *The Dispensary* (1699) was written to ridicule the opponents of a plan to establish a dispensary for the poor. In 1700 he supervised the funeral of Dryden. A Whig, he was subsequently physician general to the army and physician in ordinary to George I.

ROBERT GOULD (d.c. 1709). Gould was first the servant and then the poetical protégé of Dorset. He published a volume of *Poems, chiefly consisting of Satyrs* in 1689, and later secured a position in the household of the Earl of Abingdon. His tragedy *The Rival Sisters* was produced in 1695. A collection of his works in two volumes was issued posthumously by his widow, Martha, in 1709.

THOMAS HEYRICK (1649–94). Heyrick, grandnephew of Robert Herrick, was a native of Market Harborough, Leicestershire, and was educated at Peterhouse, Cambridge. He was ordained priest in 1681 and in 1685 returned to spend the rest of his life as parish curate of Market Harborough. His *Miscellany Poems* were published in 1691.

JOHN HOPKINS (*fl.* 1700). The author of *Amasia, or the Works of the Muses* (1700) and *Milton's Paradise Lost Imitated in Rhyme* (1699) has been identified without total certainty with John, the brother of Dryden's protégé Charles Hopkins and son of Ezekiel Hopkins, Bishop of Derry. He was an M.A. of Jesus College, Cambridge, and was ordained priest at York in September 1698.

NATHANIEL LEE (1651–92). Lee was the son of a Presbyterian divine who conformed to the Established Church after the Restoration. He was educated at Charterhouse and Trinity. Between 1674 and 1684 when he became temporarily insane he wrote ten tragedies and one comedy and collaborated in two further tragedies with Dryden. Lee is remembered for such exuberant divertisements as *The Rival Queens* (1677), however his best plays are probably *The Massacre of Paris* (written 1678, published 1690) and *Lucius Junius Brutus* (1681), historical dramas of remarkable power and originality.

His works have been ably edited by T. B. Stroup and A. L. Cooke (1955).

ANDREW MARVELL (1621–78). One of the three supreme masters of the metaphysical mode, Marvell chose in 1660 to make an entirely new start and became a trenchant and daring political satirist. The son of a clergyman, he was born at Winstead in Holderness, Yorkshire, and educated at Hull grammar school and Trinity College, Cambridge. After continental travel, he became tutor, first to Fairfax's daughter Mary (subsequently wife to George Villiers, Duke of Buckingham) and then to a young ward of Cromwell. In 1657 he was appointed to assist Milton in his Latin secretaryship. As member of parliament for Hull and the author of a number of widely read works of controversy, Marvell was one of the most influential figures in the parliamentary opposition to Charles II, his sudden death being widely, though it would seem incorrectly, attributed to the machinations of the Jesuits. His *Miscellany Poems*, containing his lyrical and reflective verse, was published after his death by a woman claiming, again incorrectly, to be his widow. His satires were circulated in manuscript and broadside form until the Revolution, when they were openly published for the first time in the various *State Poems* collections. His best known prose works were the two parts of *The Rehearsal Transpros'd* (1672 and

1673) written in opposition to the anti-tolerationist Samuel Parker, and his *Account of the Growth of Popery and Arbitrary Government in England* (1677).

The texts of the poems by Marvell in this anthology are mostly from Bodl. MS. Eng. Poet. d. 49, which consists of an uncancelled copy of the *Miscellany Poems* bound together with a transcript of the satires in a hand alleged to be that of the poet's nephew William Popple. I have followed Lord in preferring B.M. MS. Harl. 7315 as copy text for *The Haymarket Hectors* which may not be Marvell's own.

The standard edition of Marvell, that of H. M. Margoliouth (1927), suffers from its editor's involuntary ignorance of the Bodleian manuscript. A new edition has been promised from America.

JOHN MILTON (1608–74). Although the fact that Milton's greatest poetry was written after the Restoration is largely a historical accident, his influence on the age both as poet and political theorist was more considerable than is normally assumed. Nevertheless his poetry has stronger links with that of the sixteenth and eighteenth centuries than that of the age of Dryden. For this reason, no attempt has been made to represent the full range of his achievement within the present volume. The son of a wealthy London scrivener, he was educated at St Paul's School and Christ's College, Cambridge. *Comus* was written in 1634 and *Lycidas* in 1637. From the early 1640s, his main energies were diverted from poetry to controversial writing, the education of the children of some close friends, and, after 1649, the office of Latin Secretary to the Council of State. In 1652, he became totally blind. An advocate of republicanism right up to the Restoration, Milton might easily have been excluded from the Act of Oblivion. Differing accounts attribute his preservation to the intervention of Marvell, Davenant and other friends and patrons. In February 1663, with *Paradise Lost* already close to completion, he married for the third time and moved to a house in Artillery Walk, Bunhill Fields, where he continued to be visited by a wide circle of sympathizers. *Paradise Lost* was published in 1668 and followed in 1671 by *Paradise Regain'd* and *Samson Agonistes*. He died of gout.

The text of the extracts from *Paradise Lost* is that of the first edition.

JOHN NORRIS (1657–1711). Although dismissed by Locke as an 'obscure, enthusiastic man', Norris was influential in his day as a theologian, idealist philosopher, and correspondent of learned ladies. The son of a Wiltshire clergyman, he was educated at Winchester and Exeter College, Oxford, and in 1680 became a fellow of All Souls. From 1692 until his death he was rector of George Herbert's parish of Bemerton where he seems to have clashed with his Bishop, the Whig latitudinarian Gilbert Burnet. His poems appeared in *A Collection of Miscellanies* (1687).

JOHN OLDHAM (1653–83). Oldham was born at Shipton near Tedbury in Gloucestershire and died of smallpox thirty years and four months later leaving behind him a body of verse which, for all its narrowness of range, bears the impress of an original, invigorating and completely assured poetic personality. He was a graduate of St Edmund Hall, Oxford, and later took turns as schoolmaster, tutor, student of medicine, and dependent scholar. He was encouraged by the court wits, who copied such poems as the *Satyr against Vertue* and *Sardanapalus* (still unpublished) into their commonplace books, and later became friendly with Dryden who lamented his death in a famous elegy. Texts are from copies of the earliest editions in the Cambridge University Library, with the exception of the extract from the *Satyr against Vertue* which has been edited from the poet's commonplace book Bodl. MS. Rawl. Poet. 123. H. F. Brooks's long-awaited edition is now ready for publication.

JOHN OLDMIXON (1673–1742). Oldmixon made a false start as a poet before finding his true metier as a historian and polemicist. *To Chloe* is from his *Poems on Several Occasions Written in imitation of the manner of Anacreon* (1696).

KATHERINE PHILIPS (1632–64). 'The Matchless Orinda' was the daughter of a London merchant named Fowler. After his death her mother remarried and in 1647 Katherine became the second wife of James Philips, the son of her stepfather. With her husband's encouragement she founded a salon whose members addressed each other by names drawn from pastoral mythology and vowed devotion to the cause of friendship. In 1662 she travelled to Ireland where her translation of Corneille's *Pompée* was performed. Shortly after her return she died of smallpox.

The text of the poems is from the posthumous edition of 1667.

BIOGRAPHICAL NOTES

There is a modern reprint based on the edition of 1678 in the first volume of Saintsbury's *The Caroline Poets* (1905).

MATTHEW PRIOR (1664–1721). The future plenipotentiary was rescued from his uncle's wine shop by Dorset who found him reading Horace there and helped him to complete his education at Westminster School and St John's College, Cambridge. His first substantial work, *The Hind and Panther Transvers'd*, was an attack on Dryden written with the assistance of his friend Charles Montagu, later Earl of Halifax. After the Revolution, Prior was able, with Dorset's assistance, to obtain a diplomatic appointment at The Hague where he remained several years. In 1702 he cast in his lot with the Tories and superintended important negotiations with France. Stripped of his positions on the accession of George I, he managed to recoup his fortunes by the publication of his poems in a folio edition and the gift of a house from the former Lord Treasurer, Harley. By his own request he was buried beside his idol Spenser in Westminster Abbey, a circumstance which led to his unintended disinterment shortly before the second world war by a band of literary historians in search of the elegies reportedly buried with the Elizabethan.

The standard edition of Prior's literary works is that of H. B. Wright and M. K. Spears (1959). 'To the honourable *Charles Montague, Esq.*' and 'Whilst Beauty, Youth, and gay Delight' are given in their earliest (and in some ways most attractive) forms as published in *The Gentleman's Journal* for February and August, 1692. Mr R. A. Sayce has kindly checked Wright and Spears's text of *On Fleet: Shepheard's takeing away a child's bread and butter* against the manuscript in the library of Worcester College, Oxford.

ALEXANDER RADCLIFFE (c. 1645–after 1696). Radcliffe was born at Hampstead and studied law at Gray's Inn before entering the army. In 1673, he published a set of parodies of Ovid's epistles. His poems circulated widely in manuscript before being collected in *The Ramble: an Anti-heroick Poem together with Some Terrestrial Hymns and Carnal Ejaculations* (1682).

CHARLES SACKVILLE, Sixth Earl of Dorset (1643–1706). Born Lord Buckhurst, probably at Copt Hall, Essex, in January 1643, Dorset became Earl of Middlesex in 1675 and succeeded to the Earldom of Dorset on the death of his father in 1678. The friend of Buckingham, Rochester and Sedley and esteemed as a poet by both Dryden and Pope (the latter of whom preferred him to Rochester), he contributed in an even more valuable way to Restoration literature by his generous and discriminating patronage of the poets and dramatists whose portraits still hang in the 'Poets' Parlour' at Knole. Prior was educated at his expense, and Dryden compensated by him for the loss of his Laureate's pension in 1688. A Whig and one of the principal architects of the Revolution, Dorset became Lord Chamberlain under William III. The text of Dorset poses greater problems than that of any other Restoration poet except Rochester and the versions printed in this anthology are in no sense definitive. An edition promised in 1941 by the poet's biographer Brice Harris has yet to appear.

SIR CHARLES SEDLEY (1639–1701). Sedley was the civilest and the most civilized of the Restoration court wits and the outward innocuousness of much of his love poetry sometimes obscures the acuteness of the artistic intelligence at work in it. He was born in London into a cavalier family and educated at Wadham College, Oxford. In 1657 he married the sister of his dead brother's widow. Their only child, Katherine, was the witty mistress of James II. Equally famous among his contemporaries for the brilliance of his conversation and the scandalousness of his behaviour, Sedley was the subject of a great many stories, some no doubt apocryphal. The most sensational concerned his role in the Cock Tavern riot of 1663 as a consequence of which he was fined a thousand marks for indecent exposure. After an accident in 1680 when the roof of a tennis court fell on him during a game with Etherege and Fleetwood Shepherd, he grew more sober, went through a form of marriage with his mistress Ann Ayscough (his first wife, though still alive, was insane) and became a figure of some importance among the promoters of the Revolution. He was the author of three plays, *The Mulberry Garden* (1668), *Antony and Cleopatra* (1677) and *Bellamira* (1687), and was still writing fine verse in the 1690s. He died in 1701 'like a philosopher without fear or superstition'. The texts of the poems in this anthology are taken from the edition published immediately after his death by Ann Ayscough's nephew. There is a modern edition by V. de Sola Pinto (1928).

JOHN SHEFFIELD, Third Earl of Mulgrave, afterwards First Duke of Buckingham and Normanby (1648–1721). Mulgrave was, like Dorset, a descendant of Lionel Cranfield, Earl of

Middlesex, and thus a grandnephew of Suckling. An unlikeable narcissist with considerably more talent for military and political intrigue than for poetry, he was nevertheless a useful source of support for Dryden who helped him with his attack on the wits of the Rochester circle in *An Essay on Satire* and from whom he subsequently received the dedication of the *Aeneid*. In later life, as Duke of Buckingham (the title having passed from the Villiers family with the death of the second Duke) he was an influential parliamentarian on the Tory side and the builder of Buckingham Palace. His works, with further revisions by Pope, were published after his death in two absurdly luxurious folio volumes, and it is from this edition that the text of the *Essay* has been taken. An early version is available for comparison in the first volume of the Yale *Poems on Affairs of State* series, ed. G. de Forrest Lord.

SIR FLEETWOOD SHEPHERD (1634–98). Shepherd was the friend, steward and literary agent of Charles Sackville, Earl of Dorset. He was born at Great Rollright near Chipping Norton, Oxfordshire, and educated at Magdalen College and Christ Church, Oxford, and Gray's Inn. His official connexion with Dorset began in the early 1670s, however he had been known to the wits for some time before this and appears in most of the best-known stories about them. He was also the friend and financial adviser of Nell Gwyn. When Dorset became Lord Chamberlain in 1689, Shepherd superintended the sale of the offices in his gift and a few that were not. In 1694 he was knighted and appointed Usher of the Black Rod. Witty, good-natured and affable, he was the recipient of several dedications from poets too timid to address Dorset directly. His verse has never been collected.

'A dialogue between *Fleet Shepard* and *Will* the Coffee Man' was probably written by Tom Brown.

THOMAS SOUTHERNE (1660–1746). Born at Oxmantown, Dublin, in 1660, the son of a brewer, and educated at Trinity College, Dublin, Southerne was the author of ten plays of which the best are the brilliant satiric comedies, *The Wives' Excuse* (1692) and *The Maid's Last Prayer* (1693), and the tragedies *The Fatal Marriage, or the Innocent Adultery* (1694) and *Oroonoko* (1696) based on novels by Aphra Behn.

An edition of his plays is in preparation.

THOMAS TRAHERNE (1637–74). The son of a Hereford shoe-maker, Traherne studied for the ministry at Brasenose College, Oxford, and passed the remainder of his short life as rector of Credenhill near Hereford and later chaplain to the Lord Keeper of the Great Seal, Sir Orlando Bridgeman. He is the only de-votional poet of the generation of Dryden who was able to emerge from the shadow of Donne and Herbert and find a voice that was unmistakably his own. His poems remained unknown until the present century, though some of his prose meditations were published after his death through the agency of his patroness Susanna Hopton. Texts are from Bodleian MS. Eng. Poet. c. 42 and B.M. MS. Burney 392. The most recent editions of the poems are those of Gladys I. Wade (1932), H. M. Margoliouth (1958) and Anne Ridler (1966).

GEORGE VILLIERS, Second Duke of Buckingham (1628–87). Pope's 'Great Villiers', Dryden's 'Zimri', Butler's 'Duke of Bucks' and Mulgrave's 'Merriest man alive' was the son of James I's favourite who was assassinated by Felton in 1628. He was brought up with the royal children and later fought for and fled with the future Charles II. While in exile at Rotterdam he made the acquaintance of the leveller John Lilburne. In June 1657 he returned to England where he married the daughter of the parliamentary leader Fairfax. Back in favour after the Restor-ation, Buckingham became the central figure of a circle of wits including Rochester, Dorset, Sedley, Wycherley, Shadwell, Butler and Sprat, with whose aid and approbation he composed *The Rehearsal* (1672). His scandalous private life did not prevent him from holding the highest offices under Charles or from becoming the hero of the Londoners when he moved into op-position to the court party with Shaftesbury in 1674. After the collapse of the Whig cause in 1682, his fortune exhausted, Buck-ingham retired to Yorkshire where he spent his last years hunting and plotting resistance to James II. His life is related with a panache worthy of its subject in Hester Chapman's *Great Villiers* (1949).

EDMUND WALLER (1606–87). The doyen of the younger Restoration poets was born at the Manor House, Coleshill, Buckinghamshire, and educated at Eton, Kings College, Cambridge, and Lincoln's Inn. He inherited a considerable fortune which no doubt contributed to his becoming an M.P. at

18 (one account says 16). On the outbreak of the civil war, Waller, although sympathetic to the royal cause, chose the side of parliament in which his oratorical abilities had made him a figure of some consequence. In 1643 he was found to be implicated in a plot to seize London for the king and only narrowly escaped execution. Seven years of exile in France followed, after which he was pardoned and allowed to return to England where he subsequently held office under Comwell. On the Restoration he resumed his seat in the parliament from which he had earlier been barred for life. His remaining years were occupied with making himself agreeable to new generations of poets and ladies and accepting the homage paid to him as the supreme relic of the wit and politeness of the last age. Waller's poems were last edited in 1905 by G. Thorn-Drury.

SAMUEL WESLEY (1662–1735). The father of the father of Methodism was born at Winterborn-Whitchurch, Dorset. Intended by his parents for the dissenting ministry, he was sent to a private academy and later to Exeter College, Oxford, where he was induced to accept ordination in the Church of England. In the 1680s he was connected with the merry circle of the bookseller John Dunton whose style of humour is evident in both the title and the contents of Wesley's first collection of verse *Maggots* (1685). Eight years later, he published an epic in ten books on the life of Christ, the first of three lengthy works in the heroic idiom now forgotten. John Wesley was his fifteenth child.

ROBERT WILD (1609–79). Wild becomes a Restoration poet principally for his *Iter Boreale* (1660), a spirited panegyric on Monck's march from the North to break the power of the Rump. He was the son of a shoemaker in St Ives, Huntingdonshire, and a graduate of both Cambridge (St John's) and Oxford. In 1646 he was appointed rector of Aynho in Northamptonshire and remained there until he was ejected in 1662 as a non-conformist. His verse had an extremely wide public. There is a text of *Iter Boreale* in the first volume of the Yale *Poems on Affairs of State* series, ed. G. de Forrest Lord.

JOHN WILMOT, Second Earl of Rochester (1647–80). Born at Ditchley Manor House, Oxfordshire, the son of Henry Wilmot, Charles II's genial but imprudent companion on his flight from Worcester, Rochester was educated at Burford Grammar School and Wadham College, Oxford, from which he saluted the king on the occasion of his Restoration in his earliest preserved piece of verse. After making the grand tour (1661–4) in the company of a tutor who gave him a taste for intellectual pursuits which he never lost, and seeing service at sea during the Second Dutch War, he entered into the much-recounted career of roisterer, whoremaster and practical joker which has done so much damage to his reputation as a poet. In January 1667 he married an heiress, Elizabeth Mallet, whom he had earlier tried to abduct by force, and by whom he had four children. The most brilliant and the least predictable of the court wits, Rochester kept the biggest of the many surprizes he gave to his contemporaries for the last year of his life when, after a series of conversations with Gilbert Burnet, who gives a moving account of them in his *Some Passages of the Life and Death of the Right Honourable John Earl of Rochester* (1680), he renounced the 'atheistical' opinions he had maintained in aristocratic discussion circles and became a Christian.

There is no entirely satisfactory modern edition of Rochester, that of the late John Hayward (1926) suffering from editorial rewriting of indecent passages and a surfeit of spurious material, and that of V. de Sola Pinto (1953) from a respect for the text of Tonson's 1691 edition of the poems which has since been shown to be unwarranted. The texts contained in the present volume have been prepared from the *Poems on Several Occasions* of 1680, a facsimile of which has been edited by James Thorpe (Princeton, 1950), and a selection of the manuscript and printed sources listed by D. M. Vieth in his invaluable *Attribution in Restoration Poetry* (1963). Professor Pinto's *Enthusiast in Wit* (1962) is still the best introduction to Rochester the man – one of the most remarkable and most gifted men of his remarkable and gifted century.

WILLIAM WYCHERLEY (1640?–1716). Wycherley's father Daniel was steward to the Marquis of Winchester and apparently prospered in his office. When his son was about fifteen he sent him to live in the west of France where he was admitted to the company of a number of cultivated court ladies. After returning to England, Wycherley studied briefly at Queen's College, Oxford, and the Inner Temple before directing his energies towards the theatre where he won fame as the author of *The Country Wife* (1675) and *The Plain Dealer* (1677). In 1680, he married the widowed Countess of Drogheda, an act which cost him the favour of Charles II and his hopes of advancement at court. When, on her death shortly afterwards, he was unable to gain possession of her estate, he fell into the power of his creditors who had him committed to prison where he remained until he was freed by the personal intervention of James II seven years later. After his release he enjoyed the friendship of Dryden and subsequently that of the young Pope who expended considerable labour in trying to reduce his rough and ready verse to an acceptable Augustan smoothness, and, finding the task excessively difficult, persuaded him to recast a large amount of it in the form of prose maxims. Collections of Wycherley's poems were published in 1704 and 1728. The latter edited from the author's manuscripts by Theobald is the source of the poems contained in this volume. The only modern edition of Wycherley's poems is that of Montague Summers (1924).

*Index of Authors and
First Lines*

Index of Authors

Anon, 102, 112, 125, 128, 131, 144, 154, 164, 167, 172, 183, 184, 185, 225, 233, 343, 349

Banks, John, 325, 327
Baxter, Richard, 322
Behn, Aphra, 187
Blackmore, Sir Richard, 73
Brome, Alexander, 98, 171
Bunyan, John, 76
Butler, Samuel, 177, 236

Congreve, William, 200
Cotton, Charles, 41, 59, 150, 160, 174, 176, 215, 234, 245, 262, 266, 270, 277, 335
Cowley, Abraham, 37
Creech, Thomas, 193, 208
Crowne, John, 328

Darby, Charles, 60
Davenant, Sir William, 81
Denham, Sir John, 39, 93
Dennis, John, 57
Dryden, John, 80, 101, 107, 119, 127, 136, 153, 158, 161, 175, 196, 199, 204, 206, 209, 210, 217, 222, 228, 300, 309, 329, 336
Duke, Richard, 112, 168, 283
Durfey, Thomas, 264, 268

Fane, Sir Francis, 202
Flatman, Thomas, 37, 99, 140, 169, 174, 304, 319

Garth, Sir Samuel, 240
Gould, Robert, 294, 328

Heyrick, Thomas, 241, 272, 326
Hopkins, John, 345

Langhorn, Richard, 119
Lee, Nathaniel, 157

Marvell, Andrew, 91, 109, 114, 116, 302
Milton, John, 69, 74, 135

Norris, John, 78, 319, 320, 325

Oldham, John, 42, 52, 116, 117, 121, 148, 191, 247, 290, 301, 306
Oldmixon, John, 142
Orinda (Katherine Philips), 97, 149

Payne, Henry Nevile, 235
Prior, Matthew, 84, 180, 348

Radcliffe, Alexander, 40, 47, 228, 250, 256, 338, 339

Sackville, Charles, Earl of Dorset, 126, 138, 157, 159, 182, 305
Sedley, Sir Charles, 45, 56, 58, 60, 129, 137, 139, 143, 151, 152, 161, 169, 170, 186, 203, 234, 284, 290, 308, 322
Sheffield, John, Duke of Buckinghamshire, 229
Shepherd, Fleetwood, 337
Southerne, Thomas, 163

373

Traherne, Thomas, 70, 71, 79, 275

Villiers, George, 2nd Duke of Buckingham, 205

Waller, Edmund, 87
Wesley, Samuel, 293, 345

Wild, Robert, 96
Wilmot, John, Earl of Rochester, 45, 55, 58, 63, 86, 118, 137, 140, 141, 143, 147, 162, 166, 180, 183, 192, 224, 232, 250, 296, 348
Wycherley, William, 84, 176, 289, 301, 315

Index of First Lines

A Pox of this fooling and plotting of late,   121
A spouse I do hate,   176
Absent from thee I languish still,   143
After Death, nothing is, and Nothing, Death,   322
After thinking this Fortnight of Whig and of Tory,   126
Ah how sweet it is to love,   136
Ah, pity Love where e'r it grows!   185
Algernon Sidney fills this tomb   128
Alice is tall and upright as a Pine,   215
All Blisse   79
All human things are subject to decay,   309
All in the Land of *Essex*,   93
All my past Life is mine no more,   141
Almighty Crowd, thou shorten'st all dispute;   127
Almighty Vigour strove through all the Void,   73
An Age in her Embraces past,   147
An ancient Wood, fit for the Work design'd,   206
Ancient Person, for whom I,   183
And first behold the merriest Man alive   229
Andrew and *Maudlin*, *Rebecca* and *Will*   268
As I walk'd by my self   131
As some brave Admiral in former War,   45
At that so pleasant Season of the Year,   348

Base mettell hanger by your Master's Thigh!   184
Be wise, and ne'er to publick View produce   301
Before thir eyes in sudden view appear   74
Behold yon Mountain's hoary height   199
Beneath this Stone, Reader, there lieth flat   339
Bless me, 'tis cold! how chill the Air!   200
Bursting with Pride, the loath'd Impostume swells,   232
But by this time Tongues 'gan to rest;   60

But, grant thy Poetry should find success,   290
But now to chase these *Phantoms* out of sight   193

Celimena, of my heart,   158
Chloe found *Amyntas* lying   153
Chloris, whilst thou and I were free,   174
Cloris, I cannot say your Eyes   137
Cloris, I justly am betray'd   143
Come *John* sit thee down I have somewhat to say,   154
Come on ye Critticks! find one fault who dare,   305

Dear Friend, I fear my Heart will break;   45
Dear Friend, when those we love are in distress,   294
Dear skilfull *Betty*, who dost far excell   208
Dear *Tom*, how melancholly I am grown   283
Did any Punishment attend   203
Dim, as the borrow'd beams of Moon and Stars   80
Drink about till the Day find us,   58

Enflam'd with Love and led by blind desires,   157

Falsest of fair ones, swear again,   202
Farewel, too little and too lately known,   336
Farewell ungratefull Traytor   161
Fear not, my Dear, a Flame can never dye,   169
Fill a Boul of lusty Wine,   59
First, and the chiefest thing by me enjoyn'd,   117
Flight is but the Preparative: The Sight   71
For Shame your Green-wood Fires then smother,   185
Fortune made up of Toyes and Impudence   205
Freeman and *Wild*, two young hot Gallants,   57
From hence began that Plot; the Nation's Curse,   119

Good people draw neare,   112

Had she but liv'd in *Cleopatra's* Age,   228
Happy the Man, and happy he alone,   204
Happy the Man who free from Care and Strife,   293
He had been long t'wards *Mathematicks*,   236

He is not Great who gives to others Law, 84

He that is down, needs fear no fall, 77

He who writ this, not without pains and thought 300

Hee ended, or I heard no more, for now 135

Hence two miles *East*, does a fourth *Wonder* lye, 277

Here Damsel sits disconsolate, 250

Here Honest *Micoe* lies, who never knew 338

Here 337

Here stand I, 256

He's no small Prince who every day 37

How happy were good English Faces 167

How prone we are to Sin, how sweet were made 187

How sad doth *Dives* look? how deep he groans? 322

How shall we please this Age? If in a Song 290

Howe'r, 'tis well, that whilst Mankind, 84

I care not tho it be 320

I did but crave that I might kiss, 140

I, he who whileom sate and sung in Cage, 96

I saw him dead, a leaden slumber lyes 91

I sing a Woofull Ditty 114

If for thy self thou wilt not watch thy Whore, 209

If *Rome* can pardon Sins, as *Romans* hold, 188

If you walk out in Bus'ness ne'er so great, 247

I'me made in sport by *Nature*, when 241

In the milde close of an hot Summers day, 99

In this cold *Monument* lies one, 335

It must be done (my Soul) but 'tis a strange, 319

Know then with Horses twain, one sound, one lame, 266

Let Ancients boast no more 224

Let lofty *Greek* and *Latin* go, 345

Let other Poets treat of lofty Things, 272

Let others better mold the running Mass 207

Like a Dog with a bottle, fast ti'd to his tail, 169

Long days of absence, Dear, I could endure, 144

Long has he been of that amphibious Fry, 240

Long time plain dealing in the Hauty Town, 86

Love a Woman! y'are an Ass, 166
Love still has somthing of the Sea, 151

Maids need no more their Silver Piss-pots scoure, 349
Make me a Bowl, a mighty Bowl, 191
Marriage is but a Beast, some say, 177
Me-thinks already, from this Chymick flame, 107
Me-thinks, I see how the biest Swain was lay'd 345
Methinks the Poor Town has been troubled too long 138
Mistress of all my Senses can invite, 168
My dear Mistress has a Heart 140
My lodging it is on the Cold ground, 146

No, no – 'tis not Love – You may talk till Dooms day, 164
Nothing thou Elder Brother ev'n to shade, 63
Now God alone that made all things, 343
Now, now the Fight's done, and the great God of war 157
Now stop your noses Readers, all and some, 222
Now that the world is all in amaze, 37

O Father of Mercy, 119
O're the Desert, cross the Meadows, 308
Of a great Heroin I mean to tell, 225
Of all the *Grain* our Nation yields 122
Of Fire, Fire, Fire I sing, 102
Of these the false *Achitophel* was first: 217
Oh the sad Day, 319
One time, as they walk'd forth e're break of day, 52

Phillis, be gentler I advise, 180
Phillis, let's shun the common Fate, 161
Phillis, Men say that all my Vows 139
Pish! 'tis an idle fond excuse, 176
Prethee *Cloe*, not so fast, 142
Pursuing Beauty, Men descry 163

Rat too, rat too, rat too, rat tat too, rat tat too, 256
Reader beneath this Marble Stone 228

Rutt, to the Suburb Beauties full well known, 234
Ruyter the while, that had our Ocean curb'd, 109

Scrape no more your harmless Chins, 186
See! *Hymen* comes; How his Torch blazes! 170
Since thou'rt condemn'd to wed a thing, 171
Since you desire of me to know 78
Smooth was the Water, calm the Air, 152
So clear a season, and so snatch'd from storms, 97
Son of a whore, God damn you: Can you tell 348
Standing upon the margent of the Main, 150
Storm not, brave Friend, that thou hadst never yet 234
Such perfect Bliss, fair *Cloris*, we 162
Sweet Harmony of Life, just Musick flows 325

Take Time, my Dear, e're Time takes wing; 183
Tell me, abandon'd *Miscreant*, prithee tell, 306
Tell me, sage Will, Thou that the town around 233
Tell me, why Heav'n at first did suffer Sin? 81
The Cock has crow'd an hour ago, 245
The Fire of Love in youthful Blood, 182
The Poor in Wit or Judgment, like all Poor, 315
The Rabble hate, the Gentry feare 125
The utmost Grace the *Greeks* could shew, 58
The warlike Prince had sever'd from the rest 101
Then first I observe from the French-Man *Des Cartes*, 235
There lies a Broken Anker, on whose Trust 326
There wanted yet the Master work, the end 69
There was a prudent grave Physician, 56
These little Limmes, 70
Thou cursed Cock, with thy perpetual Noise, 284
Thou swear'st thou'lt drink no more; kind Heaven send 60
Thou Youngest Virgin-Daughter of the Skies, 329
Thus therefore, he who feels the Fiery dart 196
Thy Books shou'd, like thy Friends, not many be, 289
'Tis endless, Sir, to tell the many ways, 301
'Tis now since I began to die 149
To friend and to foe, 172

To *walk* abroad is, not with Eys, 275
To what intent or purpose was Man made, 40
Too happy had I been indeed, if Fate 148
'Twas a dispute 'twixt heav'n and Earth 137

Unhappy, foolish, wilful Man, 328

Vertue! thou solemn grave Impertinence, 42
Vulcan contrive me such a Cup, 192

Was ever man of Nature's framing 160
We have ventur'd our estates, 98
Well! since it must be so, so let it be, 304
Well Sir, 'tis granted, I said *Dryden's* Rhimes, 296
Were I (who to my cost already am 55
What Danger is the Pilgrim in? 78
What gives us that Fantastick Fit, 39
What *Timon* does old Age begin t'approach 250
Whatever Blessing you my Life deny, 325
When daring Blood, his rents to have regain'd, 116
When I beheld the Poet blind, yet bold, 302
When the first Broad sids were giv'n, 327
When the first Traitor *Cain* (too good to be 116
When we for Age could neither read nor write, 87
Where Oxen do low, 264
While Duns were knocking at my Door, 47
While on those lovely looks I gaze, 141
Whilst Beauty, Youth, and gay Delight 180
Whilst th'iron Hand 328
Who would true Valour see, 76
Why, let it run! who bids it stay? 41
Why should a foolish Marriage Vow 175
Why should we murmur, why repine, 174
Wou'd you in Love succeed, be Brisk, be Gay, 159

You ask from whence proceed these monstrous Crimes; 211
You Gallants all, that love good Wine, 129
You *Squires* o'th'shade, that love to tread 262
You that the *City* Life embrace, 270

MORE ABOUT PENGUINS

Penguin Book News, which appears every month, contains details of all the new books issued by Penguins as they are published. From time to time it is supplemented by *Penguins in Print*, which is a complete list of all books published by Penguins which are in print. (There are over three thousand of these.)

A specimen copy of *Penguin Book News* will be sent to you free on request, and you can become a subscriber for the price of the postage – 4s. for a year's issues (including the complete lists). Just write to Dept EP, Penguin Books Ltd, Harmondsworth, Middlesex, enclosing a cheque or postal order, and your name will be added to the mailing list.

Some other books published by Penguins are described on the following pages.

Note: *Penguin Book News* and *Penguins in Print* are not available in the U.S.A. or Canada.

THE PENGUIN BOOK OF
ANIMAL VERSE

Edited by George MacBeth

George MacBeth writes in his introduction:

'All good poems about animals are about something else
as well. It may be divine providence or it may be human
iniquity. The important point is that these qualities should
be seen *through* the nature of animals. The apparent con-
tent of the poem should at least be a part of the real
content. When Keats writes about the nightingale and
Wordsworth about the cuckoo the real subject is the poet's
wish to be at one with nature and the bird is almost en-
tirely dissolved. When Keats writes about Mrs Reynolds'
cat, on the other hand, he describes the subject clearly, as
does Wordsworth when he writes about swans.

'The main justification for this anthology can now be
clearly stated. I am on the side of those who tend to like
poems about dogs because they like dogs rather than be-
cause they like poems.'

This is an entertaining 'A to Z' of animal verse from ants
and bats to yaks and zebras.

THE PENGUIN BOOK OF
SATIRICAL VERSE

Edited by Edward Lucie-Smith

'The end of satyr is reformation,' says Defoe, flatly, in the first sentence of his preface to *The True-Born Englishman*. And this indeed is what satire has always *pretended* to be about. The mask of the reformer is the one which the satirical poet most frequently assumes; it provides him with a justification for the release of his aggressive instincts, whatever topic he chooses to touch upon. The matter is not, however, to be so easily settled. The satiric impulse is complex rather than simple.

From William Langland's *Piers Plowman* to Christopher Logue's *I Shall Vote Labour*, this anthology provides examples of satirical verse from every period of English writing.